# EDUCATIONAL TESTING

SOURCE BOOKS ON EDUCATION
(VOL. 26)

GARLAND REFERENCE LIBRARY
OF SOCIAL SCIENCE
(VOL. 607)

# SOURCE BOOKS ON EDUCATION

# EDUCATIONAL TESTING
## *Issues and Applications*

Kathy E. Green, Editor

GARLAND PUBLISHING, INC. • NEW YORK & LONDON
1991

© 1991 Kathy E. Green

Library of Congress Cataloging-in-Publication Data

Educational testing : issues and applications / Kathy E. Green,
editor.
  p.    cm. — (Garland reference library of social science; vol.
607. Source books on education ; vol. 26)
  Includes index.
  ISBN 0–8240–3336–1 (alk. paper)
  1. Educational tests and measurements—United States. I. Green,
Kathy E., 1950–   . II. Series: Garland reference library of social
science ; vol. 607. III. Series: Garland reference library of
social science.  Source books on education ; vol. 26.
LB3051.E346    1991
371'.2'6—dc20                                                    90-48938
                                                                      CIP

Printed on acid-free, 250-year-life paper
Manufactured in the United States of America

To my parents, Earl Green
and Catherine Steczkowski

# CONTENTS

# THE AUTHORS

Rita M. Baker, Ph.D., 1985, University of Denver. Dr. Baker is in private practice in Denver, Colorado. She specializes in assessment and treatment of handicapped children, adults, and hard-to-assess children. She has worked previously with the Colorado School for the Deaf and Blind.

Charlotte Webb Farr, Ph.D., 1987, University of Wyoming. Dr. Farr is an Assistant Professor, Coordinator of Teleconferencing, University of Wyoming, Laramie, Wyoming. Her research interests include assessment, learning in context, and evaluating the impact of technology on learning.

Kathy E. Green, Ph.D., 1981, University of Washington. Dr. Green is an Associate Professor, School of Education, University of Denver, Denver, Colorado. Her interests are in research methods, measurement, and statistics.

Raymond Kluever, Ph.D., 1968, Northwestern University. Dr. Kluever is an Associate Professor, School of Education, University of Denver, Denver, Colorado. His interests are assessment of special populations, educational technology, and cognition with emphasis on language development and linguistics.

Tony C. M. Lam, Ph.D., 1987, University of Washington. Dr. Lam is an Assistant Professor, Department of Educational Foundations, University of New Mexico, Albuquerque, New Mexico. His research interests are in assessment and evaluation with emphasis on cross cultural studies.

Debra J. Madsen, J.D., 1984, University of Idaho. Ms. Madsen is the Assistant Dean, College of Law, University of Wyoming, Laramie, Wyoming. Her interests include the use and validity of the LSAT and legal rights to intellectual property.

Daniel Mueller, Ph.D., 1965, University of Illinois. Dr. Mueller is a Professor, Counseling and Educational Psychology, Indiana University. His current research interests are value measurement and moral reasoning measurement. He is the author of *Measuring Social Attitudes*, Teachers College Press, 1986.

Susan F. Stager, Ph.D., 1978, Indiana University. Dr. Stager is the Assistant to the Dean, University Computing, Indiana University. She is involved in both the planning and administration of computing programs for students at Indiana University.

E. Jane Williams, Ph.D., 1983, The Ohio State University. Dr. Williams is a Supervisor of Program Evaluation for the Department of Program Evaluation, Columbus Public Schools, Columbus, Ohio. Her interests include research on teaching and program evaluation, areas in which she has presented and published papers.

Midori Yamagishi, Ph.D., 1985, University of Washington. Dr. Yamagishi is an Assistant Professor, Department of Business Administration and Information Management, Osaka International University, Osaka, Japan. She grew up in Japan and was educated in both Japan and the United States. Her major research interests are methodological and cross-cultural issues in the effects of schooling and work.

# ACKNOWLEDGMENTS

Several people helped in the process of developing this book. Marie Ellen Larcada, my editor at Garland Publishing, helped and encouraged me, gave me advice on what to expect when coordinating the work of a number of authors, and was available by phone, mail, and on special occasion in person to answer my questions. I would also like to acknowledge Joseph Braun, Jr., for introducing me to the idea of creating such a book. I would like to thank my contributors for doing their best to keep to a schedule in spite of family illnesses, job changes, and frozen water pipes. Their integrity, patience, and perseverance are appreciated. Finally, I wish to thank Carol Taylor and the Faculty Computing Laboratory staff for all of their assistance with formatting and graphics.

# INTRODUCTION

## KATHY E. GREEN

The controversy over testing continues. While criticized from many sides, testing is not only holding its own but seems to be increasing in use with federal and state legislatures becoming more invested in accountability. At the same time, major changes in test theory and technology have occurred heralding the possible availability of even more useful information that can be obtained through testing. Educational testing is one of the major components of educational reform agendas noted either by an increased presence, presence in a new guise, or by its total absence. In this climate of educational reform and legislatively mandated accountability, current knowledge of development and change in testing is akin to consumer protection. The consequences of development and change in testing will be visited upon the uninformed. It is essential that those concerned with education be cognizant of correct test interpretation. Since much score reporting uses technical jargon, this involves some understanding of terminology as well as logic.

When the opportunity to compile a book of readings about educational testing was presented to me, I jumped at it. There is a plethora of introductory tests and measurement textbooks; there are some books on understanding test scores geared to laypersons in or outside the field of education; there are extremely interesting and well-done books on psychometric theory; there are books written to inform measurement specialists of the latest developments. There are few (or no) books written for educators who do not think of themselves as professionals in testing that attempt to extend and update knowledge gained from an introductory tests and measurement course. But this is the group most likely to be affected by legislation involving testing and the group most likely to use tests frequently. This book is directed to people who use tests or who use test results but who do not consider themselves to be measurement experts.

A major task in editing this book was in selecting the most pressing topics. A number of topics of considerable interest were omitted in favor of those that seemed more immediately relevant. And some developments in testing and psychometric theory require some further work before educators "in the trenches" can easily make use of them. Some chapters that would certainly be included in a second volume would be uses of item response theory by teachers, research on teacher-constructed tests, competency and performance testing of teachers, test item construction, and linking testing to instruction.

The reader will easily recognize the different styles and orientations of the authors. All are extremely interested in educational assessment, but each has a different perspective on future directions for testing. The authors were selected primarily due to their expertise in the area but also because they have been classroom teachers or are intimately concerned with test use in their daily lives. These authors were sought for their practical as well as theoretical insights.

The book is organized into two sections. The initial section, general principles, is a review of the origins of testing and measurement theory and also reminds readers of the types of test scores they may have encountered in schools or in trying to interpret standardized test results. These chapters are brief; to get a good review of introductory tests and measurement, the reader is encouraged to study one of the textbooks referenced. The first chapter is a bit more theoretical than the remaining ones. This chapter reviews classical test theory and introduces item response theory, a comparatively new measurement model that can lead to more informative results from testing. The next chapter is included primarily as a review of terms and concepts that will be encountered throughout the remainder of the book.

The second section reviews recent testing applications and issues. Chapters 3 through 6 deal with testing of children who are exceptional in some way. Chapter 3 reviews the research and current status of the assessment of gifted children. The author of this chapter directs a university educational assessment center for gifted children, teaches graduate level assessment courses, and appears at local and national meetings to discuss gifted assessment. In this chapter, the author takes us through a brief history of gifted assessment, through current practice, and ends with a vision of future directions. The next chapter, on evaluation of hearing impaired children, provides relatively less information from the research literature, because there is relatively little research information available on the topic. The author is a statewide consultant on evaluation of the deaf and hearing impaired and is frequently called in to help evaluate both children and adults. This chapter reviews definitions and ideas about the effects of deafness, proceeds to review current practice, and closes with cautions and words of advice about testing this group. Chapter 5 reviews the research on curriculum-based assessment. Curriculum-based assessment may be a new name for an old process: testing what has been taught. Curriculum-based assessment is now presented as an alternative to standardized testing that provides ongoing assessment information rather than summative scores. It is testing closely tied to the teaching and learning process. Its origins are tied to special education although its use has expanded. Chapter 6 takes a conceptual as well as applied approach to the assessment of limited English proficient children but also reviews current practice and currently used measures. The chapter concludes with recommendations for the future and cautions about assessment of this group. The author's first language was not English, so he works from both personal and professional knowledge of the effects of English proficiency on achievement.

Chapter 7 was included in this volume due to the fascination with the Japanese educational system exhibited by many American educators. The chapter provides an international perspective from an author who has experienced both the Japanese and the American educational systems. The chapter presents a brief history of Japanese education and testing, reviews current use of tests along with criticisms of testing, and concludes with a view of the direction testing might take in Japan. The reader may be curious to note the similarities and differences between testing in Japan and the United States. And the reader may also note the reported effects of standardized testing on students in Japan. The following chapter (Chapter 8) reviews issues in the American debate on standardized testing. The chapter opens with a brief review of characteristics of standardized tests, outlines controversies in standardized test use and score reporting, and concludes with a discussion of potential trends in standardized testing.

Chapter 9 was written by a lawyer and assistant dean of a law school who has served as a guest lecturer discussing legal issues in high-stakes testing. This chapter introduces the primary constitutional grounds for legal challenges to standardized achievement testing and reviews landmark cases. The chapter concludes with a view of the future of legal challenges to testing.

Moving away from standardized testing, Chapter 10 reviews the research literature on the effects of computers in classroom testing. The potentials for gain are discussed along with criticisms of computer use. The chapter concludes with a view of future classroom testing practice. Prior to university teaching and her position as director of a major university computing facility, the first author of this chapter was a third grade teacher. The author of Chapter 5 was also at one time a third grade teacher.

The book closes with a chapter discussing the implications of one view of learning for testing. Research in cognitive psychology has begun to bear fruit useful to classroom educators. This chapter provides some background information on cognitive psychology, distinguishes the cognitive psychologist's approach from that of a psychometrician, and concludes with a view of a possible future linking these two disciplines.

We live in a time that may see great change in education including substantial changes in tests and the testing process. This time may see much more integration of learning and assessment; technological advances making more information available to teachers, students, and parents; and a redefinition of testing stemming from developments in education and psychology. The chapters herein each provide perspectives of possible futures. In this respect, the unifying theme of this book is present and future concerns in testing. Its general objective is to raise as many questions as it answers.

# Educational Testing

# MEASUREMENT THEORY

## KATHY E. GREEN

This chapter provides a brief summary of the history of testing and measurement, describes the dominant measurement model of the early-mid 1900s (classical test theory), describes item response theory models, and describes the similarities and differences among these models. This chapter reviews the theoretical structure underlying test statistics. The second chapter of this volume takes a more applied perspective and reviews common test statistics and what they mean.

### HISTORICAL DEVELOPMENT OF TESTING AND MEASUREMENT

Testing began in the twenty-fourth century B.C. in China with the use of selection tests for civil servants. China had no hereditary ruling class and relied on several levels of competitive examinations to fill positions in the civil service. Candidates for positions were examined for proficiency in music, archery, horsemanship, writing, arithmetic, and public and private rites and ceremonies. Two thousand years later (about 200 A.D.), proficiency tests were still in use and included assessment of knowledge of civil law, military affairs, agriculture, revenue, and geography. One thousand years later (1370 A.D.), tests also included tasks in composition and poetry. Candidates' examination papers were recopied and judged by two graders, with a

3

third available to reconcile disputes. (Paper making was developed as an art in China beginning in the first century A.D.)

British diplomats and missionaries in China learned about the open competition examination system and took the idea home with them. In the 1800s, trainees for British service in India were selected via examination. And the U.S. Civil Service Commission (begun in 1883) developed selection tests for various positions. France and Germany began using selection tests in the 1800s as well. By the mid-1800s written examinations were recognized in Europe and the United States as a basis for making decisions about government posts. With a growing civil service in all countries, the need for tests as tools for selection increased.

Formal examinations at universities were initially oral, such as those at the University of Bologna in 1219, but were mainly a formality. Written examinations in Europe began to be used after paper making had been learned from the Arabs in the twelfth century, the Arabs having learned it from the Chinese in the eighth century. In the 1500s, the Jesuits established rules of conduct for examinations. In 1836, the University of London was chartered as an examining organization, with no instructional program of its own. By the mid-1800s, written exams were recognized as the basis for decisions about entrance to professions and the granting of degrees.

Three unrelated events occurring in the late 1800s had a significant impact on modern testing. In 1879, the first experimental psychology laboratory was established in Leipzig, Germany, by Wilhelm Wundt. The primary purpose of this laboratory was investigation into psychophysics--the relationship between physical stimuli and the experienced intensity of the stimuli. (One of Wundt's students was an ex-British army officer, Charles Spearman, who later developed a correlation index--Spearman's rho--and a method for estimating the reliability of a lengthened or shortened test--the Spearman-Brown prophecy formula.) This laboratory spurred the development of methods of measuring sensory perceptions and their relationship to more readily measurable physical stimuli as well as new ideas about experimental design and associated statistical techniques.

In the late 1800s, after a century of increasing concern for the humane treatment of the insane and mentally retarded, the French minister of public instruction appointed a commission to examine the appropriateness of educational experiences for schoolchildren. Alfred Binet, a member of that commission, worked with French physician

Theophile Simon to develop a 30-item test measuring general intelligence and, in particular, identifying children with below-normal intellectual skills who needed alternative instruction. The Binet-Simon Scale was published in 1905. Later revised by L.M. Terman (Terman, 1916) of Stanford, a descendent of this test is still in use today.

Yet another stream of thought contributed to the demand for psychological measurement. This was Darwinian biology, as pursued by Sir Francis Galton, a relative of Darwin's. Galton was concerned with heredity and, thus, with individual differences, physical and psychological. In the 1880s, Galton began a series of studies to determine if his position stated in *Hereditary Genius* (1869, 1952) was valid. He argued that some persons possessed traits making them more capable than other persons, and these traits were mental as well as physical. This study of differences and relationships required statistical indices, one of which was developed by Karl Pearson (the Pearson product moment correlation coefficient).

By the early 1900s, there were several areas of study and practice in need of theory and methods of assessment: civil service testing, academic and intellectual achievement testing, measurement of individual similarities and differences, and measurement of sensory perceptions.

In the early 1900s true-score test theory was developed and advanced by the work of Karl Pearson and especially British psychologist Charles Spearman. Spearman criticized Pearson's 1901 studies of physical and mental traits suggesting that error in the mental trait measurement meant there was no point in recording data to four decimal places. Spearman introduced the idea of reliability in a 1904 article entitled "The Proof and Measurement of Association Between Two Things," published in the *American Journal of Psychology*. Spearman's article was referred to by E.L. Thorndike in the first book on testing, *An Introduction to the Theory of Mental and Social Measurement*, also published in 1904. Most of the true-score theory concepts were devised by Spearman and his colleagues and published between 1904 and 1922.

Extensive test development came in the years between 1915 and World War I with standardized tests developed for most school skills and content areas. The *Army Alpha* and *Army Beta* were used as group tests in World War I to test the ability of literate and illiterate adult recruits. The use of tests continued to increase in the time between World War I and World War II.

Another notable development in test theory came in 1937 when G. Frederick Kuder and Marion W. Richardson published their paper on the KR-20 internal consistency reliability coefficient. Lee Cronbach detailed Coefficient Alpha in 1951, and in 1972 Cronbach and his colleagues developed and published a book on generalizability theory.

The foundations of item response theory (or latent trait theory) were developing in tandem but were not as visible to test makers: Binet and Simon used plots of item characteristic curves (ICC) in test development in 1916, though the term ICC was not used until 1946 (Tucker, 1946). Thurstone's Law of Comparative Judgment contained the ideas of conjoint additivity present in some item response theory models. His work also highlighted the need for objectivity of measures. Richardson (1936), Finney (1952), and Lawley (1943,1944) provided early theoretical work in item response theory (IRT). In particular, Richardson (1936) explained the relationships between true-score parameters and IRT parameters. Rasch (1947) investigated the use of the logistic function in modeling intelligence and reading test item responses. In 1952, Lord investigated the application of latent trait theory to test theory analysis in his doctoral dissertation. IRT models failed to gain early currency in the field of testing, possibly due to their relative complexity and to problems with parameter estimation. With the work of Birnbaum (1957, 1958a, 1958b) and Rasch (1960, 1966a, 1966b), however, the models were made more tractable. Subsequent work, notably by Wright (1968, 1977, 1982 with Masters) and Lord (1977, 1980, 1983) has developed theory and made practice using IRT models accessible to researchers and practitioners.

In addition to work in statistics and education with IRT, logical analyses of the process of measurement were going on in related fields (psychophysics, physics). Algebraic characteristics of measurement models are described by Krantz, Luce, Suppes, and Tversky in *Foundations of Measurement* (1971) and Coombs, Dawes, and Tversky in *Mathematical Psychology: An Elementary Introduction* (1970). Measurement models with these algebraic characteristics are termed fundamental measurement models. Conjoint models are one class of fundamental measurement models with defined, axiomatized characteristics. The Rasch IRT model is an additive conjoint model.

True-score theory, item response theory, and fundamental measurement models share some common beginnings, concerns, and methods. They also share some common results. But the philosophies of measurement they represent differ substantially. Before the differences among models are discussed, the tenets and conclusions of the true-score model, the measurement model dominant in the early-mid 1900s, will be presented, followed by a cursory description of item response theory models.

## The True Score Model

The true-score model assumes that an observed test score is a fallible measure of the trait being considered. Specifically, an observed score is composed of two linearly connected parts: the true score and an error component or

$$X = T + E$$

where $X$ = observed score,

$T$ = true score of individual's position, and

$E$ = error component.

The observed score may be higher or lower than the person's true score, depending upon whether the error component is positive or negative. This is the first of several assumptions of true score (or classical) test theory. If these assumptions are not met in any specific case, the subsequent conclusions are suspect.

A second assumption of the true-score model is that the long run expected value of $X$ over repeated testing will be exactly $T$. That is, if the same person took the same test an infinite number of times and each testing session was independent of all others, we would expect the average of her scores to be her true score. Note that the model is based on the score we can expect on a given test and not on a measure of the ability the person has in whatever trait the test is measuring.

The third assumption is that true scores and error scores for any population of examinees are uncorrelated. This means that persons with high scores have no greater or less error in their scores than persons with average or low scores (which cannot in fact be true because of boundaries at zero and perfect scores).

The fourth assumption states that the correlation between error scores from independent measures (e.g., different test items or different tests) for the same examinee is zero. This assumption implies that the effects of fatigue, mood, practice, item or test dependencies, and testing conditions are negligible--at least for the duration of the test or testing sessions.

The fifth assumption of the true-score model states that error scores on one test are unrelated to true scores on another test. This assumption would be violated, as would the third assumption, if a person got low scores on two tests and had high positive error scores (e.g., guessed frequently).

Thus, the true-score model posits an additive model in which errors are random. Any systematic error under the true-score model would become part of the true score. Given these assumptions, a number of conclusions follow that allow computation of several useful quantities. One of these useful quantities is the standard error of measurement. It is equal to the test standard deviation times the square root of the proportion of unexplained or error variance:

$$SEM = S_y \sqrt{1-reliability}$$

A second useful formula is the Spearman-Brown prophecy formula. This formula allows us to estimate the reliability of a test whose length has been modified. This allows us to predict what would happen to test reliability if we shortened a test or added items to it.

Proofs of these and other formulas based on true-score model assumptions may be found in most graduate-level measurement textbooks (e.g., Allen & Yen, 1979; Magnusson, 1966).

Another index derived from the assumptions of the true-score model is the internal consistency reliability coefficient:

$$\alpha = \frac{N}{N-1}\left[\frac{\sigma^2 - \Sigma\sigma_i^2}{\sigma^2}\right]$$

where $N$ = the number of items on the test and $\sigma^2$ or it's sample estimate, $S^2$, is the variance in test scores. The remaining term, $\sigma_i^2$, represents the sum of all the individual item variances. The formula given is for Cronbach's alpha, the general case. If items are dichotomous, $S_i^2 = \Sigma p_i q_i$. With this change, one has the KR-20 which is the theoretical average of all possible split-halves of a test.

Reliability may also be estimated by the correlation between repeated administrations of a test (stability reliability), between parallel or alternate forms of a test (equivalence reliability), or split-halves of a test (internal consistency). These indices can be calculated for a test regardless of the measurement model adopted. Their interpretation under the true-score model is that the value of the correlation between test administrations or test forms represents the proportion of test variance which is true variance. Each administration of a test to a subject group has a standard error of measurement and has one or more estimates of different forms of reliability associated with it. The standard error of measurement is used to set intervals around the true score. Assuming error to be normally distributed and assuming interval measures, statements can be made about the level of confidence we have that the interval contains the observed score. However, obtained scores are generally nonlinear (noninterval) with standard errors that vary with score and thus such statements can, in fact, be misleading.

The source of variation (or error) in test scores more recently has been investigated with generalizability theory as an extension of the idea of reliability. A reliability coefficient is defined as the ratio of true to observed score variance. A generalizability coefficient is defined as the ratio of universe score variance to expected observed score variance. Generalizability is the reliability of a test when generalizing over different universes (e.g., items, raters, subjects). Thus, a test may have different generalizability coefficients which reflect its reliability over different universes.

Other measures associated with the true-score model are person score, item difficulty, and item discrimination. A person's score in the true-score model is the number correct or sum of item responses over all items or a linear transformation of that score based on a guessing correction. (The guessing correction is usually:

$$CS = RS - (NWA/NC\text{-}1)$$

where $CS$ = corrected score, $RS$ = raw score, $NWA$ = number of wrong answers, and $NC$ = number of choices.) Item difficulty is the mean item score or proportion answering the item correctly ($p$). Item discrimination is usually measured by the point biserial correlation between the item response and total test score for a person (in the case of dichotomous items) or the simple correlation between item response and total test score (in the case of graded response items). The point biserial is usually corrected for inclusion of the item score in the total score. Highly discriminating items are those with a high correlation with total test score. These test and item indices will be revisited in Chapter 2 in greater detail.

### *Benefits and Criticisms of the True-Score Model*

Test construction methods and score interpretation associated with the true-score model have been useful in calling attention to the fallibility of test scores and in providing a gross measure of test score accuracy. The *Standards for Educational and Psychological Testing* (AERA, APA, NCME, 1985) states that for each reported test score, estimates of reliability and the standard error of measurement should be provided in sufficient detail to allow users to judge whether scores are accurate enough for the intended purpose. Reliability coefficients have been used as a guide to test selection. Reliability coefficients have further been used to predict the potential reliability of lengthened or shortened tests and the validity coefficients of perfectly reliable tests (correction for attenuation). As a gross overall measure reflecting test accuracy, the reliability coefficient has seen extensive use. Various definitions of reliability (stability, equivalence) may have prompted consideration of the characteristic being studied; e.g., does this attribute remain stable over the time between measurements?

Inferences about test scores have been made using regression estimates of true scores and the standard error of measurement. The idea of homogeneity was introduced and applied with regard to a test's internal consistency. Total test score and $p$-values have been used, respectively, as indicators of a person's ability and of how difficult items are. When making ordinal comparisons within a given group, either of persons or items, this remains a useful procedure. Again, though, scores are nonlinear and lack additivity.

Finally, the true-score model is the easiest measurement model to understand for many since it is the most familiar and, in terms of computation, the easiest to use when the situation is limited to a single test given to one group. The individuals most intimately concerned with educational and psychological measurement on a day-to-day basis are classroom teachers who tend to use single tests given to just one group. Without computers, simple score counts might be the most teachers have time for. The simplicity of the true-score model approach to measurement makes it the model used by persons who are unaware that measurement models exist.

The true-score model, then, has provided some straightforward measures of person scores and item difficulty. It has also pointed out the importance of the concept of error in test scores and provided some measure of error. It has further introduced the idea of stability of test scores across time and across forms. It has also probably encouraged the development and use of tests.

The true-score model has, however, been criticized since its inception (see Walker, 1931-32), with critics' voices growing in number and strength. Some of the points of criticism are reviewed here. True-score theory provides a single standard error of measurement to reflect inaccuracy in test takers' scores, regardless of score. It has long been known that the degree of inaccuracy in scores generally increases at the extreme ends of the score distribution. The standard error of measurement may be a reasonable reflection of error at the center of the distribution but is misleading otherwise. It appears that in practice, a relationship exists between true score and the amount of error which contradicts one of the true-score model's assumptions. Since the variability in test and item score is maximized when items are of a uniform ($p$ = .5 to .65) difficulty level, advice to test constructors has been to select items of uniform difficulty. This automatically would create a test which measures most accurately at the ability level reflected by items with $p$ = .5-.65 difficulty, and less accurately at other levels.

The internal consistency reliability coefficient has been used as a measure of test homogeneity, of test quality, and so has been used for test selection. But, the value of the internal consistency reliability coefficient for any test is dependent upon (1) the item set on the test and (2) the population or sample taking the test. The coefficient also reflects the method used to assess reliability. While it is a guide to test selection, there may be better guides. Maximizing internal consistency reliability involves selecting items which are uniformly highly discriminating, or highly multicollinear. Carried to an extreme, this means selecting items which are perfectly correlated and thus completely redundant. (As the correlation between items is increased, information contained in raw scores is decreased.)

The true-score model has proven ineffective in dealing with many practical problems in testing. Person score and item difficulty estimates obtained using the true-score model are dependent on the distribution of item difficulties and person scores as are point-biserial correlations. They change when a new sample of items or persons is selected. This sample-dependence of person and item parameters makes the true-score model less than optimal for test equating, for setting a fixed mastery standard, and for providing stable estimates of person ability or item difficulty. Use of the true-score model in mastery testing, for instance, provides a migratory standard rather than a defined standard representing some judged level of competence. The true-score model also fails to provide an effective way of dealing with item bias and test design.

Finally, the true-score model does not meet one of the basic requirements of a theory: that it be testable. True scores and errors scores are not observable. There is no evaluation of fit to the model and thus the appropriateness of the model for the data can neither be supported nor disproven. The *accuracy* of use of a measure (reliability, standard error of measurement) can be evaluated numerically but not the appropriateness of the measurement model itself. The difference between the model itself and use of the model is analogous to the difference between establishing rules for *constructing* a meter stick complete with hashmarks and *using* the meter stick to measure height. The true-score model lets us assess how well we can use our ruler but doesn't inform us about its construction. The failure to generate testable propositions marks the failure of the true-score model as theory.

In summary, the sample dependence of the true-score model means that a number of test users' concerns cannot be effectively addressed (item bias, equating, item banking, standard setting). It provides an inaccurate estimate of the error in test scores, especially at the high and low ends of the score distribution. Although the approach to measurement the true-score model takes in counting the number right is simple and practical, the model itself is inadequate. An estimate of accuracy of use is available in the reliability coefficient but there is no assessment of the fit of data to the model and no guidelines for how the measure itself is constructed, how it works, or what its characteristics are. One characteristic of a measure assumed by many statistical manipulations is that of interval scaling. The true-score model does not provide interval scaling, particularly at the high and low ends of the scale. So while the true-score model has provided practitioners with an easy method of reporting test results, decades of work with true-score theory have diverted educators' attention from the basic issue of what measurement means and what characteristics a measure should have. These concerns were among those that led to consideration of different measurement models. The measurement theory receiving the greatest attention in the past two decades is item response theory. This will be briefly reviewed in the next section.


## ITEM RESPONSE THEORY


Item response theory models relate a person's amount of a trait or ability to the probability of correctly answering an item via a mathematical model. The most common application of IRT in testing is with multiple-choice items although IRT can be applied to other item types if they are numerically scored (such as true-false, completion, etc.). As was noted in the previous section, a problem with true-score theory is that the statistics derived from testing are dependent upon characteristics of the sample and of the test. IRT provides test and person statistics that are relatively invariant. This relative invariance is a major advantage if we take the task of assessing how much a person knows or can do seriously.

When people learn, we assume there is some internal store of skill and information they are building and adding to. This internal change results in changes in ability. When a test is given, we want answers to the test questions to reflect how much of the ability the person possesses. Since we cannot actually see the ability directly, the ability is sometimes referred to as a latent trait. IRT ties a person's pattern of responses to test questions to a number that represents that person's amount of the latent trait. The ability continuum extends from minus infinity to plus infinity, but in practice most values of the numbers representing ability fall between -3.0 and +3.0. (The difficulty of items and other test characteristics are also estimated in concert with person ability.) The relationship between what can be observed (the item responses) and the unobservable (the trait) is described by mathematical functions.

These mathematical models are based on assumptions about the test data; each mathematical model makes somewhat different assumptions about the data. There are currently three IRT models in common use that rest on three different sets of assumptions. The assumptions made by all IRT models are stronger than those made by true-score theory. The IRT assumptions include that of *unidimensionality*. Unidimensionality means that one dominant ability underlies test performance. This implies that other factors such as anxiety, motivation, or other abilities play minor roles in test performance. If more than one ability is necessary to numerically explain test performance, the requisite model would be multidimensional.

Multidimensional IRT models are not well developed at this time. The assumption of *local independence* is met if an examinee's responses to one item in no way affects her responses to other items. This assumption would be violated if an item had to be answered correctly to get the next question right or if one item provided a clue to other items. A further assumption of IRT models is that tests are administered with reasonable time limits (i.e., the tests are not highly speeded), that the sample of persons taking the test are a suitable group, and that examinees will answer the items correctly if they know the right answer. No test model will provide useful results if the test is totally off target for that group's level of ability or development or if examinees are careless or elect to mark incorrect answers. Other assumptions made depend upon which IRT model is selected. The most commonly used IRT model is called a one-parameter model or the Rasch model (Rasch, 1966). The mathematical function tying ability to item response is:

$$P_i(B) = e^x/(1 + e^x)$$

where $x = B\text{-}D$. $P(B)$ is the probability of getting a correct answer for this item given ability level $B$; $B$ is a person's ability; $D$ is the difficulty of the item; $e$ is the exponential function. The probability of getting the item right, then, is determined by the difference between how capable the person is and how difficult the item is *(B-D)*. If a very capable person answers an easy item, the probability of a correct answer would be high. If a less capable person answers a very difficult item, the probability of a correct answer would be low.

The Rasch model incorporates no explanatory parameters for item discrimination or for guessing. If these parameters were incorporated, we would have a two- or a three-parameter model. The Rasch model is more restrictive than the two- and three-parameter models since it requires that all items be approximately equal in discrimination and does not accommodate guessing. Presentations of two- and three-parameter models may be found in Hambleton and Swaminathan (1985) or Baker (1985).

If one plots the function $e^x/(1 + e^x)$, one obtains the following curve:

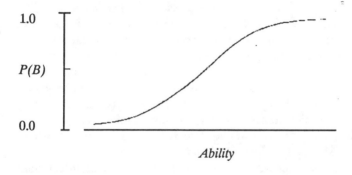

*Ability*

This curve is very similar in shape to the cumulative density function of a normal (bell-shaped) curve, but the logistic function is much easier to work with than the equation for a normal curve. As can be seen from the figure, as ability increases the probability of getting the item correct increases. So, IRT models are mathematical models that describe S-shaped curves.

With true-score theory, our measure of a person's ability is their score on the test, most often the number right. If the test is longer, the score is different than if the test is shorter. If the test has somewhat different items, the person's score may be different. The number we use to represent a person's ability, then, is arbitrary in many ways.

With IRT models, our measure of a person's ability is not dependent upon the particular set of items the person answered but the scale is still arbitrary. That is, we could equally well use a scale of 0-100 or a scale where scores could range from 100-1000. For convenience, the scale used is set to have a midpoint of zero and a practical range of -3 to +3. Lower numbers (negative values) correspond to less ability and higher numbers (positive values) correspond to more ability. Ability values on this scale may be interpreted (cautiously) in a manner similar to interpreting $z$-scores when using a standard normal curve. In IRT, ability is based upon how a person answers each item and less on an aggregate of items such as the total test score. IRT analyses give the user more information than true-score theory because each item-person interaction can be reviewed.

With true-score theory, our measure of an item's difficulty is the proportion of people who answer the item correctly. If the group taking the test is more capable, item difficulty values may be higher than if the group taking the test happens to be less capable. The number we use to represent an item's difficulty, then, is arbitrary because it changes from group to group. With IRT models, our measure of an item's difficulty is less dependent upon the particular group of persons given the test but the scale is still arbitrary. Again, for convenience, the scale used is set to have a midpoint of zero and a practical range of -3 to +3. Lower numbers (negative values) correspond to easier items and higher numbers (positive values) correspond to more difficult items. The scale used for item difficulty is the same scale used for person ability.

Thus, in IRT, answers to individual items are used to estimate person ability and item difficulty. But, how are these values estimated? If we're estimating person ability, initially an *a priori* value is used for the ability of each examinee. This value is often a function of the number of items a person gets right. Generally using an estimation procedure called maximum likelihood, the *a priori* or starting value is used to compute the probability of observing that person's particular string of responses. The *a priori* value is then altered slightly and the probability of the string of responses is recalculated. If the probability based on the second starting value is higher than the probability based on the initial *a priori* value, the second value for ability is used. The process continues until changing the starting value has a negligible effect on the probability of observing that string of responses. When maximum likelihood estimation is used, the item responses for each person are entered into a computer file and IRT software is used to obtain ability values. However, an approximation to the maximum likelihood estimate can be obtained using the following formula (Wright & Stone, 1979; p. 27):

$$B_i = H + (1 + V^2)^{1/2} ln[r_i / (L - r_i)]$$

where $B_i$ is person $i$'s ability estimate, $H$ is a measure of test difficulty, $V$ is a measure of the variance of item difficulties, $L$ is the number of test items taken, and $r_i$ is person $i$'s test score. While hand calculations may be time-consuming, all of these values can readily be calculated. If we are estimating item difficulties, the process is analogous. Wright and Stone (1979) provide a step-by-step procedure for hand calculation of ability and difficulty indices.

Since with IRT we can make predictions about how a person with ability $B$ would respond to an item of difficulty $D$, and since the person actually answers the items, we can see whether our prediction was good or poor. That is, we can assess how well the data fit our model. This assessment of fit can give us information about whether the person is responding to the test in the way we expect. For example, if a person of high ability misses the first few easy items on the test, it could be due to a start-up or acclimatization effect. We would want to consider this in our evaluation of that person's performance. Smith (1986) has identified response patterns that may stem from guessing, test anxiety, external distractions, fatigue, and plodding. The measure of fit serves as a marker to locate persons with unusual response patterns. Analogously, we can locate items to which responses are unusual.

Important features of IRT that are advantageous include: the relative invariance of person ability and item difficulty values, more precise values for error of measure, the power to estimate person ability from any reasonable set of items letting us give different tests to different persons, and the same interval scale for both persons and items. These advantages are useful in creating computer-adaptive tests, in detecting item bias, and in equating test forms as well as in better understanding the interaction between a person and an item. The disadvantages of IRT are its mathematical complexity in comparison to true-score theory and the need for computer analysis.

The next section of this chapter reviews concepts common to both classes of models described here.

## *Concepts Common to the True-Score and IRT Models*

If the true-score model is more familiar to you, it may help you to understand the concepts common to the true-score and IRT models and the ways in which they are alike and different.

First, item difficulty in the true-score model is the proportion of people answering an item correctly or the mean item score. It is not measured on an interval scale and is sample dependent. This index is also called item difficulty in IRT models but is calculated using a linearizing logistic transformation of the ratio of items right to items wrong. This transformation produces an interval scale (provided the response patterns meet the model's assumptions) and provides estimates of item difficulty independent of the distribution of person ability in the sample. The IRT item difficulty is in a one-to-one relationship with the item $p$-value. The relationship is curvilinear and involves adjusting for person ability. The logistic function $ln[(1-p_j)/p_j)]$ transforms the item $p$-value, which is not a linear reflection of the latent variable, into a new value which is linear. The logit value expresses the item difficulty on an equal interval scale with the effects of sample variance and sample mean removed.

Person ability is not really estimated by the true-score model. Expected test score is estimated by the person's raw score or number correct. Expected test score is sample dependent and not necessarily on an interval scale. The IRT model equivalent is called person ability. It is independent of the distribution of item difficulties and has interval scale properties. As with the item $p$-values, the logit function transforms the person scores which are not linear into a linear metric adjusted for test width and shifted to adjust for test difficulty level. The resulting person ability logit is freed from the effects of the test and becomes a sample-free measure.

Item discrimination in the true-score model is usually measured by the point biserial correlation. It is sample dependent. The IRT model analogue is also called the discrimination index. The discrimination index is also sample dependent; it is a measure of the linear trend of the item residuals. The value of this item discrimination index is not bounded by +1.0. This index is sensitive to items that fail to correlate with test score and also to items that correlate too highly with test score.

The index analogous to Cronbach's alpha or the KR-20 in the true-score model is called reliability of person separation in the IRT model. Its value ranges from 0.0 to 1.0 and although the computation seems different, the interpretation is the same (i.e., higher numbers indicate a higher level of reliability).

Finally, the standard error of measurement in the true-score model is based on the standard deviation of the sample of person scores and on the test reliability. It takes the same value regardless of the raw score (or true score). The standard error of measurement in the IRT model takes on a value for each different raw score, is a function of the test information, and is sample free.

Applying IRT models in test development gives us new versions of the old statistics. These new statistics contain all of the old familiar information but in a form which solves many of the measurement problems that have always beset traditional test construction.

## TEST THEORY

Item response theory is aptly named. It is a model of what happens when a person responds to an item. True-score theory is perhaps less apt; it does not qualify as theory nor does it provide a measurement model meeting practical needs. Neither item response theory nor the true-score model provides a complete theory of testing. Test theory must include a measurement model, a model to assess the accuracy of test use, and a model for assessing measure validity. No single existing theory or model provides this.

IRT models are measurement models. They are used to provide measures of ability/difficulty. The measures obtained are interval in nature provided the data fit the model. The models provide the process by which the ruler, with hashmarks, is developed. They also provide an index (standard error) noting how accurate its use will be when measuring different objects (items, persons) and indices indicating whether those objects can be measured with this ruler (item and person fit statistics).  These methods also provide information about how the measure can be improved.

IRT methods provide considerably more information than the true-score model.  What is not provided by either is evidence of validity--content, criterion-related, or construct.  Validity is an essential part of test theory.  Content validity is established by professional judgment.  IRT methods do not obviate the need for professional judgment but do provide data informing such judgment. Criterion-related validity is established by correlating different measures.  IRT methods provide better measures but they still must be correlated and the resulting matrix interpreted.  Construct validity is established using content validity and criterion-related validity together with logical analysis.  IRT methods, again, inform judgments but do not eliminate the need for judgment.

## REFERENCES

American Educational Research Association, American Psychological Association, National Council on Measurement in Education Joint Committee 1985. *Standards for Educational and Psychological Testing.* Washington, D.C.: American Psychological Association.

Allen, M.J., & Yen, W.M. 1979. *Introduction to Measurement Theory.* Monterey, CA.: Brooks/Cole.

> This book has seen frequent use as the text for psychometric theory courses. It presents classical test theory in depth but also contains several chapters outlining item response theory.

Baker, F.B. 1985. *The Basics of Item Response Theory.* Portsmouth, NH: Heinemann.

> This is a very readable book that comes with computer software providing exercises in item response theory. The software is available in both Apple and IBM versions.

Birnbaum, A. 1957. "Efficient Design and Use of Tests of Mental Ability for Various Decision Making Problems." U.S.A.F. School of Aviation Medicine, Rep. No. 58-16, Randolph, TX.

Birnbaum, A. 1958a. "On the Estimation of Mental Ability." Series Report #15, U.S.A.F. School of Aviation Medicine, Randolf, TX.

Birnbaum, A. 1958b. "Further Considerations of Efficiency in Tests of Mental Ability." Technical Report No. 17, Project No. 7755-23, U.S.A.F. School of Aviation Medicine, Randolph Air Force Base, TX.

Coombs, C.H., Dawes, R.M., & Tversky, A. 1970. *Mathematical Psychology: An Elementary Introduction.* Englewood Cliffs, NJ: Prentice-Hall.

Cronbach, L.J. 1951. "Coefficient Alpha and the Internal Structure of a Test." *Psychometrika, 16,* 297-334.

> This paper presents the algebraic development of the internal consistency reliablity coefficient used with continuous data.

Cronbach, L.J., Glaser, G.C., Nanda, H., & Rajaratnam, N. 1972. *The Dependability of Behavioral Measurements: Theory of Generalizability for Scores and Profiles.* NY: John Wiley.

> This text explains and presents examples of use of generalizability theory. Generalizability theory is an extension of the idea of reliability to provide coefficients that reflect consistency across different domains.

Finney, D.J. 1944. *Probit Analysis.* NY: Cambridge University Press.

Galton,F. 1869, 1952. *Hereditary Genius: An Inquiry into Its Laws and Consequences.* NY: Horizon Press.

Hambleton, R.K., & Swaminathan, H. 1985. *Item Response Theory: Principles and Applications.* Boston: Kluwer-Nijhoff.

> This text provides a readable introduction to item response theory (one-, two-, and three-parameter models) and also contains chapters describing IRT use in test construction, test equating, and item banking.

Krantz, D.H., Luce, R.D, Suppes, P., & Tversky, A. 1971. *Foundations of Measurement*, Vol. 1. NY: Academic Press.

> This text presents axioms and proofs underlying conjoint measurement models.

Kuder, G.F., & Richardson, M.W. 1937. "The Theory of the Estimation of Test Reliability." *Psychometrika, 2,* 151-160.

This papers presents the development of the first measure of internal consistency reliability. The KR20 is used with dichotomous data.

Lawley, D.N. 1943. "On Problems Connected with Item Selection and Test Construction." *Proceedings of the Royal Society of Edinburgh, 61,* Section A, 273-287.

Lawley, D.N. 1944. " The Factorial Analysis of Multiple Item Tests." *Proceedings of the Royal Society of Edinburgh, 6,* 273-287.

Lord, F.M. 1952. "A Theory of Test Scores." *Psychometric Monographs, 7.*

Lord, F.M. 1977. "Practical Application of Item Characteristic Curve Theory." *Journal of Educational Measurement, 14,* 117-138.

Lord, F.M. 1980. *Applications of Item Response Theory to Practical Testing Problems.* Hillsdale, NJ: Erlbaum.

In this book, Lord provides methods and examples that explain item response theory and describe how it can be usefully applied to measurement problems.

Lord, F.M. 1983. "Small N Justifies Rasch Methods." In D. Weiss (Ed.), *New Horizons in Testing.* NY: Academic Press.

Magnusson, D. 1966. *Test Theory.* Reading, MA: Addison-Wesley.

This text provides a concise introduction to classical test theory.

Rasch, G. 1947. "Recent Biometric Developments in Denmark." *Biometrics, 4,* 172-175.

Rasch, G. 1960, 1980. *Probabilistic Models for Some Intelligence and Educational Tests.* Copenhagen: Danish Institute for Educational Research; Chicago: University of Chicago Press.

Reprinted in 1980, this work presents the mathematical development of the one-parameter model.

Rasch, G. 1966a. "An Individualistic Approach to Item Analysis." In P.F. Lazarfeld & N.W. Henry (Eds.), *Readings in Mathematical Social Sciences*. Chicago: Science Research Associates.

Rasch, G. 1966b. "An Item Analysis Which Takes Individual Differences into Account." *British Journal of Mathematical and Statistical Psychology, 19,* 49-57.

Richardson, M.W. 1936. "The Relationship Between Difficulty and the Differential Validity of a Test." *Psychometrika, 1,* 33-49.

Smith, R.M. 1986. "Person Fit in the Rasch Model." *Educational and Psychological Measurement, 45,* 433-444.

This unique paper attempts to understand why people may produce unusual patterns of response to items. Smith hypothesizes several reasons for erratic item responses (such as plodding--missing items at the end of the test due to slow working speed). Smith cautions agencies using tests for placement to examine and possibly retest persons with unusual response patterns.

Spearman, C. 1904. "The Proof and Measurement of Association Between Two Things." *American Journal of Psychology, 15,* 72-101.

Terman, L.M. 1916. *The Measurement of Intelligence.* Boston: Houghton-Mifflin.

Thorndike, E.L. 1904. *An Introduction to the Theory of Mental and Social Measurement.* NY: Science Press.

Tucker, L.R. 1946. "Maximum Validity of a Test with Equivalent Items." *Psychometrika, 11,* 1-13.

Walker, D.A. 1931-32. "Answer-pattern and Score-scatter in Tests and Examinations." *British Journal of Psychology, 22,* 73-86.

Wright, B.D. 1968. "Sample-free Test Calibration and Person Measurement." In *Proceedings of the 1967 Invitational Conference on Testing Problems*. Princeton, NJ: ETS.

Wright, B.D. 1977. "Solving Measurement Problems with the Rasch Model." *Journal of Educational Measurement, 14*, 97-116.

    This entire issue of JEM addresses IRT with positions taken pro and con.

Wright, B.D., & Masters, G.N. 1982. *Rating Scale Analysis*. Chicago: MESA Press.

Wright, B.D., & Stone, M.H. 1979. *Best Test Design*. Chicago: Mesa Press.

    This book provides the first easily readable presentation of the Rasch model. It explains how item difficulty and person ability can be calculated by hand, describes fit statistics, and explains the possible uses of this IRT model.

# RELIABILITY, VALIDITY, AND TEST SCORE INTERPRETATION

## KATHY E. GREEN

This chapter provides a review of basic concepts needed to understand and use educational tests. More thorough presentations may be found in texts such as those by Sax (1989) or Anastasi (1988); more advanced information on developments in psychometrics may be found in the third edition of *Educational Measurement* (Linn, 1988). This chapter reviews the concepts of test reliability and validity and then presents a synopsis of the definition and interpretation of commonly used types of test scores.

## RELIABILITY

Reliability, whether obtained via classical test theory or item response theory, refers to the extent to which information obtained from a test is consistent. If information is reliable, it can be used confidently as the basis for making decisions about placement, grades, educational programs, etc. If information is less reliable, other sources of information in addition to a test may be sought for use in decision making.

There are several types of reliability. Consistency over time is referred to as stability (or test-retest) reliability; consistency over different test forms is equivalence (or alternate or parallel forms) reliability; consistency across raters or scorers is interrater reliability; and consistency within a single test itself is called internal consistency reliability. Stability, equivalence, and interrater reliability are each assessed by calculating the correlation between two sets of scores. (See the texts mentioned above for an explanation of correlation.) In stability reliability, the correlation is calculated between time 1 and time 2 scores; in equivalence reliability, the correlation is calculated between form 1 and form 2 scores; in interrater reliability the correlation is between (or among) raters' scores.

Factors that influence the value of the correlation include how variable the tested group is in ability (or attitude). Test reliability for groups that are more diverse will tend to be higher. This is because when differences among individuals are more striking, orderly relationships are more clearly visible. The value of a correlation depends on consistency in ordering across sets of scores.

A second major factor influencing the value of the reliability coefficient is the difficulty level of the items. If items are generally too easy or too hard for the group taking the test, the reliability will tend to be lower than if items are of moderate difficulty. The most information is obtained from tests with items that are appropriately targeted for the group (or person, with item response theory).

A third factor affecting reliability is the number of questions on the test. Longer tests tend to be more reliable than shorter tests. This is due, at least in part, to greater potential variability of scores with longer tests. Other factors such as item clarity, clarity of instructions, and freedom from distractions during the test are also important. Tests that are constructed with more care will tend to be more reliable than tests that are not reviewed and inspected before administration. When interrater reliability is of interest, reliability will be increased by providing training for raters.

Internal consistency reliability is calculated via the formula given in Chapter 1 and is termed either Cronbach's alpha or the Kuder-Richardson 20. Internal consistency reliability will tend to be higher if items are all related to the same underlying construct. That is, if internal consistency reliability is to be high, the items must be homogeneous. If multiple constructs or abilities are assessed by the same test, the overall reliability will be low. Adding apples and oranges doesn't work when constructing a highly internally consistent test. And, the factors affecting correlations mentioned previously will also affect internal consistency reliability. A form of internal consistency that preceded coefficient alpha was the split-half reliability coefficient. This was calculated by correlating one half of a test with the second half. The difficulty with this formulation lay in deciding how to divide the test since different divisions resulted in different split-half coefficients. Coefficient alpha has essentially replaced split-half coefficients. Alpha is the theoretical average of all possible split-half coefficients.

An index associated with reliability is the standard error of measurement defined in Chapter 1. The standard error of measurement is an indicator of how many points off we may be in estimating a student's "true" score. To be 95% sure we have captured a true performance value, we can form a range by adding and subtracting approximately two standard errors of measurement to and from a student's score. For example, if the obtained test score for a student was 82 and the standard error of measurement was 4 points, the range that we are 95% confident would include the student's true score is from 74 to 90. Using a range reminds us that we have imperfect measures and helps prevent over-interpretation of test scores.

All of these formulations of reliability may be applied with the results of norm-referenced or criterion-referenced tests. However, if applied to the data from criterion-referenced testing, the reliability values obtained are likely to be low since the variance of scores on criterion-referenced tests is usually severely limited. Therefore, numerous methodologies to assess the reliability of criterion-referenced tests have been developed in recent years. Berk (1984) has defined three categories of reliability: (1) reliability of mastery classification decisions, (2) reliability of criterion-referenced test scores, and (3) reliability of proportion correct scores. He suggests that one useful index is the consistency of mastery/nonmastery decisions. This is calculated by administering two mastery tests covering the same content and counting the number of consistent decisions across the two tests. When divided by the number of persons taking both tests, this forms an index of agreement.

Citations of reviews of these methodologies used to assess the reliability of criterion-referenced tests and more information about the methods may be found in Berk (1984).

# VALIDITY

Validity refers to the extent to which true statements can be made using test results. For example, if a test accurately predicts success in a future job, then we can make truthful statements about who is likely to succeed at the job and who is not. No *test* is ever valid--the results may be more valid for specific purposes, less so for other purposes, and not at all for some purposes or for some persons. Validity is a judgment based on conceptual and empirical evidence about the truth or usefulness of test scores or other assessments in making inferences. As Messick (1989) states, "...what is to be validated is not the test or observation device as such but the inferences derived from test scores or other indicators--inferences about score meaning or interpretation and about the implications for action that the interpretation entails" (p. 5).

Most validity coefficients are expressed using correlation coefficients. The higher the value of the correlation, the higher the test validity. All of the comments made above regarding factors that affect correlations apply here as well. That is, the more diverse the group, the higher the validity coefficient is likely to be. There are many types of validity, each designating appropriateness of use in a particular situation. The more commonly referenced types of validity are content, criterion-related, and construct validity. Face validity and factorial validity are also frequently used terms. Each of these is defined in the succeeding paragraphs.

Content validity refers to whether test content adequately samples some domain of content. If the content domain is roughly represented by 50% historical facts and 50% analyses of sequences of events, test content should roughly reflect this breakdown. But one rarely explicitly knows the breakdown of a content domain in terms of percent of time or material devoted to different topics, so judgments are simply made regarding whether test items seem appropriate for that domain. Breakdowns in terms of time or material are reflected by the test table of specifications.

Judgments about whether test item content reflects the domain are made by persons with expertise in the domain. These persons could be teachers, consultants, or other associated professionals. The decision about each test item could be simply "appropriate" or "inappropriate", or could be a scale value (e.g., 1 = poor, 5 = excellent). Content validity can be expressed in terms of agreement among experts or may less formally be an unquantified sense of consensus about which items are good and which are not. Teachers are probably most concerned about the content validity of the tests they themselves construct and use in their classrooms.

Criterion-related, or predictive, validity refers to how accurately a test can predict some future outcome such as job success, academic success, etc. Tests such as the Graduate Record Examination or the Scholastic Aptitude Test are intended as predictors of academic success at the graduate and undergraduate levels, respectively. If the test has higher validity, it has a higher correlation with the outcome measure. Teachers who are involved in academic or vocational counseling would be concerned with the criterion-related validity of tests. Factors affecting the value of a criterion-related validity coefficient include the time between measurement of the predictor (the test) and the outcome. Prediction tends to be more accurate over shorter than over longer time periods. A second factor is whether the test is used for selection purposes. If so, those persons not selected would be unavailable for assessment on the outcome measure. This preselection is likely to reduce the variance of scores and so reduce the criterion-related validity. The validity coefficient is also affected by the reliability of both the predictor and the outcome measure. If the individual measures are unreliable, they cannot be highly correlated except by chance.

Construct validity refers to the extent to which a test accurately measures how much of a hypothetical trait is possessed by a person. Intelligence is a construct as are creativity, introversion, and authoritarianism. Construct validation relies on clear definition of the construct, evidence about what test scores relate to and what they do not relate to, and logical analysis. If two constructs are logically related, scores on their respective measures should reflect that relationship. This is termed convergent validity. If two constructs are logically unrelated, scores on their respective measure should not be correlated. This is termed discriminant validity. Content validation and criterion-related validation are both invoked in support of the validity of a construct. While most teachers may not be directly required to validate tests of constructs, teachers use such tests or employ people who do. Whenever a student is referred for diagnostic psychological testing, the examiner makes some judgment about the construct validity of the tests used. If the tests are not judged to be construct valid, there is little point in using them. If they are judged to be construct valid, the examiner needs to understand exactly what the construct is and what the evidence is supporting its validity in order to understand what types of decisions can be made using information from the test(s).

Face validity refers to whether the test in question seems to be a reasonable measure for its intended purpose. This judgment is made based on test review for relevance and importance.

Factorial validity is determined through use of a statistical analytic technique called factor analysis. The purpose of factor analysis is to find the item (or test) groupings underlying a large number of items (or tests). These groupings are called factors. In designing a measure, the author may write items addressing various aspects of the overall test theme. For example, if creating a mathematics test, items addressing computation, story problems, and math concepts may be written. Factor analysis then determines which items empirically group together. In this example, one would expect three factors to emerge--computation, story problems, and math concepts. Factorial validation, then, is determined by how well the empirical result of a factor analysis reflects the test author's original design. Subsequent to factor analysis, the test users have a better sense of how items related empirically. Factorial validation, then, allows one to make statements about what different facets of a construct are assessed by a test. For information on factor analysis, the reader may wish to consult Cureton and D'Agostino (1983) or Tabachnick and Fidell (1989).

Standardized test scores are used with increasing frequency to report how well a school or program is doing in different academic areas. (Chapter 7 discusses issues in the use of standardized tests.) Since funding and program decisions may be tied to test scores, it is crucial to understand and accurately report scores on a school, district, and state-wide basis. The measurement process, then, has a strong connection to instructional decisions at global levels. The measurement process also has a strong connection to the instructional process within the classroom. Prior to instruction, the teacher needs to know where students are in their learning. This information may be obtained from many sources, one of them being an entry test. The question is: What will provide enough information to plan instruction for this student? Formal or informal procedures can be employed. If procedures are formal such as any type of test or quiz, the test should give reliable, valid information. If a test does not provide reliable, valid information, it should be used for research purposes rather than for decision making. If information is only moderately reliable, judgments should be tempered by this knowledge.

To maximize reliability, tests should be longer rather than shorter, have clear instructions and items, be objectively scored, have relatively easy items, and should be administered to a diverse group (not always possible, of course). To maximize the validity of a classroom test, it should be as reliable as possible and should be explicitly linked, item for item, to what has been taught.

## TEST SCORE INTERPRETATION

The number of items answered correctly is a person's raw score. This score is essentially meaningless until compared to some external referent. The external referent could be an absolute standard, as in competency testing, or a relative standard, as in norm-referencing. Even if converted to a percent correct score, the raw score has little meaning by itself--the percent correct depends upon whether the test was easy or hard.

Three ways to provide information regarding relative standing are percentiles, standard scores, and equivalent scores. Percentiles reflect the percentage of persons who scored at or below a particular score. If a raw score of 50 corresponds to a percentile rank of 78 it means that 78% of the sample taking the test received raw scores of 50 or less. To determine the percentile rank for any raw score, one must have access to the distribution of scores. One difficulty with percentiles is that the difference between two percentiles (e.g., 95 and 90, 55 and 50) is not the same at all points. The difference in raw score units between 95 and 90, for example, is greater than the difference in raw score units between 55 and 50. Thus, changes in percentile rank mean different things depending upon where on the distribution someone starts. Another difficulty with percentiles is that, as with other types of scores, they may appear to convey greater precision than they actually possess. Score reports should be accompanied by a clear statement regarding error of measurement. When explaining percentile rank to others, it could be emphasized that percentile rank is totally different from percentage correct. A major advantage of percentiles, though, is that they are easy to understand.

Standard scores express relative position as number of standard deviations away from the mean. The scale used is arbitrary--just as height can be measured in feet or meters. The person's height stays the same; the ruler or scale differs. Some commonly used standard score scales are $z, T$, deviation IQ, and GRE-SAT scales. A $z$ scale translates the test mean to take a value of 0.0 and sets the standard deviation to 1.0. To convert from a raw score to a $z$-score, one finds the difference between the score of interest and the group mean $(X-M)$ and divides this difference by the standard deviation of the scores. This results in scores that may be negative and take decimal values (e.g., -1.27). A $T$ scale translates the test mean to 50 and sets the standard deviation to 10. This eliminates negative values and most decimal values. A deviation IQ scale sets the test mean at 100 and the standard deviation at 15 (sometimes 16) while tests such as the GRE and SAT have means of 500 and standard deviations of 100. On the last two scales, scores are expressed as positive, whole numbers.

Stanines (standard nines) are scores based on scale segments rather than single points. Stanines range from 1 to 9, with 5 representing average performance. Any score falling within .25 standard deviations of the mean is given a stanine value of 5. Scores that fall between .25 and .75 standard deviations above the mean are given a stanine value of 6. The use of stanines prevents over-interpretation of small score differences.

All standard scores require that the group mean and standard deviation be known. To interpret a standard score as a percentile, it is assumed that scores on the trait are normally distributed. (Some procedures force the score distribution to match a normal distribution.) When the standard score is known and a normal distribution is assumed, raw scores can be expressed as both standard scores and as percentiles.

Scores can be interpreted with reference to different norms. Score distributions for defined groups are called norms. For instance, two groups might be (1) all high school seniors and (2) all applicants to 4-year colleges who are currently high school seniors. A student's test score could be interpreted with reference to both sets of norms.

Equivalent scores are translations of a raw score by comparison with average scores obtained by students in the same grade or at the same age. Again, it is essential to know the distribution of scores for the appropriate groups. If a test publisher were establishing grade equivalents for a test to be used with the fourth grade, samples would be tested from grade 3.0 to grade 5.9 and the score distributions plotted. Average scores for students in each group would be calculated. The average raw score obtained by third graders becomes a 3; the average raw score obtained by seventh graders becomes a 7. These scales are grade equivalents. Grade equivalents are generally reported by grade and month. A 3.0 represents September of third grade; 5.9 represents June of fifth grade.

While seemingly easy to interpret, grade and age equivalents have drawbacks. They are heavily dependent upon how well the test matches the curriculum and the sequencing of instruction at that grade level. They depend upon grade promotion practices. The grade equivalent does not indicate the level of work a student is capable of. If a third grade student has a score of 5.0 it does not mean the student can do fifth grade work. It means the third grader has scored as highly on the test as the average fifth grade student taking the same test in September. It means the third grade student did well on the test. Grade equivalents have a wider range at higher grade levels since abilities tend to become more diverse. Thus a student who was a little below the mean at grade 3 is likely to be further below the mean at grade 7 because the scale variance is not constant from grade to grade, nor is there equivalent progress from month to month. Further, grade equivalents should not be compared across tests or across content areas since, again, the variances tend to differ. Age equivalent scores have the same problems in interpretation.

Results of criterion-referenced tests are often reported as percentages. Percentages of items correct, percentages of objectives mastered, and percentages of students mastering an objective may all be reported. Many criterion-referenced test report sheets also provide norm-referenced information.

For more complete information regarding test score interpretation, the reader may wish to consult Sax (1989) or an introductory statistics text such as that by Glass and Hopkins (1984).

Facility in test score interpretation has become increasingly important in recent years as test information has been more widely publicized and used by groups empowered to make decisions affecting schools. It is also increasingly important if teachers and administrators are to take advantage of the added information available to them via use of computers and sophisticated testing software.

# REFERENCES

Anastasi, A. 1988. *Psychological Testing (6th edition).* NY: Macmillan.

Berk, R.A. 1984. *A Guide to Criterion-Referenced Test Construction.* Baltimore: Johns Hopkins University Press.

Cureton, E.E., & D'Agostino, R.B. 1983. *Factor Analysis: An Applied Approach.* Hillsdale, NJ: Lawrence Erlbaum.

Glass, G.V., & Hopkins, K.D. 1984. *Statistical Methods in Education and Psychology (2nd edition).* Englewood Cliffs, NJ: Prentice-Hall.

Linn, R.L. 1989. *Educational Measurement (3rd edition).* NY: Macmillan.

Messick, S. 1989. "Meaning and Values in Test Validation: The Science and Ethics of Assessment. *Educational Researcher, 18(2),* 5-11.

Argues that construct validity is inherent in all other types of validity. The ethics and social consequences of validation are discussed.

Sax, G. 1989. *Principles of Educational and Psychological Measurement and Evaluation (3rd edition).* Belmont, CA: Wadsworth.

Concise text presenting basic information on test selection, construction, and interpretation. Used as text for undergraduate and graduate introductory tests and measurement courses.

Tabachnick, B.G., & Fidell, L.S. 1989. *Using Multivariate Statistics (2nd edition).* New York: Harper and Row.

# ASSESSMENT OF GIFTED CHILDREN

## RAYMOND KLUEVER

Earlier chapters of this book described the historical and conceptual framework of assessment as a process. The focus of this chapter will be the applications of these processes to our work with gifted and talented (G/T) children.

This chapter includes a brief overview of some of the major historical events concerning identification of the characteristics of G/T persons followed by a model for assessing them and then some specific assessment techniques and measures used with them. The stress of the model is, first of all, on the interactive nature of children's characteristics with school, community, and cultural norms, and second, on the purposes for assessing gifted children. A major section of the chapter is a discussion of selected measures that are useful in assessing G/T children. A greater number of cognitive/achievement measures are to be found than measures in the affective or psychomotor domains. And, finally, some directions for future developments in the assessment of gifted children are suggested.

Children identified as gifted are generally thought to possess a number of outstanding abilities such as highly developed intellect, creativity, leadership skills, and special talents in certain areas. Special talents in the arts are quite common. Gifted children display a broad range of these many abilities but in different proportions. Therefore, one child's giftedness may differ greatly from another's.

In the Gifted and Talented Children's Education Act of 1978, Section 902, the following definition of gifted children was provided.

39

For the purposes of this part, the term "gifted and talented children" means children and, whenever applicable, youth, who are identified at the preschool, elementary, or secondary level as possessing demonstrated or potential abilities that give evidence of high performance capability in areas such as intellectual, creative, specific academic, or leadership ability, or in the performing and visual arts, and who by reason thereof, require services or activities not ordinarily provided by the school (Public Law 95-561, p. 2292).

Within the range of exceptionalities of children, the gifted child is beginning to receive a greater proportion of attention than in previous years. Although they are at the upper end of the continuum of abilities and are thought by some to be perfectly capable of functioning independently, they are as deserving of scarce educational resources as any other student. For all students, assessment is an integral part of the identification, curricular programming, and evaluative process of educational programs. The potential of the gifted child as a contributor to the well being of all society requires that we utilize our limited educational resources to capitalize on this opportunity. We can use our knowledge of assessment to reach this goal of providing the very best educationally enriching opportunities that are possible for gifted children so that they may become major contributors to progress in the world.

Terman's (1925) longitudinal study of a sample of 1528 gifted children represented an early venture in the assessment of this specific group of persons. He used the 1916 Stanford-Binet scale to identify them (I.Q.'s 135 to 200). Data were gathered from a number of sources to describe this sample as physically superior and as having a somewhat lesser prevalence of commonly reported social maladjustments. Their level of academic achievement was high and they had a significantly greater number of advanced degrees and educationally rewarding experiences than did persons in the general population. In follow-up studies, the group was described as producing many more publications and holding a disproportionately greater number of professional and managerial positions.

In another study of the patterns of development of gifted persons, Witty (1940) gathered data on 50 gifted children on a regular basis who were matched with a control group of 50 normally bright children. The pairs were followed from 1924 to 1940. Witty also reported observing outstanding accomplishments of gifted persons in school and in their adult life, just as Terman found. In New Zealand, Parkyn (1948) followed a group of 50 bright children and found results similar to those of Witty and Terman.

A somewhat different study was conducted by Leta Hollingworth (1942). She studied a smaller number of extremely bright persons and described them as being more solitary and probably having difficulty in relating to other persons. Their I.Q.'s were described as being among the highest one could find and their potential contribution to society enormous.

Other studies of the developmental patterns of gifted persons are similar to those reported above. Individuals with high IQ levels tend to be very successful in academic and in life pursuits and to contribute significantly to the welfare and leadership of society. It is important to identify these children early and to describe their outstanding characteristics so that we may provide optimal educational programs for their development.

## THE GIFTED ASSESSMENT MODEL

In Figure 1, a three-dimensional model for the assessment of gifted children is proposed. The purposes for assessment are noted on the front face of the model; the domains for assessment (cognitive, affective, and psychomotor) on the second face; and concerns for the within-child (internal) variables and external environmental variables are on the third face of it.

Figure 1

*Model for the Assessment of Gifted Children*

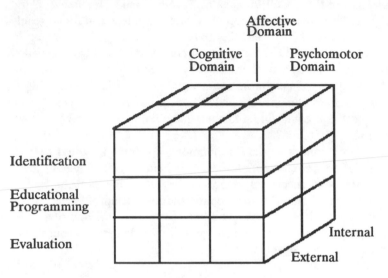

Purposes for assessment include identification for program eligibility, identification of child learning and behavioral characteristics which are important for individual program development, and finally, evaluation of child progress. For each of these three purposes, three domains of development can be specified. These are the cognitive domain, the affective domain, and the physical/psychomotor domain. The content of each of these domains has been specified; the cognitive domain by Bloom (1956), the affective domain by Kratwohl (1956), and the psychomotor domain by Harrow (1972). And, for each of the three purposes and for each of the domains, there can be internal child variables (the child's own abilities and characteristics) and external system variables (family, school, and cultural/ethnic background) which impact on all of the above considerations. That is, family, school, and community characteristics may affect the criteria used for program identification and may also be determiners of the relative importance of the child's personal characteristics considered in developing that specific educational program. The model is an interactive system with components from each of the three dimensions influencing others and presenting a complex assessment problem for the educator of gifted children.

In practice, identification for program eligibility and the determination of a child's learning characteristics are often accomplished at the same time. The nature of a child's cognitive abilities and their academic achievement are generally a major concern in these early assessment endeavors. But, concerns for the child's affective and physical/psychomotor characteristics have not received the same degree of attention in assessment. They are more likely to be determined through published rating scales or checklists, observations, and from the reports of other adults. However, the relationships among these three dimensions of the model are critically important for individual program development. Also, the interactions of the child's identified characteristics with those of the school and community system must be considered. Evaluation of children's progress is a continual, on-going process. As a result of evaluations, there is a need to update and/or change some of the earlier specified program components. Progress in the cognitive domain is frequently a major concern in evaluation but there are instances where special interest is expressed in the affective and psychomotor areas. They may be the focus of major changes rather than the emphasis on change in the cognitive domain. Social-emotional status, behavioral patterns, and physical-coordination abilities can be such that program alteration to accommodate them is most important.

Within each area, there are also internal or "within child" characteristics and "external" or system characteristics that lend direction to the assessment process. The internal characteristics are fairly well known and include descriptors from the cognitive, affective, and psychomotor/physical domain of the child. The external characteristics include system parameters; the rules of the community, school, neighborhood, and cultural norms that impact the identification process, important instructional variables, and the content of the evaluation. The internal and external variables are interactive. The important child characteristics to be identified for program eligibility or for instructional programming are the ones that the system values. Assessment processes which do not take system priorities into account are rather futile in that there will not be a good match between child characteristics and educational program goals and objectives. This mismatch may be reflected negatively in the child's perceived progress.

The assessment model described above is the conceptual basis for the assessment strategies and techniques to be described in the following sections of this chapter. Assessment of G/T children is viewed as a systematic process which takes into account the integration of child and environmental variables gathered from completed assessments and which impact on the developmental and educational progress of gifted children. Assessment is a data gathering process which facilitates decision making for program eligibility, educational program development, and evaluation of progress. Specific procedures, instruments, and approaches will be discussed in the following sections.

### *Program Eligibility*

Assessment of children for program eligibility must take the program characteristics into account. The focus of many programs is highly academically oriented but others are focused more on the arts, leadership abilities, creative abilities, or on physical coordination of individuals. And, a number of programs are a synthesis of several emphases. Assessment for program eligibility implies that children have certain defined characteristics which are different in some way from those of children in general and those persons who have these defined characteristics are eligible to participate in these uniquely designed experiences.

Norm-referenced measures can be very useful for identifying those children who meet program requirements. In the cognitive domain, measures of intellect and academic achievement status are often used as indicators of eligibility. Some of these measures are group administered and some are designed to be administered individually. In each program, a "score" or cut-off point on each instrument must be established which differentiates eligible children from ineligible children. This score may be a percentile (i.e., the 98th percentile), a stanine (i.e., the 9th stanine), or a standard score (i.e., 130) on that instrument.

In addition to norm-referenced tests, some facilities use checklists and/or rating scales to provide additional information for identification. Both published scales and scales developed within a facility have been used. Informal systems involving recommendations of self or others for participation are also in use. Performance measures with specific criteria for eligibility continue to be developed by different schools. Generally, a combination of several criteria are used to make decisions about program eligibility. These criteria are associated with the school, community, and ethnic/cultural concept of what constitutes giftedness for a particular program; i.e., the external "system" variables.

### Individual Program Planning

Differences found from child to child suggest that individualized educational programs may be valuable ways to optimize each child's educational experiences. Child management strategies based on children's affective/behavioral characteristics need to be developed to complement well planned educational programs which are generally more cognitively and achievement oriented. Assessment data for individual program planning utilize tests, observational systems, and scales just as used in the identification phase of G/T assessment but with different purposes in mind. Individual program planning takes into account both the level of performance and the unique problem solving approaches and information processing styles of children. It provides instructional guidance for teachers in terms of preferred teaching approaches to accommodate children, types and characteristics of materials, optimum length of instructional time, top-down v. bottom-up approaches, simultaneous v. sequential approaches, etc. Some children regularly produce very accurate, neatly prepared work requiring much time, but others are less concerned about detail and turn in work which was done quickly and without a high degree of precision. Test behavior and observed approaches to problem solving during assessment can identify some of these characteristics. They are important for individual program planning.

*Evaluation of Progress*

Evaluation of progress is continual and is often carried out on an informal basis through observation of children's daily work. But, more formal systems of evaluation can be conducted. Progress over time can be measured by comparing work samples from a given time to a later designated time. Normed test data, observations of performance, and specially prepared scales can be used as measures of progress. Evaluation activities serve the purpose of monitoring the progress of children to provide for changes in programs as needed to facilitate their optimal growth. And, evaluation is important to determine whether children's progress continues to parallel program objectives. That is, are these identified G/T children a good match for the nature of the educational activities that have been specially designed for them in that specific program.

The following sections provide information about the measures used in assessing various characteristics of gifted children. Most of the activity has been concentrated in the cognitive and achievement areas.

## MEASURES USED IN THE COGNITIVE DOMAIN

Some measures that have been used commonly in assessing intellectual abilities of G/T children are discussed below. The commonly used psychological tests such as the Stanford-Binet LM (Terman & Merrill, 1973) or Stanford-Binet 4th ed. Scales; Fourth Edition (Thorndike, Hagen, & Sattler, 1986) as well as the Wechsler Intelligence Scales - Revised (Wechsler, 1974) are administered by psychologists but many other measures can be administered by teachers. In a recent study comparing these two Binet scale scores for the same 51 children referred as gifted (Kluever & Green, 1989), the mean Composite Score of the SB-4 was found to be a little over 10 points lower than the mean SB-LM IQ. Only 9 of the 51 children in this sample had SB-4 Composite Scores that were the same or a little lower than the SB-LM IQ. Psychologist-administered tests will *not* be reviewed here since they have already been discussed in many other sources. Furthermore, these tests can be administered only by psychologists who have the formal preparation and the credential to use them. Reviews of the Wechsler Intelligence Scales can be found in Buros' *Ninth Mental Measurement Yearbook* (Mitchell, 1985), the SB-LM in the last several editions of Buros' *Mental Measurement Yearbook,* and SB-4 reviews will probably appear in the new 10th edition. The SB-4 technical manual has reviews of studies in which that test was used with samples of gifted children (Thorndike, Hagen, & Sattler, 1986).

Often, the teacher-administered tests are given to groups of children, but there may be special situations in which the tests will be administered to one child at a time. It will be important that the directions and time allocations be followed precisely in order to obtain valid results consistent with the test's standardization.

Multitrait systems for identifying gifted children are commonly advocated, but it is not unusual for measures of cognition to receive major emphasis in decision making for program eligibility. Group-administered tests of cognition have been used for screening for program eligibility, while individually administered tests may be used as follow-up assessments for more refined decision making and for determining a child's special learning characteristics. Group measures are efficient. They allow for screening many children in a brief period of time at minimum cost for materials and personnel time. Although these group-administered measures are efficient, there are certain precautions to be observed in using them. The typical upper limit to the norms of group tests may be a limiting factor. Small changes in the number of items correct may alter scores significantly. Children's motivation or understanding of directions may result in lower scores. Group tests typically measure a narrower range of cognitive abilities than the individually administered tests and provide less information for individual educational program development. These are, after all, group screening measures for initial identification, not highly developed clinical tools that have years of empirical research data to support them.

These measures of cognitive ability are important tools in the assessment of gifted children. The history of attempts to measure intellectual abilities can be traced to events of over a century ago. Initially, measures of physical, perceptual, and sensory abilities were thought to be very important abilities to be included in investigations of individual differences among people. But, changes in our concept of what constitutes cognitive abilities and in our approaches to measuring it have occurred over the years. Today, cognitive ability continues to be viewed as a unitary trait (one thing) as it has since the early 1900s but there is increasing interest in the research and development of scales for measurement of intellect as a composite of many different abilities. This is known as the multifactorial concept of intelligence (Cattell, 1971; Gardner, 1983; Guilford, 1956). More recently, a trend toward viewing intellect in terms of the information processing abilities of the human being has emerged (Das, Kirby, & Jarman, 1979; Sternberg, 1981). Chapter 11 of this volume reviews current thoughts about intellect from the viewpoint of a cognitive psychologist.

Commonly available measures of cognitive ability have the characteristics described above. That is, some of them are measures of intellect as one thing, but others represent multifactorial approaches to the measure of intellect, and some of them are measures of human information processing abilities. One's choice in using these measures with gifted children will be based on the purposes for the assessment and on unique program characteristics and curriculum to facilitate a good fit of child to program and on the internal/external characteristics of the model. Commonly used measures are described on the following pages.

## Checklists and Rating Scales

Checklists and rating scales are commonly used assessment devices for screening children for program eligibility. The scales can be completed quickly and provide information concerning the merits of further in-depth assessment. It is important for the respondent to know the child well in order to obtain reliable results. The theoretical basis for the scale and the content of the items are important considerations in decisions to adopt and use any particular instrument. Checklists and rating scales should be regarded as screening instruments and follow up activity with additional measures for reliable decision making should be undertaken.

Waters (1989) completed a thorough evaluation of the Silverman/Waters Checklist for Identifying Gifted Elementary School-Aged Children (Silverman, 1980). The items of the scale are based on the characteristics of identified gifted children they observed over many years of their work with them at the Gifted Child Development Center in Denver. Through continual refinement, the checklist was found to be sensitive in identifying gifted children. Outcomes of the checklist closely approximated identification based on their larger, comprehensive test battery.   This checklist, completed by parents, contains items in different areas of the child's development, learning characteristics, and topics of interest. In Waters's study, teachers also completed the checklist and comparisons were made between parent's and teacher's impressions.

The results of a validation of the checklist (Waters, 1989) indicated that the scale has acceptable psychometric characteristics. The Cognitive Abilities Test and the Gifted and Talented Screening Form were used as criteria for validation.   Waters reported a "low percentage of agreement" (p.164) between children identified as gifted on the checklist and on each of the two validating instruments.   It is possible that each instrument may be tapping somewhat different aspects of children's development.   A factor analysis of the checklist for parent responses and then for teacher responses indicated that the factor structure is somewhat different for each group.   Parent responses indicated that they tended to be more concerned with the creative, social, artistic, spatial reasoning, learning aspects of their child's talents whereas the teacher's responses seemed to emphasize the learning, social/emotional   maturity,   creative   thinking,   individualization characteristics of children. The instrument seems to be constructed and validated with care and has considerable value as a screening instrument for identifying young gifted children, although additional validation studies are indicated.

The Gifted and Talented Screening Form (Johnson, 1980) has also been used for identifying young gifted children.   The items are arranged in clusters such as a cognition cluster, etc. which represent the areas that are commonly identified as characteristics of gifted children. It is a short, 24-item self report checklist with reliability reported to be .90.   However, information concerning its validity is not reported, and no theoretical rationale or definition of giftedness is provided.

These are examples of rating scales and checklists that are available for the purpose of screening children for eligibility for programs for gifted children. Teachers need to review the  scales to determine which one(s) are most appropriate for the goals and objectives of their specific program.

## The Coloured Progressive Matrices Test

The Coloured Progressive Matrices (1984 edition) test (Raven, Court, & Raven, 1984) has been used for the identification of gifted children; especially those with different language and experiential backgrounds.  The items seem to require a more visual-spatial analytical ability with little demand for English language facility.  The demonstration used on the first test item facilitates giving directions to non-English speaking children.  It has been described by the authors as being composed of three

> Sets A, Ab, and B arranged to assess mental development up to the stage when a person is able to reason by analogy to adopt his way of thinking as a consistent method of inference.  (Raven et al., p. CPM2)

In the discussion of the validity of the test, the authors indicate that the

> CPM has a high 'g' loading with the visual-spatial 'k' factor involved to some degree.  The test is not one of "pure intelligence" but it does measure a person's intellectual output in a rather pure factorial sense.  (Raven et al., p. CPM22)

Studies by Das et al. indicate that the test loads highly on the simultaneous processing factor.

The CPM requires that children select one of six forms to complete a given visual pattern.  The test is available in both a booklet and in a formboard format and may be administered to groups of persons or to one individual at a time.   Several norm tables are supplied based on different samples of persons.  The norms are given as percentiles (5th through 95th) for children from five and one-half through eleven and one-half years using the 1982 standardization.  In addition, amended norms for ages five and one-half to eleven years and extrapolations of norms for ages three and one-half to eleven years are also given (Raven et al., p. CPM40).  The Standard or the Advanced Progressive Matrices tests rather than the CPM may be used with more mature persons. Those norms are more appropriate for their age and level of maturity.

Research in progress (Green & Kluever, 1990) on use of the CPM test with young gifted children indicates that it has much to recommend it as an appropriate instrument for them in assessing general intelligence. The items were found to be discriminating and of a sufficient range of difficulty. Over half of the subjects had CPM scores above the 75th percentile and one third of the children had scores at the 90th percentile or higher. The median Stanford Binet LM IQ of this sample of 51 children was 133. A clear trend of increase of raw score with increase in age was found. Some inconsistencies of Binet IQ's and Raven percentiles were found and may be due to the nature of the different kinds of items found on the two scales. The Binet is a more verbally oriented test while the CPM has visual spatial types of items. A three-factor solution to analysis of the item responses of these gifted children with a varimax rotation resulted in factors which resemble the characteristics that Raven described as the three dimensions of the CPM (Raven et al., p. CPM22). In summary, there is strong evidence that the CPM is quite sensitive for identification of gifted children but these children may have some different kinds of cognitive capabilities than those identified with more verbally oriented measures.

### Tests of Cognitive Abilities and Achievement

The Cognitive Abilities Test (Form 4) (Thorndike & Hagen, 1986) is a group-administered test of cognitive abilities which has been used with gifted children for some time. The three major components of the test sample an individual's verbal, quantitative, and nonverbal reasoning and problem solving abilities which are important for success both in school and in the wider environment. The Primary Battery is designed for younger children (K-3) while the Multilevel edition is for older students (Grades 3-12). Raw scores can be converted into standard scores, percentiles, and stanines. A composite score and scores from each of the three components are provided. This test is reported to be a measure of learned abilities, not innate abilities.

Scores correlate highly with the Iowa Test of Basic Skills and have value in predicting academic outcomes.

The Otis Lennon School Ability Test is another measure that can be used to describe the cognitive abilities of gifted children. Its purpose is to "provide an accurate and efficient measure of the abilities needed to acquire the desired cognitive outcomes of formal education." Test items reflect primarily the Verbal Education factor, i.e., language and academically oriented tasks. The reported psychometric characteristics suggest that it has value for use in identifying gifted children.

In the literature on gifted children, Guilford's Structure of the Intellect (SOI) concept (Guilford, 1956) is often cited as a model which is descriptive of human intellectual abilities. This SOI model is the basis for the Structure of Intellect Learning Abilities Test (SOI-LA) which has been developed to provide a profile of SOI abilities in individuals (Meeker, Mestyanek, & Meeker, 1975-81). Twenty six of the 120 factors of the SOI were selected for inclusion in the SOI-LA test. An individual's profile on each of the 26 factors is derived from the test, but a single (I.Q. like) score cannot be calculated. A special Gifted Screening form of the test using fewer than the 26 factors is available from the publisher, Western Psychological Services. Systems for intervention based on an individual's SOI profile have been designed and are used in some schools as a part of the curriculum for gifted children. Several reviewers comments concerning the SOI-LA test can be found in Buros' *Ninth Mental Measurements Yearbook* (Mitchell, 1985).

The Screening Assessment for Gifted Elementary Students (SAGES) includes three areas; aptitude, achievement, and creativity (Johnsen & Corn, 1987). It is advertised as being "helpful in identifying children who are gifted." Administration is appropriate for small groups or individuals aged seven years to twelve years eleven months. Norms are provided for gifted and for normal children. The technical characteristics and the norming of the test which are described suggest that this instrument has been carefully constructed.

Among the tests of academic achievement, a large number of choices are available. The commonly available group-administered achievement test batteries which are a part of annual school testing programs have been used as well as certain individually administered achievement tests. These tests assess the typical achievement areas such as reading, math, spelling, language arts, etc. These tests provide a relatively fast, efficient way to test many children and are cost effective, but it is not possible to observe the individual performance of a child for individual program planning. Individually administered tests are more suitable for such observations.

The Wide Range Achievement Test (WRAT), a frequently used individually administered test, was initially standardized in 1936 but has been revised several times since the original standardization (Jastak & Wilkinson, 1984). It is intended to measure reading word recognition, math computation, and spelling. The revised 1984 edition (WRAT-R) has a number of technical enhancements which reflect current test construction theory and improved format and ease of. Age norms, standard scores, and percentiles are provided for children from five years of age through adulthood.

The wide range of difficulty of the items of the test makes it attractive for assessing the level of academic attainment of gifted children. Generally, gifted children have high levels of academic achievement. A rich source of instructionally relevant information on the WRAT-R comes with observation of children's problem solving strategies. These strategies can be observed as children compute the solution to arithmetic problems, decode reading words, and sequence the letters of words dictated to them as the spelling test. The phonetic skills employed in reading and spelling, the system used in solving arithmetic problems, and their knowledge of sound-letter associations in spelling and reading are useful information in planning individualized instructional programs. Norms are useful in identifying children for program eligibility, but observations are a rich source of supplementary instructionally relevant information.

The WRAT-R can be administered in a relatively short time which is an advantage but leads to the necessity of each item contributing significantly to the total score. Since each score is based on a limited number of items, test taking behaviors become critically important variables in interpreting them. Inattentiveness, lack of persistence, and poor motivation and cooperation can be factors that may underlie unexpected low scores. Examiners need to be sensitive to these behaviors and provide some judgement of the reliability of the obtained score.

The Peabody Individual Achievement Test - Revised (PIAT-R) is an individually administered test of academic achievement which has had some limited use with G/T children at this time. It is a new test (Markwardt, 1989) patterned after the original PIAT (Dunn & Markwardt, 1970). Experience with the PIAT-R characteristics for gifted children needs to be developed. The manual contains descriptive information concerning normal and handicapped individuals but studies concerning the use of the PIAT-R with gifted children were not found. The PIAT-R has many revised and new items, updated norms, and the addition of a test of written expression.

The PIAT-R is easily administered and provides measures of achievement in the areas of general information, reading word recognition, reading comprehension, mathematics, spelling, and written expression. Standard scores, grade equivalents, percentiles, and stanines are provided for each of the areas tested. The test covers a broad range of skills (K-12) in a relatively short time. Therefore, each item contributes significantly to the total score. The written expression subtest may be omitted if desired.

The advantage of the PIAT-R is the opportunity to observe the student's problem-solving approach and to judge the reliability of the test score based on the observations of the subject's test behavior. However, testing one subject at a time is expensive and time consuming for the examiner.

Since this is a new instrument our experience with it is limited. But, it has been found that gifted children's scores on the PIAT-R were lower than on the PIAT. This often happens when new or revised tests become available. Second, the written expression subtest did not add appreciable information above that gleaned from typical classroom-assigned written expression exercises (Hafenstein, personal communication, 1989). More experience and larger samples of gifted children need to be tested with the PIAT-R to acquire a better understanding of its usefulness with this special population.

## The Stanford Diagnostic Achievement Tests

In order to develop specific educational plans for students, it is necessary to gather data to determine their present performance level and then to plan for an increase in skill development based on that initial assessment. Informal inventories of skills may be utilized to determine present performance levels or one may use published tests. Diagnostic tests have been found to be useful for this purpose. Many diagnostic tests are available and typically reflect the author's viewpoint concerning the important concepts (expressed as test items) to be measured.

An example of a series of published tests that has been useful for this purpose is the Stanford Diagnostic Reading Test (Karlsen & Gardner, 1986) and the Stanford Diagnostic Mathematics Test (Beatty, Gardner, Madden, & Bjorn, 1984) published by the Psychological Corporation. These tests can be administered to groups of children or to individuals. Each item and some clusters of items are tied to specific curricular content and educational objectives. The items represent the reading and mathematics skills that were determined by the author to be important for children to have learned. There are four levels of the Stanford test, each spanning several grade levels. The first level is for beginning learners (grades 1 and 2) while the fourth level is for high school students.

As one might expect, the four levels of the Stanford Diagnostic Reading Test vary in content from the first (primary grades) through the fourth level (high school). At the first level, there is heavier stress on reading vocabulary and reading decoding skills, but at the fourth level the emphasis is on comprehension and interpretation of reading passages. At the high school level, five different types of comprehension are tested ranging from basic literal understanding to more abstract interpretive skills. The items and clusters of items defining each of these 5 comprehension skills are defined in the test manual.

The Stanford Diagnostic Mathematics Test (Beatty et al., 1984) can also be individually or group administered. Three math tests-- number systems, computation, and applications--occur at each of the four levels (primary through high school). The major difference among the levels is an increase in the number and variety of computational items at each level. Items pertaining to the number system and numerical applications also become increasingly more difficult as one moves toward the high school level. As with the reading test described above, the curricular content of the items and clusters of items are defined in the manual and can be used for individual program development.

Although diagnostic tests are typically designed for students experiencing educational difficulties, they can have considerable value for gifted students. The profile from these tests provides a convenient, easily interpreted present performance level of gifted students. This profile is useful in planning a sequence of learning experiences which will extend and broaden a student's repertoire of skills beyond their present level. A problem associated with use of common diagnostic tests with gifted students is the difficulty level of items. The items specified for a given range of grades are often too easy for bright children, and a more advanced level of the test is needed to provide items of sufficient difficulty to establish a valid performance level for instruction. A teacher's knowledge of the student's everyday performance can adjust for this difficulty in teacher-constructed tests. In published diagnostic tests, it may be desirable to use a more advanced level of the test in order to establish a ceiling level for gifted children.

*Writing Assessment*

Writing is a highly complex cognitive linguistic task which develops gradually over many years of education. Parent's reports of their gifted child's developmental history indicates that they begin writing lists and short meaningful expressions in the preschool years (three to four years old) and then extend this skill to very complex writing patterns in later years (Kluever, research in progress). The length, complexity, and creative nature of their written expression is often rather remarkable for their age.

There are several existing systems for the assessment of written expression. Some have used global approaches which provide an over-all rating of the quality of one's written expression while others have used a more analytical approach in which specifically defined writing skills have been evaluated. The choice of approach depends on one's concept of writing assessment. In global approaches, the criteria for different ratings of the written product are defined, and raters are provided with practice to calibrate their consistency of scoring (inter-rater reliability). In general, a group (class) of children provides samples of writing which are then evaluated by an individual or a small team of raters. Assessment can be accomplished fairly quickly and economically.

Published tests which have norms for different components of writing such as the Test of Written Language-2 (Hammill & Larsen, 1988) and the Picture Story Language Test (Myklebust, 1965) have defined aspects of writing which can be assessed. In the Picture Story Language Test, for instance, writing is conceptualized via three major variables: quantity of writing, correctness of writing, and the abstractness of writing. Abstractness (the Concrete/Abstract scale) is of special interest in assessing the writing of gifted children. Twenty-five levels of increasingly more abstract story themes are described in the manual. The level that most closely approximates the child's story theme and the accompanying age norm is assigned to that child's level of story abstractness.

The combination of how much children write, the correctness, and abstractness provides valuable information to establish children's present performance level in writing and provide further direction for individual educational plans in writing. It is a critically important skill for children to develop; especially for gifted children, many of whom have the potential for outstanding accomplishments in this area.

### Creativity Measures

Gifted children's highly developed creative abilities are often mentioned in the literature. Creativity is a construct and establishing an operational definition for it has been difficult. Measures of creativity have been developed by different authors and represent their own concept of it. Measures have been developed by Torrance (1984), Meeker et al. (1975-81), Johnsen and Corn (1987), and Guilford (1971).

In the SOI-LA tests (Meeker et al., 1975-81), measures of

divergent thinking are included.   Divergent thinking is, again, a construct which seems to be highly related to creative qualities in the human being.   Components of divergent thinking that are often included in measures of creativity include fluency, flexibility, originality, and elaboration.

The Torrance Tests of Creative Thinking (Torrance, 1984) are a commonly cited measure of creativity.   There is a long history associated with them and they have been used extensively in research on creativity.   There are two sections; the Verbal tests, from which scores for fluency, flexibility, and originality are derived and the Figural Tests, from which we get measures of fluency, flexibility, originality, and elaboration.

Measures of creativity should be used cautiously and should not be over-interpreted for making major decisions concerning children's programs.   Use for research and experimental purposes may be preferable to use for individual program planning since their validation continues to be an unresolved problem.


## THE AFFECTIVE DOMAIN


There were fewer instruments and studies identified that are primarily concerned with the evaluation of gifted children's affective status than of the cognitive/achievement domain.   Tests for the assessment of gifted children's self concept, temperament, and social maturity are available.   Published and unpublished behavior checklists and rating scales have also been used as devices for describing children's behavior patterns.   Program descriptions and studies using these measures have been reported in the literature.

## Self-Concept

The Perceived Competence Scale For Children (Harter, 1982) is a commonly used instrument for assessing self concept. A study by Keeley (1989) indicated that it is conceptually sound and appropriate for gifted children. The instrument is in a rating scale format and requires a self-report from children about their opinions (self-concepts) of how they view themselves. Several areas of self-concept are measured including impressions of one's cognitive ability, social self-concept, physical abilities, general self concept, etc. A general finding of studies of gifted children's self-concept using the Perceived Competence Scale is that it is similar to that of normal, children but the area of self-concept in the cognitive area is higher than the norm (Katz, 1981). The Perceived Competence Scale can be administered individually or in small groups. It has demonstrated value for the assessment of self-concept in gifted children. But, children's protocols that vary significantly from the norm should be reviewed with a mental health professional.

The Piers-Harris Self Concept Scale (The Way I Feel About Myself) was designed for children in grades 4-12 (Piers & Harris, 1969-84). It has been used in some programs with gifted children but with some question raised about the factor structure of the Piers-Harris Scale for this group of children (Keeley, 1989). It is an 80-item self-report inventory with "yes" or "no" responses indicating that certain statements indicate the way a child feels about him/herself. The manual is well prepared and the authors' claims about the test are consistent with research findings. As with other affective measures, a mental health consultant should be available to review the results. Its use for research purposes seems warranted, but use for identification and program planning purposes should be carried out with caution.

The Coopersmith Self Esteem Inventory (Cooper, 1984) is a self-report checklist of 10 areas of self-esteem. It is recommended that local norms be developed. The Coopersmith scale has three self-report inventories that measure one's evaluation of oneself. One form is for children aged eight to fifteen years and another for the sixteen year to adult level. Although the reliability and validity studies are technically adequate, the norms that are provided are reported by reviewers to be based on an inadequate sample of subjects. Its use for research purposes would seem to be most appropriate.

Temperament is a less studied construct in gifted children than self-concept. Conflicting findings using the Martin Temperament Scale for Children (Martin, 1988) have been reported. Some relationships to I.Q. and achievement have been reported in the test manual, but in a recent study of the temperament of young gifted children based on parent report, few significant relationships were found (DeLano, 1989).

There are three forms of the scale: one for clinicians, one for parents, and one for teachers. Each parent, rating their child independently, may produce very different profiles. Similarly, any of the other raters; clinicians, parents, or teachers, may rate a child very differently than the others. These variations may reflect differences in one's experiences and/or expectations of the child. The Martin scale should be regarded as a clinical instrument and used accordingly. Further research with this scale is needed, but it has potential as an assessment instrument to extend our understanding of gifted children.

### Social Maturity

Adaptive behavior as measured by the Vineland Adaptive Behavior Scale (VABS) was defined as "the performance of daily activities required for personal and social sufficiency" (Sparrow, Balla, & Cicchetti, 1984, p. 6). In a further clarification of the definition, they stated that adaptive behavior is: 1) "age related," 2) "is defined by the expectations or standards of other people," and 3) "is defined by typical performance, not ability." The VABS is made up of 4 areas; communication skills, daily living skills, socialization skills, and motor skills. At ages above five years, the motor skills section of the test is no longer used. The test was standardized on a large sample of children and has some impressive psychometric characteristics. Through an interview process with the parent serving as the informant, the child's typical performance is described and a score for each of the areas is determined. A total score is also calculated.

A review of a large number of assessment records using the VABS suggests strongly that the adaptive behavior of gifted children is significantly above the norm. Their part scores and total scores are commonly at the 80th to 90th percentiles or higher but very few of them are below the 50th percentile. A comparison of the VABS scores of gifted and non-gifted children indicated that the major significant differences were in more highly developed socialization skills among the gifted (Sherry, Bowles, & Kluever, 1989). Other variations in gifted children's profiles may be identified on an individual by individual basis and consultation with a mental health professional may be advisable if very unusual patterns are observed. At this time, the profile of the VABS would seem be best used as a basis for educational programming, for development of behavior management strategies, and to facilitate the understanding of group dynamics.

Other adaptive behavior measures might be considered but may result in a somewhat different impressions of a child's pattern of adaptive behavior. The test items and then the clusters of behaviors (items) that constitute adaptive behavior are based on each test author's concept of this characteristic. Hence, variations in outcomes may be due to use of different tests.

The Normative Adaptive Behavior Checklist (NABC) is "a descriptive test of adaptive behavior" and indicates "how well a child compares to peers of his/her age (birth to twenty-one years) in performing skills needed for independent living" (Adams, 1984b, p. 2). The NABC is in the form of 120 item "yes-no" checklist with clusters of items in the areas of 1) self-help skills, 2) home living skills, 3) independent living skills, 4) social skills, 5) sensory and motor skills, and 6) language concepts and academic skills. Norms for "normal" students and "retarded" students are provided. The value of this instrument for gifted children may be in the extent to which the items are descriptive of their adaptive functioning within their own environment. Additional research concerning the use of this scale with gifted children is needed.

The Comprehensive Test of Adaptive Behavior (CTAB) is very similar to the NABC but has many more items (Adams, 1984a). There are 497 items for males and 527 items for females. As the title implies, it is far more comprehensive in nature than the NABC and can have value in more detailed assessments of gifted children.

The Adaptive Behavior Inventory for Children (ABIC) is a component of the System of Multicultural Pluralistic Assessment (Mercer & Lewis, 1977). There are six components in the inventory;

adaptation to family, community, peers, non-academic school roles, earner-consumer role, and self-maintenance. A parent or primary caretaker responds to a number of multiple-choice questions read to them in terms of their perception of their child's habitual adaptive behavior patterns. Differences among standard scores for each of the six areas may have diagnostic significance. The composite score for a small sample of gifted children was found to be within the mid-range of scores as usually found for normal children. This is different than findings on the Vineland Adaptive Behavior Scale where gifted children were found to score at the upper percentiles. The skills and behaviors tapped by each instrument are probably different ones.

Adaptive behavior is another aspect of functioning within the larger environment and is an indication of the extent to which one achieves independence of functioning. Assessment of these skills in G/T children is important and results can be incorporated into individual educational programs as a part of the child's learning to adapt successfully to one's community and school, the "external" part of the gifted assessment model.

## THE PSYCHOMOTOR DOMAIN

In the psychomotor domain, assessments tend to be observations of children's abilities. Gross motor skills, fine motor skills, and coordination are typically the areas that are of concern in assessments. Measures of these skills and abilities exist but are typically used by therapists, special educators, and psychologists when problems are identified or for research studies rather than for identifying or preparing educational programs for gifted children. In gifted children, motor skills may be very highly developed resulting in outstanding athletic and performance skills. These observed skills need to be nurtured just as achievement or cognitive abilities are encouraged in children.

## SUMMARY AND CONCLUSIONS

An optimal educational program for gifted children requires some assessment to determine program eligibility, appropriate educational programming, and evaluation of progress. Community, school, and cultural expectations of what constitutes an appropriate program for gifted children interacts with a child's cognitive, affective, and psychomotor characteristics to provide the structure for an individualized, educationally relevant program. A large number of choices of tests and observational systems are available for assessing gifted children's cognitive/achievement status, but tests for assessment of affective and psychomotor characteristics are far less common. Measures in the affective domain tend to be more clinically oriented and should be used with the knowledge and support of a mental health professional. Many of the decisions concerning educational programming for gifted children are generally based on cognitive/achievement data with relatively less stress on the affective and psychomotor observations.

Although effective strategies for assessing gifted children have evolved, there are some needs for further development. An important needed development concerns strategies for the assessment of gifted handicapped children. These strategies often include a concern for the unique sensory, physical, behavioral, and cognitive-linguistic information processing and coping styles of individuals. New and different instruments, observation systems, and specially developed approaches and emphases to accommodate the specific handicaps will be refined. Educational programs may need to be adapted and/or reoriented and special talents within the larger repertoire of human functions may become the target for educationally enriching activity. The need to identify gifted handicapped children for gifted program eligibility, to develop the best educational programming for them, and to evaluate their progress is important as one of their rights and must be undertaken to facilitate their optimum contribution to society.

Second, techniques for identifying and programming for gifted children with different cultural and language experiences need additional study. In the schools, a number of children, newly arrived from other countries may have limited language backgrounds and different experiences such that the commonly used assessment items and techniques are inappropriate. Although non-verbal cognitive measures have been reported as appropriate for these assessments, it may be that research in cognitive psychology, information processing styles, and critical thinking skills may hold greater promise as the basis for developing means for assessment. The processes of problem solving rather than knowledge of the language and content of items may be central to eligibility, educational programming, and evaluation of their progress.

Third, systems for assessment of children's critical thinking skills and for evaluating their information processing styles need further development. Examples of some present work include a manual, "Measuring Thinking Skills in the Classroom" was published by the National Education Association (Stiggins, Rubel, & Quellmalz, 1986). It contains a number of tables and questioning techniques which resemble the levels of Bloom's Taxonomy. The Assessment Battery for Children (Kaufman & Kaufman, 1983) has separate scores for simultaneous and successive processing skills. This work is on the frontier of research and development today. Understanding this construct and developing techniques for measurement of it are not an easy undertaking. The curricular applications of it will emerge as more work is done with it. The promise of this work is significant in promoting optimum learning opportunities for all children but with special reference here for the gifted child.

Fourth, the trend toward viewing cognition as an integration of multiple abilities seems to be more and more common and the emergence of measures of human information processing styles can be observed. Group measures of cognition which in their earliest forms resulted in single scores now have multiple components and scores representing different abilities. As is mentioned in Chapter 8, even large-scale basic skills assessments may move toward the reporting of multiple scores. Examples of tests in which multiple scores were reported were given in the previous section of this chapter. Aptitude test batteries are measures of many types of human abilities. The four SAS scores of the new Stanford Binet 4th Edition test are an attempt to define separate cognitive abilities but they are then combined into a composite score. The previous edition of the Binet scale (Stanford Binet LM) produced a single mental age and IQ score. Brief journal articles and occasional news items from test publishers hint at more refined measures of information processing that will become available. The interaction of at least three elements; time, i.e., how fast information can be processed, the extensiveness of one's knowledge/information base, and complexity of problem to be solved could be significant variables in assessing certain human processing abilities. As work in this area progresses, the form in which human information processing is assessed i.e., the specific components that are thought to be important, will become clearer. Current information processing theory will certainly contribute to this important work.

A fifth item represents a more human aspect of the assessment of gifted children. One might ask, "What does the Examiner experience in assessing gifted children?" Generally, the experience of evaluating gifted children is a truly unique one. Often, their enthusiasm and the effort they expend in responding to the challenge of difficult items are truly remarkable. They just don't give up! Their depth of response seems to reflect a wealth of knowledge and an integration of diverse and complex concepts. They may challenge the examiner and produce totally unexpected responses; something the examiner had not heard from any other child before. And perhaps a response that is not even listed in the examiner's manual! This experience can truly "make your day."

Perhaps, later editions of this volume will address some of these issues in greater depth.

# REFERENCES


Adams, G. 1984a. *Comprehensive Test of Adaptive Behavior: Technical Manual.* Columbus: Charles Merrill Publishing Co.

Adams, G. 1984b. *Normative Test of Adaptive Behavior: Technical Manual.* Columbus: Charles Merrill Publishing Co.

A checklist of adaptive behavior items.

Beatty, L.S., Gardner, E.F., Madden, R., & Bjorn, K. 1984. *Stanford Diagnostic Mathematics Test.* San Antonio: Psychological Corporation; Harcourt, Brace, Jovanovich, Inc.

This is a diagnostic test of mathematical skills for grades 1 through 12. There are four levels. The mathematical skills that students have acquired are identifiable and educational activities that will extend their skills beyond their present performance level can be planned from these profiles.

Bloom, B.S. 1956. *Taxonomy of Educational Objectives: The Classification of Educational Goals by a Committee of College and University Examiners: The Cognitive Domain.* New York: D. McKay & Co.

The educational objectives of the cognitive domain are listed. They are commonly cited in literature concerning curriculum.

Cattell, R.B. 1971. *Abilities: Their Structure, Growth, and Action.* Boston: Houghton Mifflin.

This reference provides background concerning the nature of cognition. Cattell and Horn are noted for their concept of fluid and crystallized abilities.

Cooper, S. 1984. *The Coopersmith Self Esteem Inventory.* Palo Alto: Consulting Psychologists Press.

> This is one of a number of inventories of self esteem that are available. It has potential for research purposes but should be used with caution for other decision making about children.

Das, J.P., Kirby, J.R., & Jarman, R.F. 1979. *Simultaneous and Successive Processing.* New York: Academic Press.

> A discussion of research on human information processing, especially simultaneous and successive processing.

DeLano, K. 1989. *An Exploratory Study of the Temperament of Young Gifted Children.* Unpublished Dissertation. University of Denver, School of Education, Denver.

> This is a descriptive study of the temperament of young gifted children as viewed by their parents. Many nonsignificant relationships with achievement and/or cognition were found using the Martin Temperament Scale.

Dunn, L.M., & Markwardt, F.C.,Jr. 1970. *Peabody Individual Achievement Test.* Circle Pines, Minnesota: American Guidance Services.

> This is an individually administered test of achievement of general information, mathematics, reading, and spelling.

Gardner, H. 1983. *Frames of Mind: The Theory of Multiple Intelligences.* New York: Basic Books, Inc.

> A description and discussion of the "seven intelligences" is provided in this reference. It is representative of the concept of intelligence as many faceted.

Green, K., & Kluever, R. 1990. "Structural Properties of the Raven Coloured Progressive Matrices for a Sample of Gifted Children."

Paper presented at the annual meeting of the American Educational Research Association, Boston, MA.

An item analysis and reliability study of the Raven Coloured Progressive Matrices test for young gifted children. The factor structure of the test for this sample is described.

Guilford, J.P.   1956.   "The Structure of Intellect."   *Psychological Bulletin, 53,* 267-293.

Guilford. J.P.   1971.   *Creativity Tests for Children: A Manual for Interpretation.*   Beverly Hills, California:   Sheridan Psychological Services.

A test of creativity for children based on Guilford's SOI Model (Divergent Production).

Hammill, D., & Larsen, S.   1988.   *Test of Written Language-2.*   Austin: Pro-Ed Publishing Co.

A test of written language skill for children with defined components that indicate proficiencies in different areas of writing.

Harrow, A.J.   1972.   *A Taxonomy of the Psychomotor Domain: A Guide for Developing Behavioral Objectives.*   New York: David   McKay, Inc.

A listing of psychomotor skills for which behavioral objectives may be designed as guides for individual or group instructional programs.

Harter, S.   1982.   "The Perceived Competence Scale for Children." *Child Development, 53,* 87-97.

A self-rating scale of children's perceived competence in several defined domains. The scale has very acceptable psychometric characteristics for use with gifted children.

Hollingworth, L.S. 1942. *Children Above 180 I.Q. Stanford-Binet: Origin and Development.* Yonkers-on-Hudson, New York: World Book.

This is a description of the characteristics of very highly gifted persons.

Jastak, S., & Wilkinson, G.S. 1984. *The Wide Range Achievement Test-Revised.* Wilmington, DE: Jastak Associates, Inc.

Johnsen, S.K., & Corn, A. 1987. *Screening Assessment for Gifted Elementary Students: A Method for Identifying Giftedness.* Austin: Pro-Ed Publishers.

A screening test for identifying gifted elementary students.

Johnson, D.L. 1980. *The Gifted and Talented Screening Form.* Chicago: Stoelting Co.

Another screening test for identifying gifted elementary students.

Karlsen, B., & Gardner, E.F. 1986. *Stanford Diagnostic Reading Test.* San Antonio: The Psychological Corporation, Harcourt, Brace, Jovanovich, Inc.

This is one of many available diagnostic reading tests. It has value for determining the acquired reading skills of students, i.e. their present performance level and is helpful in preparing educational programs for further educational progress.

Katz, E. 1981. *Perceived Competence in Elementary Level Gifted Children.* Unpublished Dissertation. University of Denver, School of Education. Denver.

The Perceived Competence Scale for Children was used as the instrument to study gifted children's ratings of their self-concept. Above-average ratings were found on the cognitive part of the scale.

Kaufman, A., & Kaufman, N. 1983. *Kaufman Assessment Battery for Children.* Circle Pines, MN: American Guidance Services.

> The cognitive part of the Kaufman ABC Battery includes sections that tap simultaneous and sequential processing as human information processing skills.

Keeley, R. 1989. *Validity of Two Self Concept Tests for Gifted Adolescents.* Unpublished Dissertation, University of Denver, School of Education, Denver.

> Keeley studied the psychometric characteristics of the Piers-Harris and the Perceived Competence Scale for Children and found the Perceived Competence Scale to have characteristics for gifted children that approximated those for normal children while the Piers-Harris scale showed some variation in factor structure for this same group of gifted children.

Kluever, R. 1989. "Linguistic Analysis of Young Gifted Children's Writing." University of Denver. Unpublished manuscript.

> Written stories of 15 gifted children were analyzed in terms of their syntactic and semantic components. These components were found to be at the highest norm levels and the themes were judged to be very abstract and mature.

Kluever, R., & Green, K. 1989. "Identification of Gifted Children: A Comparison of the Stanford-Binet 4th Edition and Form LM." Paper presented at the annual meeting of the American Educational Research Association, San Francisco. (ERIC Document Reproduction Service No. TM013104)

> The average Composite scores of the Binet 4th edition were 10 to 11 points lower than the average Binet LM IQ. The Verbal SAS was the highest of the 4 SAS scores on the Binet 4th ed.

Kratwohl, D.R. 1956. *Taxonomy of Educational Objectives: The Classification of Educational Goals by a Committee of University Examiners: The Affective Domain.* New York: D. McKay & Co.

A listing of educational objectives applied to the affective domain that will be useful in designing educational strategies.

Markwardt, F.C., Jr. 1989. *Peabody Individual Achievement Test-Revised Manual.* Circle Pines, Minnesota: American Guidance Services.

An individually administered test of achievement with measurement in the areas of reading, mathematics, spelling, general information, and writing.

Martin, R.P. 1988. *The Temperament Assessment Battery for Children.* Brandon, Vt.: The Clinical Psychology Publishing Co.

A series of 3 rating scales of children's temperament; one for parents, one for clinicians, and one for teachers.

Meeker, M., Mestyanek, L., & Meeker, R. 1975-81. *Structure of Intellect Learning Abilities Test.* El Segundo, CA: S.O.I. Institute.

A test of student's abilities on 26 of the 120 SOI factors resulting in a profile of SOI abilities.

Mercer, J., & Lewis, J. 1977. *System of Multicultural Pluralistic Assessment: Parent Interview Manual.* New York: The Psychological Corporation.

A structured interview scale to assess the adaptive behavior of children. It is part of the SOMPA which has a multicultural orientation to it.

Mitchell, J.V. (Ed.) 1985. *The Ninth Mental Measurements Yearbook.* Lincoln: University of Nebraska Press.

A two-volume set of references with reviews of tests.

Myklebust, H.R.  1965.  *The Development and Disorders of Written Language, Vol. 1: The Picture Story Language Test.* New York:  Grune & Stratton.

A test of children's writing skill; quantity of written output, correctness, and abstractness.

Otis, A., & Lennon, R.  1977-82.  *Otis-Lennon School Ability Test.* Cleveland: The Psychological Corp.

A group measure of children's ability.

Parkyn, G.W.  1948.  *Children of High Intelligence: A New Zealand Study.* Wellington, N.Z.: Council of Educational Research.

A study of the characteristics of gifted children in New Zealand.

Piers, E., & Harris, D.  1969-84.  *The Piers-Harris Self Concept Scale (The Way I Feel About Myself).* Los Angeles: Western   Psychological Services.

A measure of self-concept in children.

Raven, J.C., Court, J.H., & Raven, J.  1984.  *Manual for Raven's Progressive Matrices and Vocabulary Scale: Section 2, Coloured Progressive Matrices (1984 edition).* London: H.K. Lewis & Co. Ltd.

A measure of cognitive ability in children using designs of different color and pattern.

Sherry, P., Bowles, S., & Kluever, R.  1989.  "Social Maturity of Gifted Children."  University of Denver. Manuscript submitted for review.

An analysis of the social maturity of young gifted children. The within test pattern shows development of good social skills.

Silverman, L.  1980.  *Parent Questionnaire for Identifying Gifted Children.*  Denver: Gifted Child Development Center.

An inventory of characteristics commonly seen in gifted children. This is given to parents to aid in describing their children who are referred for study at the Gifted Child Development Center.

Slossen, R.L. 1981. *Slossen Intelligence Test for Children and Adults.* East Aurora, New York: Slossen Educational Publications.

A measure of intellectual ability of children.

Sparrow, S., Balla, D., & Cicchetti, D. 1984. *Vineland Adaptive Behavior Scales: Interview Edition.* Circle Pines, MN: American Guidance Services.

A measure of 4 areas of adaptive behavior of individuals from infancy through adulthood. Gifted children have higher than average levels of adaptive behavior.

Sternberg, R.J. 1981. "A Componential Theory of Intellectual Giftedness." *Gifted Child Quarterly, 25,* 86-93.

An information processing theory of human function with special reverence to gifted children in this article.

Stiggins, R., Rubel, E., & Quellmalz, E. 1986. *Measuring Thinking Skills in the Classroom.* Washington D.C.: National Education Association.

Scales for measuring thinking skills with special attention to the Bloom taxonomy.

Terman, L.M. 1925. *Mental and Physical Traits of a Thousand Gifted Children.* Stanford, California: Stanford University Press.

A study of the characteristics of gifted persons.

Terman, L.M., & Merrill, M.A. 1973. *Stanford-Binet Intelligence Scale: Manual for the Third Edition: Form LM.* Boston: Houghton Mifflin Co.

An individually administered psychological test of the intelligence. It is often used with gifted persons.

Thorndike, R.L., & Hagen, E. 1986. *The Cognitive Abilities Test (Form 4): Examiner's Manual.* Chicago: Riverside.

Thorndike, R., Hagen, E., & Sattler, J. 1986. *Stanford-Binet Intelligence Scale: Fourth Edition.* Chicago: Riverside Publishing Co.

An individually administered test of intelligence with 4 areas of ability; verbal, quantitative, visual abstract reasoning, and memory. A composite score is also computed.

Thorndike, R., Hagen, E., & Sattler, J. 1986. *Technical Manual: Stanford-Binet Intelligence Scale: Fourth Edition.* Chicago: Riverside Publishing Co.

Technical and psychometric characteristics of the Binet 4th ed. scale. Research using this scale is reported.

Torrance, E.P. 1966-84. *Torrance Tests of Creative Thinking.* Bensonville, IL: Scholastic Testing Service, Inc.

Tests of creative thinking. A large body of literature relating to use of this scale has accumulated.

U.S. Public Law 95-561. November 1 1978. Gifted and Talented Children's Education Act of 1978. *Title IX - Additional Programs, Part A - Gifted and Talented Children, Vol. 92, Part 2.*

Waters, J. 1989. *The Silverman/Waters Checklist for Identifying Gifted Elementary School-Aged Children: A Validation Study.* Unpublished Dissertation, University of Denver, School of Education. Denver.

A psychometric analysis of the Silverman/Waters checklist. Reports of item characteristics, reliability, and validity are included.

Wechsler, D. 1974. *Wechsler Intelligence Scale for Children-Revised.* New York: The Psychological Corp.

> An individually administered test of intelligence. It has 12 subtests and results in a verbal, performance, and a full scale IQ. There is a substantial body of research literature concerning the Wechsler test.

Witty, P.A. 1940. *A Genetic Study of Fifty Gifted Children.* G.M. Whipple (Ed.), 39th Yearbook (Part 2), National Society for the Study of Education.

> This is a study of the characteristics of gifted children.

# EVALUATION OF HEARING-IMPAIRED CHILDREN

## RITA M. BAKER

This chapter reviews the literature regarding the testing and evaluation of hearing-impaired children. After a description of the incidence and definition of deaf and hearing impairment, a developmental perspective of cognitive, language, and social emotional skills is presented to provide the reader with an overview of the various problems that are encountered by deaf and hearing-impaired children. Following this, the current status of assessing this population and the utility of measures of intellectual, language/academic and social-emotional abilities are addressed. The chapter concludes with recommendations regarding appropriate assessment procedures addressed.

### Incidence of Hearing-Impaired Children
### in the United States

The Bureau of Education for the Handicapped in the United States estimated well over a decade ago that there are 52,000 deaf children and 350,000 hard-of-hearing children in the public school systems (Hobbs, 1975). During the 1986-87 school year, the Annual Survey of Hearing-Impaired Children and Youth from Gallaudet College's Center for Assessment and Demographic Studies (CADS) stated 47,162 hearing-impaired children were reported, a slight drop of 3% from the previous year. Enrollment of hearing-impaired students in residential schools continued to decline with local schools reporting enrollments of larger numbers of hearing-impaired students (Gallaudet, 1988). This study reported that the percentage of hearing-impaired children reported to have handicaps in addition to their hearing impairment remained at 29% of the total; learning disability and mental retardation continued to be the most frequently reported additional handicaps. These children vary not only in degree of hearing impairment but also in the etiology and age of onset of their handicap, important factors to consider in obtaining accurate measures of ability. Commonly evaluated attributes include the children's cognitive abilities, language development and social-emotional functioning which greatly influence their ability to function in their educational program and the world. These specific dimensions of functioning account for a great deal of the variability in this heterogenous group of handicapped children.

Public Law 94-142, the federal Education for all Handicapped Children Act passed in late 1975, mandated a free appropriate education of children of school age who had been assessed and identified as having one or more handicapping conditions. A handicapping condition including the hearing-impaired was defined as a "disability interfering with the academic functioning to an extent that a child could not reasonably benefit from a regular educational program." It was mandated that these children be educated in the least restrictive environment. In general, educators have interpreted the "least restrictive" educational environment as the child's local school district or school and classroom that would be assigned if no handicap(s) was present.

*Definitions and Etiology of Hearing
Impairment/Deafness*

The term "hearing-impaired" encompasses a wide range of hearing deficiency. "Deaf" typically refers to those individuals whose hearing is disabled to an extent (usually > 69 dB ISO) that precludes the understanding of speech through the ear alone either without or with the use of a hearing aid (Moores, 1978). The term "hard of hearing" typically refers to those individuals whose hearing is disabled to an extent (usually 35 to 69 dB ISO) that makes it difficult but does not preclude the understanding of speech through the ear alone either without or with the use of a hearing aid.

Other important definitions include the term "prelingual deafness" which refers to deafness from birth or the loss of hearing before speech and language were developed and the term "postlingual deafness" which refers to loss of hearing after spontaneous speech and language were developed (Kirk & Gallagher, 1979). Congenital deafness is the term typically used to refer to persons who were born deaf, while the term adventitiously deaf refers to those persons who were born with normal hearing but in whom the sense of hearing became nonfunctional later through illness or accident (Committee, 1938).

The etiology or cause of hearing impairments is an important consideration. This is due to the fact that many causes of deafness are associated with neurological impairment. For example, maternal rubella, encephalitis, and meningitis are conditions which are often associated with brain impairment or organicity as well as deafness. It is important to screen for residual effects of these conditions when completing a psychological evaluation. If deficits are observed in nonverbal, performance test results then a referral for a more comprehensive examination such as a neuropsychological examination is appropriate.

## DEVELOPMENTAL PERSPECTIVES

### Cognition

One of the most widely accepted theories of intelligence applicable to the deaf and hearing-impaired population was presented by John Horn and Raymond B. Cattell (1967). Their innovative theory of the structure of intelligence identified two types of intelligence referred to as "fluid" and "crystallized" intelligence. The former consists essentially of nonverbal, relatively culture-free mental efficiency while crystallized intelligence is primarily comprised of acquired skills and knowledge dependent upon exposure to educational, cultural, and other environmental stimulation resulting in environmental learning.

Kaufman (1979) noted that the difference in verbal and performance IQs may be indicative of discrepancies in fluid and crystallized ability, although the verbal-performance and fluid-crystallized dichotomies are not perfect. Fluid ability reflects incidental learning which is typically gained indirectly from life's experiences; therefore, hearing-impaired children can gain much of this information by observing through their intact visual senses. Crystallized ability, however, reflects much direct and deliberate training via the auditory channel, and by virtue of their handicap, deaf children are unable to receive this information.

Fluid intelligence may be measured by performance in such tasks as figural classifications, figural analyses, number and letter series, and paired associates. Crystallized intelligence is measured by such tasks as abstract and word analogies, mechanics of language, general information, and vocabulary (Horn & Cattell, 1967). Although well-known cognitive measures such as the Wechsler Intelligence Scale for Children-Revised, Wechsler Adult Intelligence Scale-Revised, and Stanford-Binet are composed of tasks measuring both fluid and crystallized components of intelligence, an item analysis of these individually administered intelligence tests yields a relatively clear assignment of the individual subtests or subtasks into one of the two identified categories. Deaf and hearing-impaired children as a group possess normal levels of fluid intelligence but have difficulty acquiring crystallized intelligence to a degree comparable to their hearing counterparts. Kirk and Gallagher (1979) indicated that the auditory deficit depresses environmental learning which precludes normal development in the verbal areas. This delay in verbal learning acquisition, generally referred to as crystallized intelligence by Horn and Cattell in their research, suggests that hearing-impaired children would exhibit obvious verbal deficits but may display more normal or even accelerated fluid abilities.

Hearing-impaired children are thus penalized due to their handicap on many of the tests typically given by school psychologists.

That is, many of the cognitive or intelligence tests administered are verbally weighted, and as the hearing-impaired child is delayed in the area of verbal function, these children will be unable to perform well on these tests. Scores from such tests are obviously discriminatory and are invalid indicators of actual cognitive ability.

There is considerable agreement among authorities about cognitive assessment instruments to use with hearing impaired children. The performance scales of the Wechsler Intelligence Scale for Children-Revised (Wechsler, 1974) was mentioned most often in the literature reviewed. Wisland (1974) reviewed instruments appropriate for use in assessing physically handicapped, language-impaired children; the Hiskey-Nebraska Test of Learning Aptitude (Hiskey, 1966) and the Leiter International Performance Scale (Leiter, 1969) were recommended as appropriate instruments for assessing multiply handicapped children.

Other intellectual tests that have been used with deaf and hearing-impaired children include the Bayley Scales of Infant Development (selected nonlanguage items), Columbia Mental Maturity Scale, human figure drawings, Merrill-Palmer Scales of Mental Abilities, Raven's Progressive Matrices, and the Smith-Johnson Nonverbal Performance Scale. Not all of these tests have norms and are seen as screening, supplementary, or supportive measures to be used in conjunction with other tests.

*Language*

The verbal and language abilities of nonhandicapped children increase as their experiences in the environment become cumulative; this observation is less valid for hearing-impaired children. The development of crystallized intelligence (acquired skills and knowledge via the environment, culture, and regular education) may be severely depressed for deaf children. Although deaf children develop a normal pattern of vocalizations (e.g., babbling, crying, cooing) until about six to nine months of age their ability to communicate orally decreases after this time (Suppes, 1974). The acoustically handicapped child's relative inability to master language is displayed in the child's depressed performance on tests of intelligence, educational and school achievement examinations requiring verbal (or spoken) and written reception of information, and language tests requiring written verbal expression.

Perhaps one of the most comprehensive studies of written language was reported by Myklebust (1964) with a thorough comparative analysis of stories written by 200 deaf children in residential and day schools and 200 hearing children matched for age and intellectual level (IQ score) utilizing the Picture Story Language Test. The deaf student's stories were consistently shorter in length than those written by the hearing students; the syntactical structure (use of tense, articles, omissions, substitutions, and word order) was vividly different for the two groups; and the use of abstraction by the deaf was less frequent. The deaf student sample wrote "more about the actual circumstances portrayed in the picture, more about what can actually be observed." The deaf students' stories were deemed to be substantially more concrete than those produced by the hearing students. A higher proportion of nouns was found in the stories of the deaf at all levels ranging from seven to fifteen years. The most commonly found parts of speech in the 200 compositions written by deaf children were as follows, ranging from most to least frequent occurrence in the compositions; nouns, verbs, articles, pronouns, adjectives, prepositions, adverbs. The hearing child's written productions consisted primarily of nouns, verbs, and articles. The use of pronouns, prepositions, adjectives, and conjunctions was markedly delayed in the deaf group and only rudimentary use of adverbs was attained by fifteen years of age.

A brief motion picture used by Heider and Heider (1940) to elicit written language samples from hearing and deaf children attending the Clarke School for the Deaf in Massachusetts yielded 1,118 compositions. The following conclusions were drawn: the deaf use simpler and shorter sentences than the hearing; generally speaking, the compositions of the deaf resemble those of less mature, hearing children, although no significant differences were found in the total length of the actual compositions. When different forms of subordination in sentence structure were analyzed relative to difficulty, the more difficult forms were used less by the deaf than by the hearing group.

Because of the child's retardation in language development, opportunities for communication with hearing peers and adults are minimized.  Odom, Blanton and Lankhuf (1973) suggested that the decreased social interaction levels of deaf children may be related to their lessened opportunities to receive interpretations and verbal explanations of the emotions of others in their environment.  This leads us to the next area of focus--social-emotional functioning.


## Social-Emotional Functioning


Obviously, the hearing-impaired group with reduced communicative abilities is greatly helped or hindered by variations in child-rearing practices, overprotection from parents, fostered dependence on primary caretakers, and experiences associated with a variety of additional environmental facts that influence their social and emotional maturation.

Researchers working with the deaf and hearing-impaired have continued to confirm high rates of reported behavioral and emotional problems within the deaf, school-age population.  The incidence of behavioral disturbances among deaf and hearing-impaired youth in the United States has been estimated to range from a low of 7.9% in a National Survey of Hearing Impaired Children (Jensema & Trybus, 1975) to a high of 22.5% in a survey of the Psychological Status of Deaf School Admissions 1953-1964 (Vernon, 1969).  Incidence studies between the years of 1969 through 1980 indicated that the rate of emotional or behavioral disturbances ranges from 7.9% to 22.5% dependent upon the population included in the survey, the definition used for identifying behaviorally and emotionally disturbed deaf children, and the identity of the professionals responsible for diagnosing the children.  These rates appear to be from three to ten times higher than for comparable groups of hearing children; however, the methodological problems associated with the collection of such information and the impact of the handicapping condition must be taken into consideration when evaluating such research.

## TESTING HEARING-IMPAIRED CHILDREN

### *Intellectual Testing*

Many well-known cognitive instruments contain language or verbally oriented test items. When these tests or subtests are administered to a hearing-handicapped child, any results become a measure of his or her residual hearing acuity and receptive language abilities as well as his/her actual performance on the test. In addition, if a verbal or written response is required for obtaining a correct score then the test is also a measure of the child's ability to expressively communicate to the examiner. For these reasons, such tests as the Stanford-Binet and verbal scales of the Wechsler Intelligence Test for Children-Revised yield invalid intelligence scores. The results of such measures are representations of the child's hearing acuity, receptive language comprehension, and expressive communication skills. Thus, a verbal intelligence quotient (as well as the full scale intelligence quotient) from a Wechsler scale should never be reported as an accurate cognitive estimate for a hearing-impaired child as it provides an estimate of the degree to which the child has mastered verbal concepts.

### *Stanford-Binet*

This very popular individual measure of intelligence has been administered to a variety of children with handicapping conditions. As noted above, invalid intelligence scores may be reported. An obvious inappropriate usage of the Stanford-Binet was reported by Vernon and Brown (1964) in which a young deaf girl was committed to an institution for the mentally retarded on the basis of a Stanford-Binet intelligence quotient of 29. After a five-year period this deaf youngster was re-evaluated using a nonverbal performance intelligence test which yielded an intelligence quotient of 113.

In summary, the Stanford-Binet (Terman & Merrill, 1973) is typically deemed to be particularly inappropriate for use with deaf children because of its heavy emphasis on language fluency. However, in the hands of knowledgeable, experienced psychologists who work routinely with deaf and hearing-handicapped individuals results may be helpful in assessing a student's verbal abilities and potential for integration into regular classroom programming.

*Wechsler Intelligence Scale for Children-Revised (WISC-R)*

The performance scales of the Wechsler Intelligence Scale for Children-Revised (Wechsler, 1974) are deemed to be the most appropriate estimate of a hearing-impaired child's cognitive abilities. The Wechsler Intelligence Scale for Children-Revised, a measure of intelligence for children ranging in age from six to sixteen and a half years, is a very well-known test due to its excellent standardization; in addition, it is one of the most researched scales for children. However, by administering only the performance subtests to deaf children, the sample of behavior obtained is halved; this should be taken into consideration when reporting the performance intelligence quotient for deaf children as this score could be an underestimation of actual cognitive ability.

The Office of Demographic Studies at Gallaudet College published the Standardization of the WISC-R Performance Scale for Deaf Children (Anderson & Sisco, 1977) to improve the psychometric evaluation of deaf children. The Wechsler performance subscales were standardized on a national sample of 1,228 deaf children from residential and day schools for the deaf located throughout the United States. The deaf children were found to perform similarly to hearing children on all performance subtests except Coding and Picture Arrangement although the mean IQ was 95.70 on the WISC-R performance scale. The subtest mean scores ranging from the easiest to most difficult were: Object Assembly (M = 10.32), Mazes (M = 10,03), Picture Completion (M = 9.51), Block Design (M = 9.48), Picture Arrangement (M = 8.71), and Coding (M = 8.03). The normative tables for deaf children from the Gallaudet College publication (November 1977) should be used in reporting and interpreting WISC-R results for deaf children.

Although the performance tests can be administered to most deaf children without a great deal of adaptation some younger and/or lower-functioning children experience difficulty in understanding the concepts of missing, order, and time. Examiners who have had a great deal of experience with deaf/hearing-impaired youngsters often briefly review the concept (e.g., missing/most important, story order, match/the same) prior to administration of the subtest. A research project (Ray, 1979) has attempted to develop a series of adaptations of instructions for the WISC-R which are available for purchase which might be helpful. In addition, a variety of modified instructions for administration of the WISC-R performance scales to deaf children including pantomime instructions are reviewed by Sullivan and Vernon (1979).

## Leiter International Performance Scale (LIPS)

The Leiter International Performance Scale (Leiter, 1969) is an untimed measure of non-verbal intelligence for children ranging in age from two to eighteen years. Unlike the Wechsler Intelligence Scale for Children there are no standardized instructions available for use with the deaf; however, this does not appear to be a major concern as the instructions are entirely non-verbal and the child only needs to have the concept of "sameness" in order to respond to a series of tasks arranged in order of successive difficulty. The Leiter International Performance Scale is composed of tasks in which a series of one-inch cubes are matched to a variety of stimulus strips attached by the examiner to a wooden frame; this physical presentation allows children who have motor problems to respond more easily. The speed of response is not important on this test; therefore, the motorically involved hearing-impaired child is not penalized for slow performance.

Disadvantages of the Leiter International Performance Scale include the fact that no deaf norms are available; however, the Arthur Adaption of the Leiter International Performance Scale does provide normative data for the age range of two to twelve years. Technical information on reliability, validity, and item analysis is limited for the Leiter.

*Hiskey-Nebraska Test of Learning Aptitude (HNTLA)*

The Hiskey-Nebraska Test of Learning Aptitude (Hiskey, 1966), a non-verbal test of learning aptitude for deaf and hearing children ranging in age from three to eighteen and a half years, yields a learning quotient (LQ) for the deaf. The revision of the Nebraska Test of Learning Aptitude was standardized on children and youth from two years and six months to seventeen years and five months; there were final totals of 1,079 deaf children and 1,074 hearing children tested. The deaf children came from ten widely separated states extending from New York to Utah to Florida with the majority of the deaf children coming from state schools for the deaf. The coefficients of reliability were .947 and .918 for deaf children ranging in age from three to ten and age eleven to seventeen, respectively; for hearing children the reliability coefficients were .933 and .904 for children ranging in age from three to ten and age eleven to seventeen, respectively (Hiskey, 1966).

The Hiskey-Nebraska Test of Learning Aptitude contains standardized instructions for deaf as well as for hearing children. Instructions for the deaf involve pantomime and pointing. The HNTLA is often preferred by many in the educational setting due to the fact that many areas (e.g., visual discrimination, visual matching, classification, spatial reasoning, nonverbal memory) applicable to the educational setting are assessed and reported through the subtest scores. A study (Hirshoren, Hurley, & Hunt, 1977) sampling 59 prelingually deaf children who were tested with both the Performance Scale of the Wechsler Intelligence Scale for Children-Revised and the Hiskey-Nebraska Test of Learning Aptitude yielded a Pearson product-moment correlation of .89, a high correlation suggesting that both tests measure very similar abilities. As a note of comparison, the Wechsler manual (Wechsler, 1974) reports a correlation of .90 between the Performance Scale and the Total Scale for the Wechsler standardization sample.

Although many professionals have found the HNTLA to be most helpful in assessing a variety of language-handicapped children, significant disadvantages of the HNTLA include the length of time required for administration of the test, poor visual representation of many of the picture test materials, as well as several technical problems (e.g., reliability of each subtest is unknown, and a minimal raw score difference can result in a difference of up to 2 1/2 years in the learning age).

*Kaufman Assessment Battery for Children (K-ABC)*

This individualized intelligence test which has recently joined the ranks of cognitive tests available to psychologists was standardized on a large sample of "normal" and exceptional children ranging in age from twenty months to twelve and one-half years (Kaufman & Kaufman, 1983). This instrument also includes a nonverbal scale which is administered via pantomime and requires the subject to respond motorically, circumventing the receptive and expressive communication components of testing that penalize most hearing-impaired children. The one validity study reported by Kaufman and Kaufman indicated that the results of the K-ABC Nonverbal Scale with hearing-impaired children correlated .63 with the Performance IQ of the Wechsler Intelligence Scale for Children-Revised performance scale. It was reported that the sample of 40 hearing-impaired children (ranging in age from eight to eleven years, eleven months of age) scored highest on the Gestalt Closure subtest of the Kaufman Assessment Battery for Children and significantly below hearing children on the Matrix Analogies, Photo Series and Hand Movements subtests. A later study by Porter and Kirby (1986) comparing different modes (American Sign Language versus mime and gesture) of communicating test instructions for the K-ABC Nonverbal Scale reported a significant correlation between the Kaufman and the performance subscales of the WISC-R although the scores on the K-ABC were significantly lower than on the WISC-R. This implies that the K-ABC would underestimate the true abilities of hearing-impaired children.

A subsequent study (Ulissi, Brice, & Gibbins, 1989) which attempted to address some of the foregoing controversy regarding the feasibility of using the K-ABC with hearing-impaired children. Their sample of 50 (26 male and 24 female prelingually hearing-impaired children ranging in age from six to twelve years, five months) yielded the following Pearson correlations between the K-ABC and the WISC-R: Sequential = .670; Simultaneous = .845; NonVerbal = .859; Mental Processing Composite = .836. Results indicated that both the Simultaneous Processing Scale and the Nonverbal Scale seemed appropriate for hearing-impaired children whose scores were similar to those of the test's normative sample. The Sequential Processing Scale involving meaningful symbols (e.g., words and numbers) was more problematic for hearing-impaired children. It was also noted that the K-ABC was significantly related to school achievement while the Nonverbal score correlated most highly with reading and math scores and the Sequential Scale correlated most poorly. It is concluded that only continued field testing and use by professional psychologists can determine the role the Kaufman Assessment Battery for Children will play in evaluating this special population.

## *Raven's Progressive Matrices (RPM)*

This test which can be administered individually or in a group setting, has been used frequently with deaf persons; hearing norms are reported for ages eight through sixty-five years of age. The actual test booklets contain a series of 60 matrices or designs in which the subject is required to choose the correct missing insert (from six to eight alternative choices). Reliability coefficients of .83 to .93 are reported for adult subjects; criterion-based validity coefficients range from .40 to .75 (Foulds & Raven, 1950)

The Raven's Progressive Matrices are accepted as a supplementary or adjunct test of nonverbal intelligence due to ease of administration and lack of communication necessary when giving the test to deaf individuals. However, it is important that the examiner be cautious about impulsive responding from deaf examinees.

## *Language and Academic Skills Evaluation*

By virtue of their handicap deaf and hearing-impaired youngsters do not develop language consistent with their non-handicapped peers. The academic achievement of deaf/hearing-impaired children is much depressed below that which could be expected from their performance on intelligence tests with reading comprehension being the lowest. The degree of receptive and expressive language development is dependent upon the factors previously noted (i.e., the onset and degree of their impairment, the etiology or accompanying conditions). However, in an educational system it is important to assess the actual functioning abilities of deaf/hearing impaired children in the area of language and general academic abilities in order to appropriately develop an individualized educational program and address the feasibility of their being integrated into other "regular" classes.

Tests that are frequently and routinely administered to deaf and hearing-impaired youngsters in order for school systems to make decisions regarding their programs are reviewed below.

*Stanford Achievement Test (Special Edition for Hearing-Impaired Students)*

The Stanford Achievement Test is a standardized achievement test normed on a national sample of 275,000 school children in grades one to nine; this sample was chosen in accordance with the 1970 U.S. Census and was stratified proportionally according to ethnic minority, geographic region, parental income, educational level of the community, and major school characteristics. The Special Edition for Hearing Impaired Children (SAT-HI) is an adaption of the Stanford Achievement Test designed for hearing impaired students; norms are based on the performance of a carefully selected random sample of 6,873 hearing impaired students in 119 special education programs throughout the United States (Allen, 1986). This sample included gifted as well as academically slow, hearing-impaired children. Age-based percentile norms for hearing-impaired students were developed from this sample. The SAT-HI is a full-range achievement test consisting of six different batteries: Primary Level I, Level 2, Level 3, Level 4, Level 5, and Advanced Level. The core areas tested are Vocabulary, Reading Comprehension, Mathematical Concepts, and Mathematics Computations.

The SAT-HI version includes practice tests for subtests and procedures for choosing the appropriate reading levels for hearing-impaired children with raw scores converted into grade equivalent scores, scaled scores, and percentiles. The grade equivalent scores obtained range from kindergarten through the ninth month of twelfth grade and the scaled scores reported range from 42 through 300, making the hearing-impaired child's results on the SAT-HI comparable to the hearing SAT standardization group. Advantages of this test include the fact that this is the best available ongoing assessment of basic skills from elementary through high school levels with periodic restandardizations (i.e., 1974, 1983, in process 1990). This test can also be administered in group settings although, as with all group testing with deaf and hearing-impaired children, relatively low examiner-examinee ratios are necessary in order to administer the test and instructions in the clearest manner possible. Ample time and attention must be available to assure understanding of test instructions and application of meaningful pre-test practices for the hearing-impaired examinees.

Jensema (1978) presents complete reliability information on the Stanford Achievement Test for Hearing Impaired children. A reliability coefficient of .83 was reported by averaging the reliability coefficients for all subtests in the different test SAT-HI batteries; the standard error of measurement (SEM) which was derived from the average of all the SEMS of the SAT-HI subtests of the different test batteries is 3.0. No studies of validity specifically for the SAT-HI are reported in the literature. Because test items of the SAT-HI and the SAT are the same, it is assumed that content validity will not vary between the two tests.

*Social and Emotional Evaluation*

The social and emotional assessment of deaf/hearing-impaired children is extremely difficult by standard means. Self-report measures require verbal skills and projective testing instruments presuppose confidence between the subject and the examiner, a rapport which is typically unattainable when an examiner does not possess the skills to communicate with the child. Fluency in manual communication is mandatory in administering such tests as the Rorschach and Thematic Apperception Test (TAT). Other factors for consideration include: the question of norms being applicable as most projective tests are standardized with hearing child populations, the lack of exposure of deaf/hearing-impaired subjects to many objects and situations presented, the interference of a sign language interpreter in the testing situation. Test scores obtained by a psychologist not familiar with the deaf population are subject to more error. Commonly used measures are reviewed below.

*Meadow-Kendall Social-Emotional Assessment Inventory for Deaf Students*

This scale, a fifty-nine item teacher checklist, consists of social adjustment, self-image and emotional adjustment scales (Meadow, 1983). It was standardized on hearing-impaired children in the United States enrolled in public and residential schools in the 1970s. Advantages of this test, which is geared for hearing handicapped children ranging in age from seven to twenty-one years of age, include its standardization on over 2,000 hearing-impaired/deaf children and its ease of administration by teachers.

Of the 2,365 completed Meadow-Kendall research edition inventories received, 1,793 were from residential schools and 572 were from day programs in the United States. Three factors were justified by the factor analysis and inspection by the investigators supported face validity. The three factors were labelled as follows: Scale 1, Social Adjustment; Scale 2, Self Image; Scale 3, Emotional Adjustment. The inter-item reliabilities of the three scales (using Cronbach's alpha) were: Scale 1 = .96, Scale 2 = .94, Scale 3 = .91. Interrater reliabilities from the classroom teacher and counselor yielded the following results: Social Adjustment .93, Self Image .66, and Emotional Adjustment .58. Correlations of this instrument with the Walker Problem Behavior Identification Checklist were reported in the manual as follows: Social Adjustment .79, Self-Image .67 and Emotional Adjustment .54 (Meadow, 1983).

As noted in the foregoing paragraph the disadvantages of the Meadow-Kendall include low reliabilities for some subscales and only moderate validity. Probably interrater reliability is low due to the vague criteria for scoring.

*Human Figure Drawings/House-Tree-Person*

Well-known tests such as the Draw-A-Person and House-Tree-Person are frequently used with the deaf. There are no norms for the deaf for either test although some studies do report more common responses (e.g., enlarged ears on human drawings) among deaf and hearing-impaired children. Such tests are seen as adequate screening tests for severe emotional problems among the hearing handicapped population as they are relatively non-verbal and can serve as a non-threatening "warm-up" exercise.

An extensive study using the Human Figure Test, an essentially nonverbal technique, was reported by Myklebust (1964) in an attempt to investigate the possible effects of early life deafness on self-perception, person perception, and identification. The drawings (i.e., man, father, mother, self) were obtained from 830 children in schools for the deaf (511 children in residential deaf schools, 319 in day schools) in the United States. The Draw-A-Man subtest was administered to 274 hearing children as a control group in the study. The basic comparisons were of residential versus day school students, males versus females, and deaf versus hearing children. Myklebust provided an extensive review of the findings. Although indications of immaturity and emotional problems with the deaf children were indicated when comparing their protocols with the hearing control group, results indicated advantages and disadvantages for each type of school program related to identification and self-image issues. The day school children showed more emotional stress, conflict, and frustration in comparison with both the residential deaf group and the normal hearing group. More children were identified as disturbed in the day school sample of deaf children. Myklebust reported that the deaf child's more frequent contact with deaf peers and deaf adults in the residential setting is a fundamental factor in developing feelings of belonging and of general well-being as reflected on the Human Figure Test.

Disadvantages of the human figure projective tests continue to include their questionable validity and reliability and subjective interpretations. Misinterpretation has been observed to result in the misdiagnosis of deaf/hearing-impaired children.

*Minnesota Multiphasic Personality Inventory (MMPI)*

This very popular and well-researched self-report personality test requires a high level of reading and a thorough understanding of English idiomatic structure. The majority of deaf and hearing-handicapped individuals lack both of these requirements. A study by Sullivan and Vernon (1979) reports the results of MMPI administration to all entering students in a preparatory class at Gallaudet College, a population of intellectually elite deaf students. All MMPI profiles suggested extreme levels of psychopathology with the deaf subjects. Without adaptation, this measure seems to be inappropriate for use with a deaf population.


# SPECIAL CONSIDERATIONS IN EVALUATION OF HEARING-IMPAIRED CHILDREN


## Examiner Characteristics


Testing children with impaired hearing requires a high degree of skill and wide experience with deaf children. Examiners who are familiar with the evaluation of deaf and hearing-impaired children typically use a total communication approach in administering test batteries. The term "total communication" refers to a combination of speech, lipreading, and amplification (i.e., hearing aids, Phonic Ear) along with the simultaneous use of a manual sign system (Meadow, 1980). Examiners who work with hearing-impaired youngsters not only need special communication skills to communicate with deaf and hearing-impaired youngsters but should possess a working knowledge of how the deaf child's lack of hearing acuity has impacted his or her ability to adequately interpret the environment. In addition, it is imperative that the examiner have an understanding of and respect for the world of deafness as it relates to deaf culture.

When a deaf or hearing-impaired child relies on total communication as the primary mode of learning, then total communication should be used by the examiner to ensure the greatest reliability and validity when administering tests. Research indicates that overall performance of deaf children was higher when subtests on the WISC-R were administered through total communication (Sullivan, 1982).

As hearing-impaired children rely to a greater extent on visual cues than hearing children, it is important for the examiner to be particularly sensitive to subtle body language, facial expressions, movements of the hands, and any other nonverbal communications that may cue the child or result in the child responding in a certain way. The examiner should also be aware of the fact that many hearing-impaired children give the impression that they understand a direction or question when, in reality, they do not. This tendency to acquiesce is frequently observed during normal communications as well as in testing situations and probably results from their learning a role to avoid confrontations and potentially embarrassing situations.

Frequently, psychologists or other mental health professionals may use a sign language interpreter in assessment situations. It is important to use a Certified Sign Language Interpreter. Obviously, the introduction of a third party into any situation can lead to interpreter-related distortions such as inadequate translation of psychological/psychiatric concepts or a self-imposed role and attitude towards either the client or clinician (Gallaudet, 1988). It has been this examiner's experience that much meaningful information may be lost when using an interpreter for three reasons--the client may have had previous negative experience with professionals utilizing interpreters, the examiner feels uncomfortable in attempting to communicate such "personal and intimate" questions and communications via a third party, and the interpreter feels frustrated in being bound by the limits of being only a "translator" who is unable to elaborate or add to the deaf individual's communication expressed according to Ethical Code of Certification as a Sign Language Interpreter.

Ideally it is best to locate a psychologist who possesses sign language skills and is experienced in evaluating and treating hearing-impaired children possessing differing degrees of hearing loss occurring at different ages. Beware of the examiner who has taken one or two sign classes and has evaluated only a few hearing-handicapped youngsters; it is important that the examiner not only be able to communicate with the deaf or hearing-impaired child in a comfortable manner but that the professional has an understanding of the impact of this major sensory impairment on cognitive, educational, and psychosocial functioning. It is also important to have an examiner who is accepting of the expertise of available, knowledgeable resources (i.e., teacher of the deaf/hearing-impaired, audiologist, speech and language pathologist) who are experienced in working with deaf and hearing-impaired children. If a psychologist is unavailable within your local school system, then consultation with your state-wide educational consultant for deaf/hearing-impaired children or state department of education may be useful. Another valuable resource could be Centers on Deafness which provide interpreting services and lists of available resources for the deaf within respective local areas.

## *Environmental Considerations*

Environmental considerations include the need to be in a testing environment that minimizes extraneous visual and auditory stimulation. Full visual attention from the child should be obtained as it is imperative that the child watch the examiner's face as well as manual communication while test instructions and questions are being read. Lighting in the room should be appropriate without shadows or glare; any glare on the examiner and interpreter's faces as well as in the child's eyes and on test materials should be minimized. The examiner should speak in short, simple sentences (particularly if the child is relatively young); speech should be clear and distinct but should not be exaggerated.

Obviously the child should be wearing his or her typical amplification aids and communication of directions should be in the communication system typically used in the classroom to meet the needs of the individual child. Examiners should be aware that testing deaf or hearing-impaired children takes more time than evaluating hearing children and plan accordingly.

## Family and Educational Factors

Questions to consider when evaluating the family of a hearing-impaired child would include but not be limited to: Where are the family members (e.g., parents, siblings, extended family) in the grief process? In many situations parents have not accepted the child's handicap and continue to focus on intensive training in compensatory (i.e., speech training, language skills instruction and tutoring, speech-reading) skills in an attempt to make the child like a "hearing" child versus accepting the child's handicap and allowing the child to develop as normally as possible as a hearing-impaired individual. How have members of the family adjusted to the communication difficulties posed in trying to communicate with the hearing-impaired child? Have family members begun to learn sign language if that has been deemed an appropriate channel? Do family members actively include the child in the natural family communications or is the child left to visually adapt to his environment as he/she observes the actions of others?

Educational factors to consider when evaluating a hearing-impaired child include the time of onset of special education programming relative to the diagnosis of the sensory disability as well as the type of communication utilized. When was amplification, i.e., hearing aids, applied, if appropriate? Does the child benefit from amplification during extended day as well as during school hours? Is the child's program individualized to meet his or her special needs in the school environment? What is the type of program--oral or total communication--that would best meet the child's needs? How much is she or he integrated into the normal "mainstream" of the school environment and the quality of those experiences? How does the child's academic functioning levels compare with the extent and duration of his or her hearing loss and mode of instruction?

## FUTURE CONSIDERATIONS

It is anticipated that by using presently existing psychological instruments that determinations can be made regarding the appropriateness of their use in identifying the extent to which the "psychological world" of deaf persons is similar to or different from that of persons who hear. In addition, through research perhaps more appropriate standardized psychological tests can be developed specifically for this unique population. This process is a slow and tedious one; however, as time progresses more research continues to be conducted.

A variety of research projects (Gallaudet College, 1988) are underway in an attempt to assess the utility of psychological tests with deaf children and adults. For example, the Beck Depression Inventory, Barrett-Lennard Relationship Inventory, Tennessee Self-Concept Scale, Symptom Check List 90 (Depression Scales), Psychiatric Epidemiology Research Interview, Social Adjustment Scale, Life-Events Questionnaire, General Life-Functioning Scales, Carroll Rating Scale, Dysfunctional Attitude Scale, Medical Check List, and Minnesota Multiphasic Personality Inventory (MMPI), are twelve self-report psychological instruments under study. These instruments are being presented in American Sign Language (ASL), the language used by the majority of the American prelingually deaf adult population; results are being compiled regarding the reliability of response to different Certified Sign Language Interpreters as well as the reliability and validity of the translated test items.

## SUMMARY

The evaluation of hearing-impaired children as well as adults is a complex undertaking. Several salient facts must be taken into consideration when attempting to obtain the most valid and reliable estimates of functioning possible. These include, but are not limited to, the following: (1) Traditional assessment measures cannot easily be administered and interpreted due to the fact that most tests do not contain normative data for the deaf and hearing-impaired populations. (2) Much test data are invalid due to the fact that language is required for the hearing-impaired youngster's understanding of the task or performance of the task. Therefore, test results are not a measure of what the test was intended to measure but a measure of the subject's receptive and/or expressive language abilities. (3) Unless the examiner possesses an adequate understanding of the etiology, extent, onset and impact of a hearing loss, adequate conclusions cannot be made by the examiner about the validity of level of performance. (4) Professionals should be sensitive to and understanding of "deaf culture," the impact of being isolated and oftentimes rejected by hearing peers and family, and the need to identify with a like group of individuals with whom they can communicate and interact freely and comfortably.

As more and more deaf and hearing-impaired children are integrated into public school systems throughout the nation, it is imperative that conscientious practitioners not only gain a comprehensive understanding of the appropriateness (as well as inappropriateness) of standard instruments for use with this population but also gain an understanding of deaf culture and the social and emotional impact of this major sensory handicap on their total existence.

**REFERENCES**


Allen, T.E. 1986. *Understanding the Scores: Hearing-Impaired Students Stanford Achievement Test (7th edition).* Washington, D.C.: Gallaudet Research Institute, Center for Assessment and Demographic Studies.

Anderson, R.J., & Sisco, F.Y. 1977. *Standardization of the WISC-R Performance Scale for Deaf Children.* Washington, D.C.: Office of Demographic Studies, Gallaudet College.

> This standardization sample of congenitally or prelingually deaf (70 dB or greater pure-tone average hearing loss in the better ear) students ranging in age from six to sixteen years, eight months, was used to provide Wechsler Intelligence Scale for Children-Revised performance subscale scores. This group was deemed to be a representative sample of deaf children in the United States.

Committee on Nomenclature 1938. "Conference on Executives of American Schools for the Deaf. *American Annals of the Deaf, 83.*

> Report from the members of the executives of the American schools for the deaf in the United States denoting their recommendations for definitions of terms commonly used in describing deaf and hearing-impaired children.

Foulds, B.A., & Raven, J.D. 1950. "An Experimental Survey with Progressive Matrices." *British Journal of Psychology, 20,* 104-110.

> General reference for the Raven's progressive matrices, a nonverbal test of intelligence.

Gallaudet College 1988. *A Tradition of Discovery: The 1987-88 Annual Report of the Gallaudet Research Institute.* Washington, D.C.

A source of factual information on the status and achievements of hearing-impaired children and youth in the United States published by the Gallaudet Research Institute since July, 1974.

Heider, F., & Heider, G.M. 1940. "Studies in the Psychology of the Deaf", No. 1. Psychological division, Clarke School for the Deaf. *Psychological Monographs, 52,* No. 232.

A report comparing 1,118 written language samples of hearing children with students at the Clarke School for the Deaf yielding significant differences across a variety of written language dimensions.

Hirshoren, A., Hurley, O.L., & Hunt, C. 1977. "The WISC-R and the Hiskey-Nebraska Test with Deaf Children." *American Annals of the Deaf, 8,* 392-394.

This research article reports the outcome of 59 prelingually deaf children on the Performance Scale of the Wechsler Intelligence Scale for Children-Revised and the Hiskey-Nebraska Test of Learning Aptitude.

Hiskey, M.S. 1966. *Hiskey-Nebraska Test of Learning Aptitude Manual.* Lincoln, NE: Union College Press.

The restandardization and revision of the Nebraska Test of Learning Aptitude for Young Deaf Children which was standardized on 1079 deaf children and 1074 hearing children in the United States ranging in age from three years to seventeen years. Technical information and standardization statistics along with general instructions for administering the test to deaf and hearing children as well as scoring is presented in the manual.

Hobbs, N. 1975. *The Futures of Children: Categories, Labels, and Their Consequences.* San Francisco: Jossey-Bass.

Horn, J.L., & Cattell, R.B. 1967. "Age Differences in Fluid and Crystallized Intelligence." *Acta Psychologica, 26,* 107-129.

The theory of the structure of intelligence including the percepts of "fluid" and "crystallized" intelligence is presented by its originators.

Jensema, C.   1978.   "A Comment on Measurement Error in Achievement Tests for the Hearing Impaired." *American Annals of the Deaf, 123(4)*, 496-499.

A research report noting the results of the Stanford Achievement Test for hearing-impaired school-age children in the United States.

Jensema, C., & Trybus, R.J.   1975.   *Reported Emotional-Behavioral Problems Among Hearing-Impaired Children in Special Educational Programs: United States, 1972-73.*   Series R, Number 1. Washington, D.C.: Gallaudet College.

The compilation of survey form results obtained from various educational settings (i.e., public school programs, state schools for the deaf) in the United States noting the number of hearing-impaired children judged to display emotional-behavioral problems.

Kaufman, A.S.   1979.   *Intelligence Testing with the WISC-R.*   New York: Wiley.

A comprehensive test addressing the use of the Wechsler Intelligence Scale for Children-Revised.

Kaufman, A., & Kaufman, N.   1983.   *Interpretive Manual.*   Circle Pines, MN:  American Guidance Corporation.

The examiner's manual for the Kaufman Assessment Battery for Children (K-ABC).

Kirk, S.A., & Gallagher, J.J.   1979.   *Educating Exceptional Children (3rd edition).*   Boston: Houghton Mifflin.

A classic textbook which addresses a variety of handicapping conditions among school-age children including auditorially handicapped students with conductive and sensorineural hearing losses versus adventitiously deafened.

Leiter, R.G. 1969. *General Instructions for the Leiter International Performance Scale.* Chicago: Stoeling Company.

The examiner's manual describing the appropriate procedures for the administration and scoring of this nonverbal intelligence test ranging from the two-year to eighteen years, six months levels.

Meadow, K.P. 1980. *Deafness and Child Development.* Berkeley: University of California Press.

A leading research professor and director of the Child Development Research Unit at Gallaudet College Research Institute in Washington, D.C. surveys the primary research published on the linguistic, cognitive, social, and psychological effects of profound deafness in children.

Meadow, K.P. 1983. *Revised Manual: Meadow-Kendall Social-Emotional Assessment Inventory for Deaf and Hearing-Impaired Students.* Washington: Gallaudet College.

The manual describing the rationale for the Meadow-Kendall Social-Emotional Assessment Inventories for Deaf and Hearing-Impaired (SEAI), development of test items, collection of data, and statistical analyses as well as the procedures for administering, scoring and interpreting the inventories.

Moores, D.F. 1978. *Educating the Deaf: Psychology, Principles, and Practices.* Boston: Houghton Mifflin.

Myklebust, H.R. 1964. *The Psychology of Deafness: Sensory Deprivation, Learning, and Adjustment (2nd edition).* New York: Grune and Stratton.

This comprehensive textbook about deafness--including the nature and extent of deafness, deafness and psychological processes, language-speech, speech-reading, reading and writing, other handicaps, special abilities, and aptitude--is a classic in the field of deafness.

Odom, P.B., & Blanton, R.L. 1967. "Phrase-learning in Deaf and Hearing Subjects." *Journal of Speech and Hearing Research, 10,* 600-605.

Odom, P.B., Blanton, R.L., & Lankhuf, C. 1973. "Facial Expressions and Interpretation of Emotion-arousing Situations in Deaf and Hearing Children." *Journal of Abnormal Child Psychology, 1,* 139-151.

A study confirming the observed decreased social interaction levels of deaf children in comparison with hearing children indicating the impact of lessened opportunities of deaf children to receive interpretations and explanations of the emotions of others within their environment.

Porter, L.J., & Kirby, E.A. 1986. "Effects of Two Instructional Sets on the Validity of the Kaufman Assessment Battery for Children-Nonverbal Scale with a Group of Severely Hearing Impaired Children." *Psychology in the Schools, 23,* 37-43.

A study investigating the effects of explaining the instructions of the Kaufman Assessment Battery Nonverbal scale via American Sign Language (ASL) versus mime and gesture which concluded that although there was a significant correlation between the K-ABC Nonverbal scale and the WISC-R the scores on the Kaufman were significantly lower than on the Wechsler Intelligence Scale for Children-Revised.

Ray, S. 1979. *An Adaptation of the Wechsler Intelligence Scales for Children-Revised for the Deaf.* Nitchitoches, LA: Northwestern State University of Louisiana.

A manual describing the use of supplemental materials designed by Dr. Ray to minimize the adverse effects of certain handicapping conditions when administering the Performance Scales of the Wechsler Intelligence Scale for Children--Revised.

Sullivan, P.M. 1982. "Administration Modifications on the WISC-R Performance Scale with Different Categories of Deaf Children." *American Annals of the Deaf, 127(6),* 780-788.

Reviews acceptable methods/techniques utilized in the administration of directions to deaf children on the Wechsler Intelligence Scale for Children-Revised.

Sullivan, P.M., & Vernon, M. 1979. "Psychological Assessment of Hearing-impaired Children." *School Psychology Digest, 8(3),* 271-290.

This article presents an overview of the present status of psychological services and general test taking considerations in testing hearing-impaired children along with a review of commonly used intellectual, behavioral/personality, academic, neuropsychologic, communication/language, and vocational interest/aptitude assessment areas with this school age population.

Suppes, P. 1974. "A Survey of Cognition in Handicapped Children." *Review of Educational Research, 44,* 145-176.

Reviews the development of abilities with handicapped children.

Terman, L.M., & Merrill, M.A. 1973. *Stanford-Binet Intelligence Scale: Manual for the Third Revision, Form L-M.* Boston: Houghton Mifflin.

The manual for the administration and scoring of the Stanford-Binet Intelligence Scale (Form L-M) along with the description of the standardization group and statistical properties of this well-known test.

Ulissi, S., Brice, P., & Gibbins, S. 1989. "Use of the Kaufman Assessment Battery for Children with the Hearing Impaired." *American Annals of the Deaf, 10,* 283-287.

A study of 50 hearing-impaired elementary school students at the Kendall Demonstration School in Washington, D.C. utilizing the Kaufman Assessment Battery for Children, the performance scales of the Wechsler Intelligence Scale for Children-Revised, and the Stanford Achievement Test-Hearing-Impaired Edition. Scores on the K-ABC were correlated highly with performance scores of the WISC-R and the Simultaneous Processing Scale and the Nonverbal Scale of the Kaufman seemed appropriate for use with hearing-impaired children.

Vernon, M. 1969. *Multiply Handicapped Deaf Children: Medical, Educational, and Psychological Considerations.* Washington, D.C.: CEC Research Monograph.

Vernon, M. 1976. "Psychological Evaluation of Hearing Impaired Children." In L. Lloyd (Ed.), *Communication, Assessment and Intervention Strategies* (pp. 195-223). Baltimore: University Park Press.

Vernon, M., & Brown, D.W. 1964. "A Guide to Psychological Tests and Testing Procedures in the Evaluation of Deaf and Hard-of-hearing Children." *Journal of Speech and Hearing Disorders, 4,* 414-423.

Wechsler, D. 1974. *Manual for the Wechsler Intelligence Scale for Children-Revised.* New York: Psychological Corporation.

This book reports the rationale, standardization, and statistical properties as well as the directions and scoring of the Wechsler Intelligence Scale for Children-Revised, a test standardized on 2,200 subjects (boys and girls ranging in age from six years, six months through sixteen years, six months) including black and other nonwhite groups in the same proportions reported in the 1970 census.

Wechsler, D. 1981. *Wechsler Adult Intelligence Scale-Revised Manual.* New York: Psychological Corporation.

The manual reports the rationale, standardization, and statistical properties for a sample of 1,880 adult subjects ranging in age from sixteen years through seventy-four years, eleven months selected according to the current U.S. Census data and tested between 1976 and 1980. Directions for administration and scoring of the WISC-R are also included in the manual.

Wisland, M.V.  1974.  *Psychoeducational Diagnosis of Exceptional Children.*  Springfield, IL:  Charles C. Thomas.

# CURRICULUM-BASED ASSESSMENT

## E. JANE WILLIAMS

The controversy around testing continues. There are many who contend that: standardized tests are of limited use for teachers for daily instructional planning, especially with low-achieving students (Galagan, 1985; Gickling & Thompson, 1985; Tucker, 1985); they do not adequately measure change or learning (Marston & Magnusson, 1985); they do not adequately sample the curricula from which instruction occurs (Deno, 1985; Gickling & Thompson, 1985; Marston & Magnusson, 1985; Neisworth & Bagnato, 1986); and the traditional pre-post test change scores in educational measurement are unreliable (Marston & Magnusson, 1985; Salvia & Ysseldyke, 1985, cited in Marston & Magnusson, 1985). However, there are others who feel that this is not the case, that if a standardized test is selected to match the curriculum by a committee of educational specialists, such as teachers, administrators, and testing specialists, then the issues above are less likely to be troublesome. There are also those who contend that classroom testing serves little purpose other than providing a measure for assigning grades--that tests are not integrated with instruction.

Curriculum-based assessment (CBA) is called an alternative to standardized achievement testing by its supporters, or, if not considered an alternative, then a supplement to standardized achievement testing (Deno, 1985; Fuchs & Fuchs, 1986). CBA is also considered an alternative to traditional classroom testing since it is directly integrated with instruction. This chapter will explain what CBA is, how it has been used, and what the research tells us about CBA. This chapter also provides suggestions for implementation and recommendations for future research.

## WHAT IS IT?

From 1977 to 1983 a program of research was undertaken at the University of Minnesota to develop and test the effectiveness of measurement and evaluation procedures that teachers could routinely use for instructional planning. The purpose of the research program was to determine whether or not teachers using such a system (experimental) would be more effective than teachers using a conventional special education evaluation treatment (contrast). Thirty-nine special educators, each having three to four pupils in the study, were randomly assigned to experimental and contrast groups. Analyses of covariance revealed that experimental teachers effected greater student achievement (Deno, 1985; Fuchs, Deno, & Mirkin, 1984). The set of design characteristics that guided this research program required that the measures be reliable and valid, simple and efficient, easily understood, and inexpensive. Curriculum-based assessment was the emerging assessment method.

Curriculum-based assessment was defined by Gickling (1981, cited in Tucker, 1985), as "a procedure for determining the instructional needs of a student based upon the student's ongoing performance within existing course content." CBA has some similarity to criterion-referenced assessment, which permits a check on what skills a child already has, what skills are to be acquired, and what skills have been mastered within an instructional program. CBA is a type of criterion-referenced assessment but uses the material to be learned as the basis for assessing the degree to which the material has been learned (Neisworth & Bagnato, 1986; Tucker, 1985). Assessment rather than summative evaluation is the goal. CBA is characterized by frequent, brief assessments, direct measurement, standardized procedures, and direct links to instruction. (See Salvia and Hughes, 1990, for in-depth development of CBA.)

A distinction has been made between CBA and curriculum-based measurement (CBM). The purpose of assessment is to find whether the student has learned the specific task just taught; the goal of CBM is to find whether the student can perform specified aggregate tasks. For example, CBA might find whether a child knows how much 2 + 7 is; curriculum-based measurement might find whether the child can add single digit numbers he/she has not directly been taught. CBM, then, is conceptually closer to criterion-referenced assessment. With CBA the assessment methodology is totally congruent with the program objectives (Neisworth & Bagnato, 1986). CBA provides a way of matching student ability to instruction, thereby reducing low achievement and poor student-behavior responses in the school setting (Thompson, Gickling, & Havertape, 1983, cited in Tucker, 1985).

There are several basic assumptions which are critical to an understanding of CBA. First, each student's needs are best defined in terms of the context of his/her specific local educational program or course of study (Tucker, 1985). Neisworth and Bagnato (1986) note that "CBA can be no better than the curriculum it employs. A curriculum with relatively few objectives, large gaps between objectives, omissions in important areas, or disproportionate emphasis in one or two domains will not provide the optimal base for individualized programming" (p. 181). Clearly, the choice of an appropriate curriculum is fundamental. Neisworth and Bagnato present guidelines for selecting or building curricula.

Secondly, CBA can only occur when the expected curricular outcomes are known and measurable and where there is a method for the ongoing measurement of student progress in terms of those outcomes. At this time, outcome measures, for the most part, refer to student achievement proficiency in basic school skills (Deno, 1985). Tasks that cannot be broken down into small, independent units, such as critical thinking skills, may be less amenable to CBA procedures. Lastly, in order for CBA to be effective, good teaching practices, which are basic to sound instruction, must be used (Tucker, 1985).

## RESEARCH FINDINGS:  IS CBA EFFECTIVE?

CBA measures of classroom performance developed at the University of Minnesota Institute for Research on Learning Disabilities have been used as research tools, to examine such things as differences in student classroom performance between learning disabled and low achieving students, as well as serving as a research base.  Recent research indicates that CBA techniques provide time- and cost-efficient, as well as valid and reliable, measures of student performance and rate of improvement in reading, spelling, and writing; are sensitive to long- and short-term changes in student performance; and produce relevant information for instructional and program planning (Shinn, Ysseldyke, Deno & Tindal, 1986; Ysseldyke, Thurlow, Graden, Wesson, Deno, & Algozzine, 1982 cited in Galagan, 1985).  Shinn et al. (1986) found CBA techniques sensitive to differences between learning disabled and low achievers on weekly performance measures of reading, spelling, and spelling accuracy on a written expression task when no meaningful differences had been found between their performances on several commonly used norm-referenced tests.  CBA performance measures were administered weekly over a 5-week period to 71 fifth-grade students.  No significant differences were found in their rates of improvement over the 5-week period.  These findings support the hypothesis that teachers' referral decisions are based on classroom observations and "the subsequent administration of norm-referenced tests may reflect an inefficient confirmatory process" (p. 545).

Fuchs and Fuchs (1986) make an important point based on findings from a meta-analysis of eighteen controlled studies that used CBA.  Studies were included that employed a "control group to evaluate the effects of curriculum-based monitoring on academic achievement. Such monitoring was defined as curriculum-based data collection that occurred at least twice weekly, with decisions concerning the adequacy of programs formulated on an individual, not group, basis" (p. 71). Factors such as instrumentation, methodological rigor, and adequacy of decision making were coded as variables.   Their research examined the effect of measuring student progress toward long-term v. short-term goals on contrasting outcome measures of student achievement, i.e., probelike v. global achievement tests.  Results of the studies were transformed to estimates of effect size which, in turn, were converted to an unbiased effect size. No statistically significant associations were found between measurement goal or outcome measure and duration of treatment. However, an important interaction effect was noted when the effect of type of outcome measure within each of the goal conditions was examined. "When progress was measured toward long-term goals, effect sizes calculated on global outcome measures were higher than the probelike outcomes. On the other hand, when progress was measured toward a series of short-term goals, effect sizes were lower on global than on probelike outcome measures" (p.78). The authors explain this in terms of the relative strengths associated with the different goal measurement strategies. Long-term goal measurement corresponds better with global measures of reading skills, including tests of decoding, word recognition, and comprehension than with instructional activities (Deno et al., 1982, cited in Fuchs & Fuchs, 1986). On the other hand, with short-term goal monitoring, there is a one-to-one relationship between instruction and measurement.

This finding may be especially important in the education of handicapped students, who typically have poorly developed strategies for maintaining and transferring skills. Short-term goal measurement focuses on specific instructionally related tasks; the measurement and instructional focus changes upon mastery of that material. The authors note that this may be problematic because of the intent of short-term goal measurement. The close connection between instruction and measurement may discourage teachers from sufficiently reviewing material to allow long-term skill transfer. The more global, long-term goal approach to measurement may encourage teachers to incorporate instructional procedures that better allow for skill maintenance and generalization.

Teachers may prefer short-term goal measurement because it is easier to understand and it guides instruction by providing information about when to progress from one skill to another (Fuchs, Wesson, Tindal, Mirkin & Deno, 1982, cited in Fuchs & Fuchs, 1986). In fact, evidence suggests this to be teachers' predominant monitoring strategy (Fuchs, Fuchs, & Warren, 1982 cited in Fuchs & Fuchs, 1986). Nevertheless, short-term goal measurement may be misleading. Students may master a series of instructional objectives but still exhibit insufficient achievement on more global indices, which better represent the true desired outcome performance. Consequently, Fuchs and Fuchs

(1986) prescribe caution for teachers who monitor mastery of short-term objectives: A valid assessment of pupil performance may require monitoring of long-term goals as a supplementary strategy.

Because of the newness of CBA, research on or with CBA is limited. However, from the studies reviewed, CBA techniques have been found to be effective means for instructing and monitoring pupil progress and program impact with both preschool and school-age children.

## CURRICULUM-BASED ASSESSMENT MEASURES

Bagnato, Neisworth and Capone (1986) and Neisworth and Bagnato (1986) summarize CBA early childhood assessment methods and measures. Bagnato et al. (1986) classify CBA instruments into five types: normal-developmental, based on developmental milestones using nonhandicapped children as the reference group; adaptive, developmentally sequenced objectives designed for specific disabilities; handicap-specific, which address the unique needs of a particular impairment such as visual or neuromotor disabilities; strategy-matched, which suggest techniques for achieving the objectives such as behavioral methods; and curriculum-referenced, comprised of norm- and criterion-referenced scales that are frequently standardized. Because of their generic/hybrid character, curriculum-referenced scales are not as precise as specific curriculum-embedded measures, but they do offer a normative assessment and provide an estimate of curriculum-entry points. Neisworth and Bagnato classify and review the measures according to three types: multidimensional batteries, adaptive skill assessment measures, and adaptive process measures. The multidimensional batteries are those which integrate both norm- and criterion-referenced features; the adaptive skill assessment measures assess specific disabilities; and adaptive process measures "emphasize the shaping and generalization of distinct behavioral capabilities within a curricular format" (p. 193), such as child performance scales, clinical judgment scales, and adaptive diagnostic toys to assess the cognitive, adaptive, affective, and social capabilities of young exceptional children.

While the authors' classification systems vary, the majority of the instruments reviewed in each article are identical; however, each review includes several assessment measures not included in the other. The reader should find it helpful to review both since the tables provided include some different features. In addition to providing the age range, domains/components, target population, and special features for each instrument, Neisworth and Bagnato include the amount of time needed to administer the measure, adaptations of the measures, and the publisher of each, while Bagnato et al. include the theoretical basis for each measure.

## RECOMMENDATIONS FOR IMPLEMENTATION

Although CBA has been implemented mainly in special education classrooms, it has also been implemented in the regular classroom, usually at the elementary level. Several authors have provided recommendations for the implementation of CBA based on their research and experiences (Blankenship, 1985; Coulter, 1985; Germann & Tindal, 1985; Marston & Magnusson, 1985; Rosenfield & Rubenson, 1985).

Germann and Tindal (1985) present a model of special education which uses an integrated approach to the entire decision-making process. This model employs a direct and repeated measurement and evaluation system for student identification, program planning, program implementation, and instructional evaluation, as well as the documentation of program effects on groups of students. This model was found "effective" for special education programs at both the individual and system level, where effectiveness was operationalized "as either improvement toward an IEP goal or with performance more commensurate with that exhibited by peers" (p. 256). Two domains are described by Germann and Tindal: academic skills and social behaviors. Germann and Tindal's model incorporates two essential principles.

First, a behavioral approach is applied to identifying and remediating educational problems, i.e., attention is given to student behavior and school environmental demands rather than to categorizing students into disability classifications. The argument has been advanced that categorization alone does not provide for remediation and may be detrimental to the child's educational future. This model assumes that the present educational environment is a critical influence upon how and what a child learns and how he/she behaves. Second, the model makes use of a repeated measurement evaluation paradigm, i.e., the development of a continuous data base across all educational decisions, including initial program selection, program planning, program implementation and evaluation, and program certification. The delivery system focuses on reducing discrepancies between the student's performance and the specific environmental demands in the various skill areas (e.g., academic skills: reading, spelling, written expression, and mathematics; social behaviors: noise, out of place, physical contact, and off-task) by adjusting programs to reduce these discrepancies for specific educational behaviors. Germann and Tindal place special emphasis on the idea that social problems need to be considered within the environment in which they occur.

Blankenship (1985) describes the essential characteristics of CBA, provides suggestions for developing them, and describes procedures for using CBA data for instructional decision making. In concluding, she recommends that teachers who are applying this method for the first time go slowly. By starting with the assessment of basic skills the teacher can become familiar with the process and then expand CBA to a variety of academic subjects. Having teachers work in pairs or teams is suggested as a cost- and time-saving method.

Research conducted on the implementation of CBA in special and regular education settings in Minneapolis Public Schools was reported by Marston and Magnusson (1985). CBA was found to be a viable alternative for monitoring pupil progress. Within this school system, CBA procedures were found to be efficient and accurate in the screening, identification, program planning, and progress monitoring of mildly handicapped students who received special education services. In general CBA was found to be a feasible assessment model. When implementing this model, Marston and Magnusson remind the reader that it is critical that there be a strong commitment from the school administration which may entail a need for thorough reorganization.

Rosenfield and Rubinson (1985) examined CBA through the lens of consultants in school systems implementing the new system of assessment. In order to implement such a change successfully, there must be a thorough understanding of the school culture, i.e., "the characteristics of the situation, the people in it, their shared experiences and their prejudices" (Checkland, 1981, p. 181, cited in Rosenfield & Rubinson, p. 282). The authors explain that a major source of resistance to CBA is that one of its basic underlying principles--that material should be at the child's instructional level--conflicts with a widely held basic assumption of many teachers, an assumption held in spite of research to the contrary. CBA opposes curriculum-driven planning. Teachers who are bound to "covering the material" within their units may be initially uncomfortable with CBA. Consultants need to be sensitive to the cultural regularities of the particular school and should examine teacher resistance to CBA from this perspective. In addition, Coulter (1985) noted that "CBA cannot be fully implemented unless appraisal professionals accept its need and rationale. If appraisal professionals do not accept CBA as a legitimate component of the appraisal process, its use may become perfunctory or inconsequential" (p. 279).

Rosenfield and Rubinson (1985) present four stages for introducing CBA to teachers. First, create a need for it--teacher commitment and input is essential for success. Second, establish a support and reward structure for teachers as they begin to implement CBA, i.e., establish a process whereby teachers can network with one another when implementing CBA. Third, provide teachers with "guided practice," specific feedback on their behavior in the classroom after attempting to implement CBA. The usual inservice training format provides for imparting knowledge, but guided practice or shadowing is essential for skill attainment (Coulter, 1985; Rosenfield & Rubinson, 1985). Fourth, be available to assist teachers to allow for individual adaptations. Consultants must make use of dissemination/diffusion techniques that may make the process more successful with CBA-like models requiring significant changes in teacher attitudes, skills, and behaviors (Rosenfield & Rubinson, 1985).

Along this same theme, Fuchs and Fuchs (1986) noted that care should be taken to select goal-monitoring methods to promote the type of outcome that special educators desire (i.e., global growth v. mastery of discrete curriculum units). More specifically, the curricular and content validity of their measurement procedures must be addressed as practitioners develop their programmatic or IEP goals and objectives and related curriculum-based assessment procedures. This can only be done when practitioners write IEP goals and objectives, which relate well to the true desired outcome performance.

## RECOMMENDATIONS FOR FUTURE RESEARCH

More research needs to be conducted evaluating the short- and long-term effectiveness of CBA in different content areas at different grade levels. Germann and Tindal (1985) cited a limitation of their work: serious research needs to be conducted to address the manner in which effectiveness is operationalized and defined. The data presented were based on only one system for defining and implementing a special education system.

Additionally, Rudman (1987) noted that the research offers little solid evidence of the potential for improving classroom teaching by reviewing test results. Studies were cited to support both sides, i.e., those for and against the use of tests in teaching; however, there have been no comprehensive, experimental studies that systematically contrast test use by classroom teachers who are trained and who have substantial classroom experience with those who are not trained in measurement and have little classroom experience. Until this is done, teachers will have to rely on intuition. Knowledge from such studies will assist educators to better understand the teacher decision making process linking assessment and teaching, which will in turn provide for better training of teachers.

At this time, research studies on the stability estimates of reliability, criterion-related validity, and transfer of learning and generalizability of CBA still need to be conducted (Deno, 1985). In the meantime, CBA should be explored as a supplement to current assessment practices.

## REFERENCES

Bagnato, S.J.; Neisworth, J.T.; & Capone, A. 1986. "Curriculum-based Assessment for the Young Exceptional Child: Rationale and Review." *Topics in Early Childhood Special Education, 6(2),* 97-110.

This article provides a topology and reviews a variety of CBA assessment measures available for specialists serving the handicapped child.

Blankenship, C.S. 1985. "Using Curriculum-based Assessment Data to Make Instructional Decisions." *Exceptional Children, 52(3),* 233-238.

Blankenship describes the essential characteristics of CBA, provides suggestions for developing them, and describes procedures for using CBA data to make instructional decisions.

Bullard, P., & McGee, G. April 1984. "Developing and Norming a Curriculum-based Assessment in Reading." Paper presented at the annual convention of the Council for Exceptional Children, Washington, D.C. ERIC ED 245481.

Coulter, W.A. 1985. "Implementing Curriculum-based Assessment: Considerations for Pupil Appraisal Professionals." *Exceptional Children, 52(3),* 277-281.

Coulter presents the efforts of New Orleans public schools in implementing CBA into their assessment practices in accordance with Louisiana rules and regulations.

Deno, S.L. 1985. "Curriculum-based Assessment: The Emerging Alternative." *Exceptional Children, 52(3),* 219-232.

Deno provides background and illustrations of CBM in special education.

Fuchs, L.S., & Deno, S.L.  August 1981.  "A Comparison of Reading Placements Based on Teacher Judgment, Standardized Testing, and Curriculum-based Assessment."  (Institute for Research on Learning Disabilities).  Minnesota University, Minneapolis, MN.  ERIC ED 211603.

Fuchs, L.S., Deno, S.L., & Mirkin, P.K.  1984.  "The Effects of Frequent Curriculum-based Measurement and Evaluation on Pedagogy, Student Achievement and Student Awareness of Learning."  *American Educational Research Journal, 21(2),* 449-460.

Fuchs, L.S., & Fuchs, D.  April 1986.  "Effects of Long- and Short-term Goal Assessment on Student Achievement."  Paper presented at the Annual Meeting of the American Educational Research Association, San Francisco.  ERIC ED 268169.

Fuchs, L.S., & Fuchs, D.  1986.  "Curriculum-based Assessment Progress Toward Long-term and Short-term Goals."  *Journal of Special Education, 20(1),* 69-82.

> This article summarizes results of a meta-analysis of 18 controlled studies which evaluated the effects of curriculum-based monitoring on academic achievement.

Galagan, J.E.  1985.  "Psychoeducational Testing:  Turn Out the Lights, the Party's Over."  *Exceptional Children, 52(3),* 288-299.

> Examines the legal problems associated with standardized testing and demonstrates the legal imperative for incorporating and implementing CBA in special education evaluation systems.

Gattullo, M.    1987.    "Marking Strategies in Italy."    *Studies in Educational Evaluation, 13,* 43-47.

Germann, G., & Tindal, G.  1985.  "An Application of Curriculum-based Assessment:  The Use of Direct and Repeated Measurement."  *Exceptional Children, 52(3),* 244-265.

Germann and Tindal present a model of special education for developing effective educational programs incorporating both academic skills and social behaviors. The model is based on the use of direct and repeated measurement.

Gickling, E.E., & Thompson, V.P. 1985. " A Personal View of Curriculum-based Assessment." *Exceptional Children, 52(3)*, 205-218.

Goldsby, C. 1988. "Norm Referenced Test Customization: Curricular Considerations." Mathematics Unit, New York City Board of Education, NY. ERIC ED 300430.

Green, D.R. April 1987. "Local versus National Calibrations." Paper presented at the Annual Meeting of the American Educational Research Association, New Orleans. ERIC ED 300450.

Haertel, E. 1987. "Scores and Scales for School Achievement." *Studies in Educational Evaluation, 13*, 61-71.

Hofmeister, A.M., & Preston, C.N. September 1981. "Curriculum-based Assessment and Evaluation Procedures-Revised." Minneapolis: National Support Systems Project.

Marston, D., & Magnusson, D. 1985. "Implementing Curriculum-based Measurement in Special and Regular Education Settings." *Exceptional Children, 52(3)*, 266-276.

Two studies are presented which utilize CBM for decision-making with children with learning difficulties: one in an elementary school, the other in a large school-based resource program for mildly handicapped children.

Neisworth, J.T., & Bagnato, S.J. 1986. " Curriculum-based Assessment: Congruence of Testing and Teaching." *School Psychology Review, 15(2)*, 180-199.

Numerous CBA instruments are presented and summarized that are available to the school psychologist for use with preschoolers.

Rosenfield, S. & Rubinson, F. 1985. "Introducing Curriculum-based Assessment through Consultation." *Exceptional Children, 52(3)*, 282-287.

> The authors examine four stages for a consultant to consider when helping teachers adopt and develop a model CBA program.

Rudman, H.C. 1987. "Testing and Teaching: Two Sides of the Same Coin? *Studies in Educational Evaluation, 13*, 73-90.

> Rudman discusses the use of tests by American teachers and the link between assessment and teaching. This discussion is research-based rather than philosophical in nature.

Salvia, J., & Hughes, C. 1990. *Curriculum-based Assessment: Testing What is Taught.* New York: Macmillan.

> This text describes how to develop tests and other assessments that directly reflect instruction.

Seidenberg, P.L. April 1986. "Curriculum-based Assessment Procedures for Secondary Learning Disabled Students: Student Ctr. and Programmatic Implications." (Long Island University Transition Project. Learning How to Learn) Brooklyn, NY: Long Island University.

Shinn, M.R.; Ysseldyke, J.E.; Deno, S.L.; & Tindal, G.A. 1986. "A Comparison of Differences between Students Labeled Learning Disabled and Low Achieving on Measures of Classroom Performance." *Journal of Learning Disabilities, 19(9)*, 545-552.

> Shinn et al. present findings on a study conducted at the University of Minnesota Institute for Research on Learning Disabilities administered weekly over 5 weeks to low achievers and LD students on measures of reading, spelling, and written expression.

Stodden, R.A. & Ianacone, R.N. July 1986. "Curriculum-based Vocational Assessment Handbook: A Guide to the Implementation of Curriculum-based Vocational Assessment Activities. Revised." Vocational Assessment Project, Contract No. DAJA 37-85-M0461, U.S. Department of Defense Dependents Schools, Washington, D.C. ERIC ED 288303.

Sugai, G. 1988. "Educational Assessment of the Culturally Diverse and Behavior Disordered Student: An Examination of Critical Effect." From a paper presented at the Ethnic and Multicultural Symposia, Dallas, TX. ERIC ED 298706.

Taleporos, B., Canner, J., Strum, I., & Faulkner, D. 1988. "The Process of Customization of the 'Metropolitan Achievement Test' (MAT-6) in Mathematics for New York City Public School Students." Office of Educational Assessment, New York City Board of Education, NY. ERIC ED 301586.

Tamir, P. 1987. "Testing and the School Curriculum: Evolving Trends." *Studies in Educational Evaluation, 13,* 3-6.

Tucker, J.A. 1981. "Non Test-based Assessment: Trainer Manual." Minnesota University, Minneapolis, MN: National School Psychology In-Service Training Network. ED 236864.

Tucker, J.A. 1985. "Curriculum-based Assessment: An Introduction." *Exceptional Children, 52(3),* 199-204.

Tucker, J.A. Fall 1987. "Curriculum-based Assessment is No Fad." *The Collaborative Educator,* 4-5.

# TESTING OF LIMITED ENGLISH PROFICIENT CHILDREN

## TONY C. M. LAM

Lam Chiu Ming, a twelve-year-old, is a recent immigrant whose family migrated from Taiwan a year ago. Chiu Ming's native language is Chinese, and he speaks hardly any English. During his school years in his native country, Chiu Ming attended a school that used only Chinese as language of instruction. Also, he has never taken a test in which he had to select the one correct answer and darken the appropriate bubble on an answer sheet. Chiu Ming has difficulty following and understanding the lectures even though he has a bilingual tutor to help him. Recently, Chiu Ming sat with his English-speaking peers and took the district-mandated achievement test battery. Not only did he do poorly on the test but the testing experience was very unpleasant for him.

Although hypothetical, Lam Chiu Ming represents one of the hundreds of thousands of youngsters currently enrolled in the United States school system who have difficulty functioning in school because their English proficiencies are limited and because their socio-cultural and educational experiences are markedly different from those promulgated and rewarded by the American school system.

In addition to recent immigrants or new arrivals from foreign countries, other limited English proficient (LEP) students include American-born children whose low acculturation to the dominant culture has prevented adequate development of English-language skills.

Native Americans exemplify this second group of LEP children. It is important to recognize that LEP children have a variety of socio-cultural and educational backgrounds; hence the educational needs of these children are diverse.

A student with a non-English background is identified as "educationally disadvantaged" in an English-language environment. In fact, it is one of the five interdependent indicators of "educationally disadvantaged" identified (Pallas, Natriello, & McDill, 1989). The other key indicators are "minority racial/ethnic group identity, living in a poverty household, living in a single-parent family, [and] having a poorly educated mother" (p. 17). This educationally disadvantaged population suffers deficiencies in enriching experiences from the school, the family, and/or the community which subsequently lead to their generally low academic achievement. Children residing in ghetto areas, for instance, tend to have poor academic performance and not to graduate from school (Pifer, 1979). Findings from a recent National Assessment of Educational Progress (NAEP) survey have shown that Hispanic, Asian, and Native American children who are not competent in English are not as successful as their white peers in our educational system (Baratz-Snowden, Rock, Pollock, & Wilder, 1988). Another analysis of the educationally disadvantaged status of LEP children demonstrates that their low level of acculturation into mainstream society has denied them equal access to educational and economic opportunities because they are handicapped in test taking. As Olmedo (1981) points out, "acculturation is also related to testing issues because it involves the acquisition of language, values, customs, and cognitive styles of the majority culture--all factors that may substantially affect performance on tests that have been standardized according to majority norms" (p. 1082).

A few census studies have projected an overwhelming increase in future years in the LEP population or individuals with non-English language background. In one study, the number of LEP individuals was estimated to increase from 2.5 million in 1976 to 3.4 million in 2000 (Oxford-Carpenter et al., 1984). This is a 36% increase over a period of 25 years. Of this LEP population, Spanish LEPs will increase from 1.8 million  (71%) in 1976 to 2.6 million (77% increase) in 2000. The U.S. Bureau of the Census (1986) reported that the number of newborn to seventeen year-olds who speak a primary language other than English (PLOTE) was just under two million in 1982, or 2.5% of all the children in that age range. The number of PLOTE children is projected to increase to 6 million by 2020, which is 7.5% of all children in that age range. The increase is roughly 200% within a period of 39 years. Regardless of which study one refers to, the growth rate of school-age students with limited or non-English backgrounds (especially that of the Hispanic population [Macias, 1977]) is expected to exceed that of the general population (Oxford et al., 1981). Given this trend, equal educational opportunity for LEP students will increasingly become a priority issue for educators in this nation. Meeting the diverse needs of these children from diverse educational, social, cultural, and linguistic backgrounds is presenting the greatest challenge that American educators have as yet had to face.

Assessment of learning and aptitude are vital and integral to the educational process. Testing, especially standardized testing, has been the gatekeeper of equal access to educational, social, and economic opportunities in American society. Test performance has been used for making decisions about entering and placing existing students from special programs, graduating students from high school, admitting students into institutions of higher education, obtaining scholarships, certifying professionals, securing jobs, and receiving promotions. Aggregated to the group level, standardized test results have been used to hold accountable educational performance of programs, districts, and states, which ultimately guide policy and administrative decision making, such as appropriation of federal or state funds.

Since linguistic factors are a major determinant of performance on standardized tests in all content areas, and since testing controls access to educational and economic opportunities, language competency indirectly controls these opportunities. Therefore, a need exists for sound and accurate testing of LEP students for the purposes of assessing academic achievement, diagnosing special educational needs, and predicting academic success. In testing as in teaching, it is important to understand the social, cultural, and linguistic backgrounds of LEP children. Much progress is needed in the development and implementation of unbiased assessment methods and instruments for minority students, especially for language minority students.

This chapter provides an overview of some key issues in the testing of LEP children in grades K-12 with the goal of reducing misuse of testing with this population. The chapter will discuss legal requirements in the assessment and education of LEP children, problems and potential strategies in the assessment of LEP children for accountability purposes and for instructional purposes (Cole, 1988), and recommendations for some alternative, sounder and more valid, it is to be hoped, practices for testing this population of students, and potential directions for future research and development.


## LEGAL REQUIREMENTS IN THE EDUCATION
## AND ASSESSMENT OF LEP CHILDREN


As legislators, lawyers, and public pressure groups helped develop national awareness of issues related to educational equality, language became increasingly recognized as a unique and strategically primary component. Title VII, the 1968 Bilingual Education Act passed by Congress in the form of an amendment to the Elementary and Secondary Educational Act (ESEA) of 1965, encourages and funds bilingual education programs for the purposes of (1) increasing English language skills, (2) maintaining and perhaps increasing mother tongue skills, and (3) supporting the cultural heritage of the student. In 1970, the Department of HEW issued a memorandum defining the obligations of school districts to language minority children. The Equal Educational Opportunity Act of 1974 included legislation to prevent educational agencies from failing to take appropriate action to overcome language barriers impeding equal participation by students in their educational programs. In addition to specifying equitable education for language minority children, guidelines for the assessment of this group of children were prescribed in public laws and resolutions from court cases.

According to Public Law (P.L.) 94-142, the Education for All Handicapped Children Act, testing and evaluation procedures are to be fair and nondiscriminatory. Specifically, the Law prescribes that, in order to assure equal educational opportunity for all types of students, tests and evaluation materials must meet four criteria (Jones, 1979):

(1) they must be provided and administered in the child's native language; ( 2) they must have been validated for the purpose for which they are used; (3) they must be administered by trained personnel; (4) they must be tailored to areas of specific educational need.

The law and its accompanying guidelines were established to safeguard misdiagnoses and misplacement of students into special education programs. The content of P.L. 94-142, including assessment directives, applies to minority students since court decisions holding that biased assessment instruments were in large part responsible for the overrepresentation of minority group children, especially those labelled mentally retarded, in special education classes.

Two well-known court cases related to education and assessment of students with limited or no English backgrounds are *Diana v. State Board of Education* and *Lau v. Nichols.* In 1973, in *Diana v. State Board of Education* charges were brought and upheld against the California board of education for misclassifying Mexican-American children as mentally retarded, based on their performance on standardized IQ tests. A major provision of the out-of-court settlement was the stipulation that testing of children with non-English-speaking backgrounds must be conducted in the children's native language as well as in English. The following year, in the proceedings of the San Francisco court case of *Lau v. Nichols* the U.S. Supreme Court, on behalf of the Chinese-American students, upheld the 1968 and 1970 HEW guidelines stating that it was the responsibility of the school system to ensure equal educational opportunities to all students, regardless of their background. In 1975, an appointed task force of the Department of Health, Education and Welfare (HEW) developed remedies to the "Lau" decisions (commonly referred to as the "Lau Remedies"). Part of the remedies require that a school district, in order to meet the responsibility of providing education for LEP students, must assess the degree of each of its student's English-language ability (dominance) with sufficient accuracy to place him or her in one of the following categories: 1) monolingual speaker of a language other than English; 2) speaker of a language other than English predominantly; 3) bilingual speaker; 4) speaker of English predominantly; 5) monolingual speaker of English ("Task Force Findings Specifying Remedies Available for Eliminating Past

Educational Practices Ruled Unlawful Under *Lau v. Nichols,*" D/HEW, Summer 1975, p. 2.). These "Lau" categories of language proficiencies in two languages are based on relative performance in the two languages. Hence, a student classified as bilingual can be illiterate (pseudolingual) or highly proficient (dual bilingual) in both languages (Dulay & Burt, 1980). This relative measure of language dominance is not adequate for determining 1) an effective pedagogical approach utilizing the two languages and 2) the language or languages with which a student should be tested in order that the knowledge or abilities that the test is designed to measure can be accurately measured with minimum language interference. For instructional purposes and for accurate assessment of psychological and educational attributes, it is important that absolute, rather than relative, proficiency levels in both languages be assessed.

## PROBLEMS IN THE IDENTIFICATION OF LEP CHILDREN

Assessment of language proficiency is made difficult by two interrelated factors: 1) conflicting views of the nature of language, and 2) the inadequate quality of instruments available to measure language proficiency.

### *Definition of English-Language Proficiency*

Although it is agreed that language proficiency can be expressed in the areas of listening, oral production, reading, and writing, there is little agreement among linguists regarding the nature of language proficiency. The number of dimensions underlying the language proficiency construct has been a controversy issue. On the one hand, it has been argued that language proficiency is a unidimensional construct and that a single factor is sufficient for explaining language proficiency (Oller, 1979). An opposing view proposes that language proficiency is determined by multiple factors or competencies

(Bachman & Palmer, 1981). Other perspectives of language proficiency are "social" versus "academic" and discrete-point versus integrative view. These different points of view of language proficiency have direct bearing on the language assessment procedures and testing considerations for LEP children.

Cummins (1980) distinguishes two forms of language competency: Basic Interpersonal Communication Skills (BICS) and Cognitive Academic Language Proficiency (CALP)[1]. BICS refers to skills in surface aspects of language used primarily for social discourse, while CALP refers to mastery of language components, such as vocabulary, grammar, and syntax, which are necessary for learning in academic settings. According to Cummins (1980), a LEP student may need up to two years to gain conversational (BICS) skills in English and up to seven years to acquire academic (CALP) skills equivalent to his or her native English-speaking peers. It would be inappropriate to rely on a child's BICS for instructional placement and to decide whether or not he or she should be exempted from testing or what language should be used to test him or her. As noted by Padilla (1979), "a basic misconception concerning bilingualism is that because someone can speak a second language they can be tested in the second language" (p. 236).

Other perspectives on language proficiency that have major influences on language testing are the discrete-point and the integrative view. From the discrete-point view, language proficiency is perceived as ability to control discrete features of the language such as grammatical rules and phonemes. The Language Assessment Scale (LAS) is an example of a discrete-point language proficiency test (the LAS also has an integration component). The integrative view, on the other hand, defines language proficiency as simultaneous control of the various discrete features of the language. Instead of assessing proficiency in discrete skills such as knowledge of synonyms or antonyms, integrative testing would require an examinee to generate stories based on pictures presented. The Basic Inventory of Natural Language (BINL) is an example of an integrative language proficiency test.

*Assessment of Language Proficiency*

In addition to and related to the problem of the lack of a universally accepted conceptualization of the language proficiency construct, instrumentation problems further compound the difficulty of accurate identification of LEP children.  Although there are many commercial and locally developed language proficiency tests available (for instance, see Lange & Clifford, 1980; Pletcher, Locks, Reynolds, & Sisson, 1978; Stansfield, 1981; and Thorum, 1981), most of these tests' psychometric properties (reliability and validity) have not been determined.  The unknown quality of these tests, together with the diverse definitions of language proficiency, has generated a serious lack of consistency in the classification of students into the various English proficiency categories (Gillmore & Dickerson, 1980; Ulibarri, Spencer, & Rivas, 1981; Wald, 1981).  For example, the most recent study funded by the Department of Education (Pelavin, 1986) revealed that even between two commonly used commercial language proficiency tests, as many as 80% of the students classified as English Proficient by one test were classified as limited English Proficient by another.  Since results from this proficiency assessment will very often determine whether or not the student will be exempted from standardized testing, such inconsistencies between proficiency test results suggest that students may be exempted or not exempted from testing or may be tested in English or in their native language partly because of the language test used by the particular school district.  Another problem in using currently available language proficiency tests to identify LEP status is that these test results usually reflect a child's listening and speaking skills, which are BICS skills, and, as stated above, are not necessarily good indicators of the extent to which the child is ready to be tested in paper and pencil tests written in English (Lam, 1987).  In selecting a language test, the key is to clearly define the purpose of conducting such testing:  that is, how the test results will be used.

Another problematic area in the testing of LEP children develops out of the ease with which a child may be diagnosed as doing poorly in classroom and testing situations because of limited language skills when the real cause is an underlying learning disability.  Certainly such disabilities may result in language deficiencies that superficially resemble those of LEP students.  One indicator of a potential underlying learning disorder is a diagnosis of deficiency or slow development in both the native language and in English (Greenlee, 1981). As R. L. Jones (1979) suggests, determination of the native language proficiency of a LEP student becomes important when advancement in English is slower than that of other students with similar bilingual backgrounds. Jones also suggests that LEP students should be assessed in time to identify learning problems that exist from the beginning and that could hinder acquisition of a new language. Such a practice could also intercept problems of potentially greater magnitude. Another indicator of possible learning disability and hence one that justifies further diagnosis is deviation in a LEP child's test performance profile from that characteristic of his or her ethnic group (Cummins, 1982), for example, a performance as weak in arithmetic as in vocabulary.

The primary cause of learning disabilities may be inherent in the individual child rather than in his or her patterns of acculturation. However, testing instruments and other methods of assessment, including the initial referral process, that are sufficiently sensitive and complex to determine such conditions usually require administration by teams of experts and adequate assessment instruments. Once again, time, expense, and lack of competent bilingual school psychologists or translators/interpreters, inadequate cooperation from family members and the community and supportive research often prohibit adequate solutions to complex problems. Hence, although it is widely recognized the team approach is the best method for the assessment of LEP children with special needs (e.g., see Cheng, 1987), to implement such an approach requires much work and efforts to overcome the difficulties and obstacles listed above.

There is abundant need for research designed to improve current practices in assessing language proficiency. One general recommendation is to employ a multi-method approach, including, in addition to language testing, teachers' ratings, observation, and student background information. If instruction in children's native languages is to be provided and if one is to follow the PL 94-142 and "Lau Remedies" testing guidelines, a LEP child should be tested in his or her native language, and hence proficiency in his or her native language should be assessed. Currently, there is a dearth of such assessment instruments for languages, other than Spanish. Research and development of adequate instruments for the assessment of native language proficiency (including Spanish) therefore appears to be necessary.  However, the extent of what is needed is strongly affected by the political climate and current attitudes toward the education of LEP children.


## DIFFICULTIES AND PROBLEMS IN THE TESTING OF LEP CHILDREN


A test is psychometrically sound if the scores it produces are both reliable and valid.  A test is reliable if it can consistently produce the same scores for the same individuals because of low measurement error.  Validity refers to the extent to which the test is measuring the attribute that it purports to measure and not other irrelevant attributes or factors.  For example, a mathematics story problems test is designed to measure a student's application of mathematical skills, which is the target attribute.  If a child's performance on the test is affected by other irrelevant attributes, such as verbal and test-taking skills that the test is not intended to measure but by which the test score is nevertheless affected, then validity of the test is lowered.  Hence, a test is a psychometrically sound instrument if it can consistently measure only that attribute which it is intended to measure.

When differences in test performance between groups are found, it does not automatically prove test bias because it is possible that the observed differences in test performance do indeed reflect true group difference in the attribute the test measures.  An item is considered biased if two groups of individuals with equal abilities have different probabilities of  answering the item correctly (see Hills, 1989, for methods for identifying biased test items).  A test is biased and discriminatory against a certain group of children if, for that particular group, measurement error and the extent of contamination by extraneous factors, due to biased items contained in the test, is higher than for other groups to the extent that the target group's test scores are unfairly deflated.  This lowered reliability and validity, or test bias, is a result of the interaction between the children's background, the format and content of the test, and the manner and context in which the test is administered. This bias may exist to the extent that the test for the linguistic minority group no longer measures the same construct since the factorial structure differs significantly from that of the majority group   as determined by confirmatory factor analysis. Differential reliability and validity, including cross-cultural equivalence of measurement, must be determined in order to test LEP students with different socio-cultural and educational backgrounds (Brislin, Lonner, & Thorndike, 1973).   Use of test results that are not comparable across groups is unfair and discriminatory. Test bias is also dependent on the appropriateness of the purpose for using the test (Cole & Moss, 1989). A test used to measure reading comprehension of LEP children may be valid for that purpose, but the same test may not be appropriate for assessing learning potential of these children, and hence the scores are invalid for the second purpose. In this case, it is not the test itself, but rather, the interpretation of the test results that is biased.

The various factors that can contribute to bias and  unfairness in the testing of LEP children are described next. I then will discuss potential strategies for the solution of these inequities, taking into consideration the difference between standardized testing primarily for accountability purposes and classroom testing for instructional purposes (Cole, 1988).

*English Proficiency*

The most prominent irrelevant factor in the testing of LEP children in content areas other than language arts and proficiency that can contaminate validity of test scores is, of course, language skills.  It is an assumption in non-language testing that test performance is not affected by linguistic barriers. That is, the examinee is "able to follow instructions and to understand the questions, and [is] not slowed down in reading and answering questions to the point the test is no longer a 'power' test for them because they lack familiarity with English" (Lam, 1987, p. 4).   Violation of this assumption will make it difficult to determine the extent to which low scores are due to lack of knowledge in the content area (say, mathematical skills) or to language difficulty, which, in this case, is an irrelevant attribute.  For students with limited English proficiency or with proficiency substantially lower than that of their peers, the likelihood of violating this assumption is rather high. To quote from the *Standards for Educational and Psychological Testing* (AERA, APA, NCME, 1985) regarding testing of linguistic minorities,

> for a non-native English speaker and for a speaker of some dialects of English, every test given in English becomes, in part, a language or literacy test.... Test results may not reflect accurately the abilities and competencies being measured if test performance depends on these test takers' knowledge of English. (p. 73)

Regardless of how one conceptualizes, defines, and measures language proficiency, the consensus is that, except for tests designed to measure language skills, limited English proficiency handicaps and invalidates performance on tests in which instruction is given and content is written in English. Therefore, examinees with equal abilities or knowledge may receive significantly different scores if their levels of English proficiency differ (Blakely, 1986). It is with this observation that the *Standards for Educational and Psychological Testing* call for tests designed to "minimize threats to test reliability and validity that arise from language differences" (pp. 73-74). The following are some solution strategies to the language problem in testing LEP children.

1) Determine if the LEP child, particularly if he or she has some but not quite full proficiency, is suitable for testing. The decision to test or not to test a LEP student, that is, whether or not the student is testable (Lam, 1987), will depend primarily on the severity of his or her language deficiency and secondarily on other factors to be discussed later in this chapter. For standardized testing such as district or statewide achievement testing or psychological assessment, established guidelines for exempting LEP students should be followed cautiously. (The examiners should be prepared to challenge the credibility of prescribed procedures.) If no guidelines are available, administrators should establish such guidelines using multiple criteria such as language proficiency scores, student prior educational history and use of language, teacher observational ratings, and parental consent. These guidelines can be generalized to classroom testing. Those children who failed to meet the criteria for taking tests written in English can either be exempted from testing altogether or tested with comparable tests

written in the native language. It should be noted that exempting students from taking a test does not imply that the attribute measured by the test is not of importance; it normally means that the instrument is not appropriate for those particular students either because of the language, content, and format of the test or because the students are not expected to possess the target attribute (for example, recent immigrant high school students are not expected to have knowledge of American History). When exemption from testing is due to inappropriate test structure, alternative methods of assessment should be explored.

2) Translate tests from English to the child's native language. In locating a test written in the child's native language, the order of preference, particularly for standardized tests, should be the use of, first, an existing instrument; second, a translation of an existing instrument originally written in English; and third, construction of a new instrument. Given the dearth of instruments available in different languages, translation of existing instruments appears to be the most viable option. However, test translation is not without its shortcomings.

In test translation, an equivalent test is technically defined as one that has reliability, difficulty, and item by total-test score correlations equal to those of the original test (Clark, 1965). The most highly recommended procedure in test translation is back translation (Oakland, 1977; Valdes, Barera, & Cardinas, 1984). In this procedure, the test that has been translated into the second language is translated back into the original language. The two versions in the original language are compared, and modification is then made to items that show apparent discrepancies. After that process is completed, the revised version goes through another back translation. At least three back translations, each conducted by a different translator, are generally recommended (Brislin et al., 1973). Also, a decentering process is encouraged in which content is modified in both the original and the second language versions (Chapman & Carter, 1979). Back translation and decentering enable production of a translated test that is functionally rather than formally equivalent (Chapman & Carter, 1979). A formally equivalent test is a result of an exact and direct translation of items, the major shortcoming of which is distortion of meaning through translation because of basic dissimilarities between two languages. While accurate translation is more easily achieved if the two languages are closely related linguistically, it is always possible that a concept or word central to one culture may not have an exact counterpart in the other culture or that a word which has a single meaning in one culture may have multiple or opposite meanings in the other (Hyness, 1970). Hence, direct translation may actually introduce more language bias. Unfortunately, back translation, although a reliable method of reducing such bias, is costly and time-consuming, and very often it is difficult to find competent translators. There is, of course, far greater possibility for the introduction of language bias when translating a content area from the social sciences, for instance, than from mathematics. The quality of the translated test should be determined by establishment of the psychometric properties of the test (AERA et al., *Standards for Educational and Psychological Testing*, 1985). Invariance of performance on translated items can also be assessed through the use of item response theory (Hulin, Drasgow, & Parsons, 1983).

There are numerous other potential pitfalls with the use of test translation (DeAvila, 1973; Oakland, 1977; Samuda, 1975; Sechrest, Fay, & Zaidi, 1972). For example, the translated test may be technically comparable to the original test but the content may still be culture-bound (Olmedo, 1981). Also, the translated test may not be appropriate for subgroups with different dialects. For example, a Spanish translated test for Mexican children may not be appropriate for children from Puerto Rico. Perhaps one immediate realistic solution to the difficulties inherent in producing an appropriately equivalent test for use in crosscultural and subcultural situations is awareness of the pitfalls inherent in translations generally. Such awareness, while perhaps not resulting in adequately replicated test instruments, may provoke alternative solutions to assessment needs.

It is important to keep in mind when considering test translation that the basic goal of testing the child in his or her native language is to maximize the ability to understand what is required and to be able to express his knowledge and skills without language interference. As mentioned earlier, one cannot assume that, just because a child is not fluent in English but is conversant in his or her native language, he or she has sufficient academic native language proficiency to prevent language interference when tested in the native language, which may suggest learning disability or a lack of academic preparation.

Along with the guidelines for exempting LEP students or administering tests in the child's native language, there should also be guidelines for testing LEP students once they are judged testable in English (Lam, 1987). Some suggested recommendations are listed below.

3) Assure that the LEP students understand the test instructions by modifying and simplifying them and, if necessary, translate the instructions into the child's native language and present both language versions. Adequacy of instruction has been found an important source of test bias (Scheuneman, 1987, p. 166).

4) Extend the time limits to compensate for the extra time the LEP students need to read and respond to the items due to linguistic barriers.

5) Simplify wording by replacing non-content words that are unfamiliar to the children with those more familiar to the children. It is possible that even if a single word in an item is ambiguous to a student, the meaning of the item can be altered for him.

6) If a test proctor who speaks the children's native language is available, train the proctor to check and respond to questions regarding instruction and wordings that are not clear to the children but without unduly giving hints to the answers. For upper grade students, dictionaries should be permitted.

Test modifications, including the use of a native language speaker proctor, are potentially subject to stakeholder bias or bias due to the subjective nature of the procedures. To guard against these pitfalls, one should (1) have at least one non-stakeholder to verify the modifications to assure that the changes do not change the difficulty of the items; (2) document all the modifications; (3) if the same test is used for pre- and post-testings, make sure the same modifications are made to both testings; and (4) document and train proctors regarding what is permissible in assisting the LEP children in taking the tests. Also, it is important to remember that, if norm-referenced tests are used, test and procedural modifications will invalidate the norms, that is, the normative data usually derived from the test are no longer valid. However, at the same time, test reliability and validity are enhanced. The trade-off is, in the author's opinion, a favorable one. If normative information is used with a modified test, one should use it cautiously, keeping in mind that because the normative population is significantly different than the LEP population, the norms are inappropriate for evaluating LEP children's academic abilities and aptitude in the first place.

A potential solution to low norm validity for the LEP population is development of local or regional norms with standardization samples made up of students with similar linguistic, social-cultural, and educational backgrounds. While these specialized norms have the advantage of providing rough estimates of no-treatment expectations for program evaluation and guidance in the selection of tests with appropriate difficultly levels (Cleary et al., 1975), they have two major shortcomings. First, it is an immense and impractical task to devise norms for each language group and its subgroups in different regions (DeAvila & Havassy, 1974). Also, a comparison of LEP children with children of similar backgrounds negates the reality that these LEP children will eventually be competing with their English-speaking middle-class peers for educational and economic opportunities. Unless regional norms are also developed for college entrance and employment tests and job performance is compared only to individuals within each ethnic group, the special regional norms for school-age students may in fact perpetuate the tendency to underprepare these students to function successfully in American society. Research on the effects of test modification on test and norm validities for LEP and other special population is needed.

In addition to the language factor, as mentioned above, the social-cultural and educational backgrounds of LEP children introduce other difficulties to the assessment of this special population. The most significant background variables that have become extraneous factors in the testing of LEP children are cultural and educational experience, test sophistication, and test context.

## Cultural and Educational Experience

If the answers and the content of a test, such as vocabulary, examples, stories, and illustrations, are based on the middle-class culture, values, and experiences (that is, the test is ethnocentric), then it is likely that examinees with other cultural and educational backgrounds will be penalized in taking the test because of their lack of familiarity with the middle-class culture and values. Such culture bias in standardized testing has been a major criticism against the use of standardized testing because of its adverse effects on minority students (for example, Cole & Bruner, 1971; Laosa & Oakland, 1974, Neill & Medina, 1989). As a result, test publishers have been making a concerted effort to remove such bias from their tests by having the tests reviewed by experts for content that may be biased and offensive to students from different cultural and ethnic backgrounds and to use statistical procedures to detect biased items (see, for example, Cole and Moss, 1989). Since cultural and educational experiences are rather diverse in the LEP population, steps should be taken to avoid such bias on an individual basis and in classroom testing. Standardized tests should be reviewed for cultural bias for the particular cultural group in question by teachers and those who know these students. If judged necessary, modifications should be made to the test content, as discussed above, to increase its relevance for the group. The diversity of ethnic-cultural groups in American society also calls for item bias reviewer-teams of commercial test publishers, consisting of reviewers with understanding of the different languages and cultural backgrounds (Lam, 1988).

At times, the educational level of some LEP students may be lower than that of their grademates. In those cases, testing these students at grade level with standardized achievement measures may be too difficult for these students. An option to exempting these students from testing is to conduct out-of-level testing, that is, administer a test at a level lower than the students' grade level. The validity of the out-of-level testing procedure is controversial in nature (Lam, 1987). Recognizing that major problems with out-of-level testing are reduced face and curricular validities, the author believes that for content areas such as mathematics and language arts, testing students one level below or above is a viable option for increasing the reliability of test scores.

*Test Sophistication*

One of the explanations of the poor test performance of some LEP students is that they do not have test taking skills. Test taking skills, or testwiseness, is defined as "a subject's capacity to utilize the characteristics and formats of the test and/or the test-taking situation to receive a high score" (Millman, Bishop & Ebel, 1965). These skills include both those related to efficient test-taking behavior, such as effective utilization of time, and those related to "beating the test" through such strategies as identifying flaws in the item construction (for instance, choosing the longest option as the correct answer). While one can hardly question the legitimacy of efficient test-taking skills, arriving at correct answers on the basis of test structure characteristics rather than knowledge of the content can be viewed as "tricks" to test-taking that should not be encouraged. Nevertheless, low, not high, test-taking skills introduce measurement error (Ebel, 1965).

The literature has shown that testwiseness is related to performance on standardized tests (Callenbach, 1973; Gaines & Jongsma, 1974; Oakland, 1972). Also, a limited amount of research evidence suggests that minority students tend to be less testwise than their majority peers because they lack familiarity with objective tests containing primarily multiple-choice items (Millman & Setijadi, 1966). As expected, if LEP students are not familiar with a test's format, procedures, and vocabulary, they will have difficulty demonstrating their knowledge and comprehension by their test performance (Blakely, 1986). Also, testwiseness has been found to have a positive correlation with verbal skills (Diamond & Evans, 1972). Because of these findings, it seems logical to assume that, at least for some types of LEP student, such as recent immigrants from countries that do not emphasize standardized objective testing, lack of test taking skills is likely to be an extraneous factor that can lower both their test performance and its validity.

Fortunately, research has also suggested that testwiseness can be developed through training (see, for example, Gibbs, 1964; Moore, Schutz, & Baker, 1966; Langer, et al., 1973; Sarnacki, 1979; Slakter et al., 1970) and abundant training materials are available. (See e.g. Caswell, 1982, for a partial list.) It appears that given the limited resources and time constraints often encountered in school settings and the legitimacy of the two types of test-taking skills discussed above, teaching to improve efficient test-taking behavior of LEP students should be the focus of test-taking skills training. Practice tests designed to familiarize examinees with the test accompany most standardized tests. Minimally, LEP students judged as naive test-takers should be given practice tests. If circumstances permit, a test-taking skills program should be established. No matter what training one offers, three caveats should be noted. First, the interval between training and testing should not be long, probably less than two weeks. If students' improvement across time is being assessed, training should occur just prior to the first pre-test rather than the post-test, so that the post-test scores will not be inflated (or the pre-test scores deflated), hence inflating the change scores. Finally, for extremely test-naive children, more than one training period may be needed, especially if the training is brief (as in simply administering the practice test). These recommendations apply to standardized objective testing for accountability or instructional purposes.

*Test Content*

A test should be administered in such a manner to elicit maximal performance of all examinees. LEP children with low socio-economic family backgrounds may have low motivation to succeed in school because of their pessimistic view of the future rewards of their efforts. This negative attitude will probably introduce a negative bias in their attitudes toward testing. Motivation to do well on tests can be enhanced through explanation of testing purposes and by use of the procedures discussed above to improve the appropriateness of the tests for them. Another way of motivating them to do well on tests is by reducing the procedural bias of the context in which testing takes place, especially in regard to characteristics of the examiner.

In a series of research investigations conducted by Fuchs and associates on the effects of examiner familiarity (defined as level of acquaintance) on test performances of language-handicapped children, the researchers found that

> language-handicapped children obtain higher scores when tested by familiar, rather than by unfamiliar, examiners and that this performance appears robust.... Moreover, it appears that unfamiliar examiners depress the performance of language-handicapped, but not unhandicapped, children ..., indicating that examiner unfamiliarity is a source of systematic error or bias in the assessment of language handicapped children. The importance of this finding is underscored by the fact that most examiners are strangers to their examinees. (Fuchs & Fuchs, 1989, p. 304)

In a meta-analysis of examiner familiarity effects on Caucasian, Black, and Hispanic students' test performances, Fuchs and Fuchs (1989) found that examiner familiarity effects raised Caucasian and minority examinees' tests performance by .05 and .72 standard deviations respectively.

Research on effects of the examiner's race on minority students' test performance has found both significant (e.g., Jacobs & DeGraaf, 1972; Mishra, 1980) and negligible effects (e.g., Graziano et al. 1982; Jensen, 1974; Sattler, 1973; Shuey, 1966). Upon close examination, it appears that the personal characteristics of the examiner and the consequent rapport established between examiner and examinee are more important than whether or not they have the same racial or cultural background, although ease of establishing rapport and cultural match are probably related. Since negative examiner effects arise from anxiety and uneasiness induced by the examiner, especially in individualized testing, an examiner who is receptive, warm, caring, and responsive, and who gains the trust of the examinee, should reduce the examinee's apprehensiveness. Such trust may be more readily achieved if the examiner also has the same ethnic and linguistic background as the examinee's. If a monolingual examiner is used, especially in individualized testing, it may be important to include a bilingual interpreter. (A bilingual interpreter is also important for standardized testing if one is to follow the procedures recommended above.) In addition, testing LEP students in a familiar classroom environment also contributes to students' high motivation. If student progress is to be assessed, it is important that the testing environment remain the same at pre- and post-testings in order to avoid distorting the assessment of change due to differential examiner effects. When there is room for subjectivity in scoring, such as rating of writing samples, efforts should be made to conceal examinees identities in order to avoid unduly negative expectation of their performance due to examiner's knowledge of the examinees' language status and cultural backgrounds.

## SUMMARY

For consideration of the best methods for testing cognitive abilities, academic achievement, and affective growth of LEP children, accurate assessment of their language proficiencies is essential. However, identification of LEP children is made difficult by various theories and definitions of language proficiency and the lack of sound assessment instruments and procedures, especially when testing also entails the determination of learning disabilities. In view of these problems, a multiple-method approach to assessing language proficiency is recommended.

In conducting educational and psychological testing, implicit assumptions are made about the examinees. To the extent that these assumptions are not met, reliability and validity of the test scores will suffer. In testing LEP children, four test assumptions could be violated because of the test-takers' language background and its socio-cultural and educational correlates. These assumptions are: 1) that there are no language barriers that will hinder the examinees' test performances, 2) that the cultural and educational experiences of the examinees are those of the middle-class mainstream population, 3) that the examinees have the necessary test-taking skills, and 4) that the testing context, in particular the characteristics of the examiner and the examiner's family background, do not inhibit the examinees' motivation to do their best on the test. Potential practical solutions to these problems in the testing of LEP children proposed and discussed in this chapter include test translation, minor modifications of test content and procedures, test review for cultural bias, teaching of test-taking skills, use of examiners who understand the children's language and cultural experience, and testing conducted in environments familiar to the children.

## CONCLUSIONS AND DISCUSSION

With the rapid growth of the LEP population, educational administrators and teachers face an increasing need to muster adequate resources and sound instructional approaches with which to combat the unprecedented and proliferating difficulties in the education of LEP students in the American school system. Without concerted effort to stem this growing failure on the part of our educational system, the country's economic, social, and political stability may be threatened (Levin, 1985).

In response to these educational needs, there is an increasing demand for psychometrically sound educational, linguistic, and psychological assessment instruments and procedures for use with the population of LEP children. Also, "the sheer growth rate of the population with non-English backgrounds is likely to force schools and communities to rely even more on testing and assessment as a crucial tool in making decisions about which educational services to offer these students" (Duran, 1989, p. 582). Although currently there is intense interest in the research and development of adequate testing practices for language-minority children, much progress is needed to improve the quality of the tests, the conditions under which they are administered, and the way in which test results are used. Without such advancement, negative effects of inappropriate and premature testing will perpetuate, including intellectual and emotional harm (deflated self-esteem) due to the frustration, feelings of helplessness, and humiliating experiences that derive from test taking. Misuse of test results in reaching inappropriate instructional decisions include student placement and lowered teacher expectations based on labels associated with poor test performances. These harmful testing effects can mitigate against the academic success of LEP children and must be eliminated. As noted by Macdonald (1975), evaluation of students without consideration of "the emotional impact,. . . [the] full awareness of its reward function, . . . [and] the consequences of evaluation upon the total lives of the students" (p. 19) is immoral evaluation.

For improvement in the testing of LEP children, the need to construct sound assessment instruments is obvious. Also, as implied by the above discussion on strategies for improving testing practices of

LEP children, efforts must be made to develop policy for testing, to train competent examiners, and to explore alternative ways of testing.

### Policy for Testing LEP Children

As discussed above, consideration must be given as to whether or not a LEP child should be exempted from testing and, if tested, in which language and with what procedure the test should be administered. Policy that sets guidelines for testing LEP children is much needed to avoid subjective and arbitrary decisions and stakeholder bias (selection of students for testing for the purpose of raising or lowering average group scores), both of which can cause substantial damage to the child's psychological well-being and educational opportunities. Testing policies for LEP children must be technically sound, logical, and research-based. Currently, there is a demand for work that will lead to establishing sound policy for testing LEP students. Based on a national survey of state policy for LEP student testing, Lam, Tonigan and Panofsky (1989), in their preliminary analysis, found that about half the states that returned the questionnaires did not have any guidelines for exemption of LEP students from standardized testing. The recently published *Code of Fair Testing Practices in Education* (Joint Committee on Testing Practices, 1988), in which codes for fairness are delineated, represents an attempt to generate guidelines for testing children from different linguistic and cultural backgrounds. However, this effort is inadequate as a guide, as the codes are much too superficial to be useful in applied situations. Sound state and district policies for testing LEP students with specific step-by-step guidelines are necessary.

### Training of Competent Examiners

One of the factors discussed above that contributes to adequate testing of LEP children is the appropriateness and competency of the examiner. In individualized cognitive and psychological assessment of LEP children, not only must the examiners be skilled in proper test selection and administration and in interpretation of test scores, but they must also be knowledgeable in linguistics, bilingual special education, and cross-cultural counseling, and have either background in or understanding of other languages and cultures. Given the scarcity of school psychologists with bilingual assessment specializations, university-based training programs should be developed to train and produce new school psychologists with the skills and experience to work effectively with LEP children (Figuerosa, Sandoval, & Merino, 1982; Rosenfield, 1982). In addition to training programs, in-service training should be provided for teachers and school psychologists who conduct testing of LEP children. The primary purpose of in-service training is to enhance the examiners' sensitivity to and awareness of the cultural and linguistic differences of LEP children. The least preferred method of bilingual assessment is the employment of interpreters to assist monolingual examiners in testing. For less common languages, bilingual assessors are less apt to be available; the use of an interpreter may be the only option. These interpreters should be trained in language interpretation and testing skills. In sum, training of new bilingual school psychologists, provision of in-service training for existing school psychologists and teachers, and recruitment and training of interpreters of various languages are crucial for the improvement of testing practices of LEP children.

## Alternative Methods of Assessing LEP Children

One approach to improving the quality of LEP testing, (that is, being able to measure the target attribute with a minimum of confounding influences by irrelevant factors) is the exploration of alternatives to traditional methods of testing, which usually involve a single testing with either a paper and pencil test or an oral examination. These alternatives may either be non-test assessment options, such as observation, or, modification of existing testing procedures, some of which I have discussed above, or new testing procedures. Here, alternative methods of assessing LEP children in the areas of language proficiency, academic achievement, and special education are briefly considered. These alternative assessment methods can either replace or supplement the existing assessment procedures.

In addition to the techniques used in tests to assess different areas of language proficiency, such as measuring oral production by presenting a picture to the examinees and asking them to produce stories, other more indirect or disguised methods have been proposed in the literature. These methods include, for example, sentence repetition (Natalicio, 1976), reaction-time tests of bilingualism, in which examinees are asked to recall in a specific period of time as many words as possible in their native language and within the same period of time as many words as possible in English (Johnson, 1953), and others (see Fishman & Cooper, 1969). These alternative methods and others yet to be explored (for example, the time it takes to count backwards in the two languages), may be useful for determining language dominance or as supplemental data to language proficiency test scores.

For the assessment of academic achievement, traditionally either norm-referenced or criterion-referenced tests are used. Norm-referenced testing evaluates students' performance by comparing it to the performance of their peers (norms). Criterion-referenced testing utilizes pre-determined criteria to evaluate student mastery of specific educational tasks. While norm-referenced tests are suitable for accountability purposes, such as for determining federal and state program eligibility or assessing program effects, they are usually not as sensitive to the curriculum as criterion-referenced tests. Because of the prescriptive and diagnostic nature of criterion-referenced testing, it has been recommended for bilingual handicapped children in educational program planning (Mowder, 1980). Currently, there is growing dissatisfaction with current testing practices, and a strong interest in fair and valid assessment of educational quality is developing. This movement is exemplified by the recent (October 1989) international "Quality Indicator Forum" sponsored by the Center for Research on Evaluation Standards and Student Testing (CRESST), which took place on the UCLA campus. A major target of criticism in current testing practices is the use of the highly structured objective test format which, educators claim, cannot adequately measure learning because of the mismatch between how the information is learned and how it is tested (for example, using multiple-choice items to measure reading skills). Also, even with criterion-referenced testing, the overlap between curriculum and test content or the linkage between instruction and assessment is not as high as it ought to be. There is a trend toward employing performance testing, in which learning is evaluated through observation and examination of the quality of a task or project (for example, a writing sample or oral presentation) completed by the student.  In this way, academic progress is assessed by examining a portfolio of student work instead of their written responses to items in standardized achievement tests.  Although this method of assessing student knowledge has always been used by teachers, it is the first time attempts have been made to employ it to replace accountability testing such as  statewide achievement testing or special program eligibility testing.  The implementation of this "authentic" assessment broadly and uniformly is expectedly a nontrivial task.  For example, training of teachers, resource limitations, and federal stipulations on the use of norm-referenced tests are some of the problems encountered by the state of North Carolina  in its recent effort to implement this new assessment.

Curriculum-based measurement (Salvia & Hughes, 1990), which combines the advantages of both commercial achievement tests and teacher observation (Deno, 1985), falls in line with this trend toward behavioral assessment of educational achievement (Shapiro, 1987). This testing approach, which has been used in special education, focuses on direct assessment of curriculum and close monitoring of student progress through routine and tailored testing (Blankenship, 1985; Marston & Magnusson, 1985) and hence holds the greatest promise to test what's being taught.   The curriculum-based measurement approach appears to concur with the advocation of the use of computer to conduct continual diagnostic assessment of student learning for the purpose of guiding instruction (Green, 1988).

The shortcomings of this approach are twofold.  First, as with criterion-referenced testing, curriculum-based assessment requires substantial understanding of the pedagogical approach and curriculum used for instruction (Reynolds et al., 1984).  Second, it is difficult to use the results for between-individual or between-group comparisons; hence they may not be immediately useful for accountability purposes, such as program evaluation.  Nevertheless, curriculum-based measurement has far more potential advantages than weaknesses, and future research is clearly warranted.   Chapter 5 of this volume provides a review of curriculum-based assessment.

It seems that curriculum-based measurement not only can be applied to the regular education setting but could also be a viable alternative to standardized achievement tests for the LEP population because of its flexibility of adjustment to individual student backgrounds and needs.   Thus far,  the  applicability of  curriculum-based measurement outside of special education, especially for minority students, has not been explored and should be, given the promise of its present applications. Similarly, portfolio assessment and computer diagnostic assessment appear to be effective alternatives or supplement to standardized paper and pencil testing not only for the mainstream student population but also for the LEP children. Future research is needed to test this observation.

The dissatisfaction with the highly structured educational assessment practices and the quest for valid assessment options or quality indicators are exacerbated by the need to develop procedures for assessing thinking as a response to the current emphasis in education to teach higher order cognitive functioning (See the special issue of *Educational Researcher* on educational assessment, Nickerson, 1989). As noted by Nickerson (1989), for the assessment of high-level cognitive abilities, currently "there is not a consensus...as to precisely what kinds of tests should be constructed or how they should be used" (p.3). Some proposed assessment procedures such as interviews, observations, and justification of answer selection, all focus on understanding the process an examinee employs in arriving at the solution to a question presented to him or her. In comparison to the traditional assessment approach, this cognitive approach should enable the examiner to more easily disentangle the language difficulty of the LEP children from the attribute being measured.

In special education assessment of language minority students, as it is with other types of testing, in addition to the obvious language bias, the socio-cultural backgrounds of these students also present potential bias that can invalidate the test results; in particular, the opportunity to learn the skills, knowledge, and values measured by the test. A solution to cultural bias has been the construction of culture-free tests. This effort has not met with success as test developers have realized that tests are not capable of measuring their target attributes and at the same time devoid of culture. As noted by Sattler (1988): "Every test is culturally loaded to some extent. Thus it is important to distinguish between a test that is culturally loaded and one that is culturally biased" (p.579) since "learning takes place in a social-cultural environment" (Barnett, 1983, p. 40). As an alternative to culture-free tests and as a supplement or alternative to the traditional intelligence tests such as the WISC-R, various models have been developed which either integrate or take into consideration the socio-cultural differences of the language minority students and their influences on test performance (Cummins, 1984). These models include the System of Multicultural Pluralistic Assessment (SOMPA) (Mercer & Lewis, 1977), the task analysis model of assessment (Mercer & Ysseldyke, 1977), the Cartoon Conservation Scales (DeAvila & Havassy, 1974), the Kaufman Assessment Battery for Children (Kaufman & Kaufman, 1983), the Learning Potential Assessment Device (LPAD) (Feuerstein, 1979). The LPAD and its variant, the Budoff Learning Potential Assessment Techniques, commonly referred to as the dynamic assessment technique, utilize the test-teach-retest strategy to assess individual ability to learn new information or skills, and hence their potential to learn. (See Jones, 1988, for a description of these techniques). The techniques appear to be promising for assessing learning disabilities of LEP children. As noted by Duran (1989), "Adaptation of these techniques for use with United States children of non-English backgrounds has not been investigated and merits intensive attention" (p. 582). Due to the fact that the dynamic assessment techniques and other assessment models are costly and time-consuming, investigation of the appropriateness of established non-verbal or culture-fair tests, such as the Block Design subtest of the WISC-R, the Raven's Progressive Matrices, and Cattell's Culture-Fair Intelligence Tests, and new non-verbal tests such as the test of Nonverbal Intelligence (TONI), is in order for special education assessment of LEP students. Although these non-verbal tests have been used in that capacity due to a lack of more appropriate alternatives, research is needed to support the appropriateness of such usage of the tests; especially in view of the unsettled question: "Can content of a test and the process tested be equally common to all cultures?"

Testing, especially testing of language minority children, has been a controversial issue in the history of testing. As noted by Nickerson (1989), "some people object to testing in principle, others believe that too little of it is done" (p. 5). Regardless of the opposition, educational and psychological assessment, together with their inherent problems, will endure as long as civilization continues to flourish. To avoid misuse of testing of LEP children, as it is for testing of all children, we must conduct careful and in depth analysis of the purposes of testing and their associated negative side effects. (See Cole and Moss, 1989, for a guideline.) Teachers' knowledge and competency in the construction and use of tests and other assessment instruments must be enhanced. More importantly, we must be cognizant at all times that regardless of whether assessment is performed for instructional or accountability reasons, the mission of testing is to assure equal educational and economical opportunities and to enhance quality of life for all children, including those children whose English proficiency is limited.

# REFERENCES

American Educational Research Association, American Psychological Association, and National Council on Measurement in Education 1985. *Standards for Educational and Psychological Testing.* Washington, D.C.: Author.

> This revision of the 1974 *Standards for Educational and Psychological Tests* was developed in response to increasing social concern about the role of standardized testing in achievement of socioeconomic equity. Technical advances and new applications in the general area of testing also required accountability through more clearly articulated criteria for evaluation of tests, testing practices, and the effects of test use.

Bachman, L.F., & Palmer, A.S. 1981. "The Construct Validation of the FSI Oral Interview." *Language Learning, 31,* 67-86.

Baratz-Snowden, J., Rock, D., Pollock, J., & Wilder, G. 1988. "The Educational Progress of Language Minority Children: Findings from the NAEP 1985-86 Special Study." Princeton, NJ: National Assessment of Educational Progress/Educational Testing Service.

Barnett, D.W. 1983. *Nondiscriminatory Multifactored Assessment: A Sourcebook.* New York, NY: Human Sciences Press, Inc.

Blakely, M.M. February 1986. "Teaching Test-taking Skills to Elementary LEP Students." National Clearinghouse for Bilingual Education Forum.

Blankenship, C.S. 1985. "Assessment, Curriculum, and Instruction." In J.F. Cawley (Ed.), *Practical Mathematics Appraisal of the Learning Disabled*, 59-79. Rockville, MD: Aspen Systems.

Brislin, R. W., Lonner, W.J., & Thorndike, R.M. 1973. *Cross-cultural Research Methods.* New York: John Wiley & Sons.

Callenbach, C. 1973. "The Effects of Instruction and Practice in Content-independent Test-taking Techniques upon the Standardized Reading Test Scores of Selected Second Grade Students." *Journal of Educational Measurement, 10,* 25-30.

Caswell, M.S. Spring 1982. "A Guide to Test Taking: As Easy as 1-2-3." *Educational Measurement: Issues and Practice, 1(1),* 20-23.

Chapman, D.W., & Carter, J.F. 1979. "Translation Procedures for the Cross-cultural Use of Measurement Instruments." *Educational Evaluation and Policy Analysis, 1(3),* 71-76.

> The authors analyze methods of verifying and validating translations of tests, questionnaires, and other measurement devices for cross-cultural use.

Cheng L-R.L. 1987. *Assessing Asian Language Performance: Guidelines for Evaluating Limited-English-Proficient Students.* Aspen Publication Inc., Maryland: Rockville.

> In these guidelines for evaluating LEP Asian minority students, Dr. Cheng treats with knowledge and understanding those cultural constraints and linguistic differences that greatly complicate efforts of language assessment and intervention. Numerous instruments, formal and informal, provided throughout the book should prove of considerable use to evaluators.

Clark, J. 1965. "Item by Item Parallel Achievement Test for Different Foreign Languages." *Journal of Educational Measurement, 2,* 77-83.

Cleary, T.A., Humphreys, L.G., Kendrick, S.A., & Wesman, A. 1975. " Educational Uses of Tests with Disadvantaged Students." *American Psychologist, 30,* 15-41.

Cole, M., & Bruner, J.S. 1971. "Cultural Differences and Inferences about Psychological Processes." *American Psychologist, 26,* 867-876.

The "deficit hypothesis" often used to account for the intellectual inferiority of minority groups when measured by American middle-class standards is criticized by Cole and Bruner. Environmental conditioning yields differences, not deficits, as demonstrated by studies by Labov and others summarized in this article. The idea of competence needs more accurate theoretical development and more enlightened experimental applications.

Cole, N.S. 1988. "A Realist's Appraisal of the Prospects for Unifying Instruction and Assessment." In *Assessment in the Service of Learning: Proceedings of the 1987 ETS Invitational Conference.* Princeton, N.J.: Educational Testing Service.

Cole, N.S., & Moss, P.A. 1989. "Bias in Test Use." In Linn, R.L. (Ed.), *Educational Measurement (3rd edition)*. New York: Macmillan.

This paper discusses the definition of test bias in the context of validity, methods of investigating bias, and procedures for a broader evaluation of test use other than technical validity evidence.

Cummins, J. 1980. "The Cross-lingual Dimensions of Language Proficiency: Implications for Bilingual Education and the Optimal Age Issue." *TESOL Quarterly, 14(2)*, 175-187.

Cummins, J. 1982. "Tests, Achievement, and Bilingual Students." *Focus: National Clearinghouse for Bilingual Education, 9*, 1-7.

Cummins, J. 1984. "Bilingualism and Special Education." In C. Rivera (Ed.), *Language Proficiency and Academic Achievement*, 71-76. Avon, England: Multilingual Matters.

DeAvila, E.A. 1973. "I.Q. and the Minority Child." *Journal of the Association of Mexican-American Educators, 1*, 34-38.

DeAvila, E.A., & Havassy, B. 1974. "The Testing of Minority Children--A Neo-Piagetian Approach." *Today's Education, 63*, 71-75.

Deno, S.L. 1985. "Curriculum-based Measurement: The Emerging Alternative." *Exceptional Children, 52(3),* 219-232.

This paper described curriculum-based measurement (CBM) as an alternative to both commercial standardized tests and informal teacher observations. Illustrations focus on the use of CBM in special education.

Diamond, J.J., & Evans, W.J. 1972. "An Investigation of the Cognitive Correlates of Test-wiseness." *Journal of Educational Measurement, 9(2),* 145-150.

Dulay, H., & Burt, M. 1980. "The Relative Proficiency of Limited English Proficient Students." *National Association for Bilingual Education (NABE) Journal, 4,* 1-24.

Duran, P.D. 1989. "Testing of Linguistic Minorities." In Linn, R.L. (Ed.), *Educational Measurement (3rd edition).* New York: Macmillan.

Complications of adapting and implementing valid assessment procedures for persons with non-English backgrounds are related to the population validity of tests and to the legitimacy of test-development and test-administration practices. Selected studies that examine effects of language background and proficiency on the validity of test use in education are reviewed.

Ebel, R.L. 1965. *Measuring Educational Achievement.* Englewood Cliffs, NJ: Prentice-Hall.

Feuerstein, P. 1979. *The Dynamic Assessment of Retarded Performers.* Baltimore: University Park Press.

Figuerosa, R.A., Sandoval, J., & Merino, B. 1982. *Preparing School Psychologists to Serve Bilingual and Limited English Proficient Children.* Davis, CA: University of California, Dept. of Education.

Fishman, J.A. & Cooper, R.L. 1969. "Alternative Measures of Bilingualism." *Journal of Verbal Learning and Verbal Behavior, 8,* 276-282.

Frederiksen, N. 1984. "The Real Test Bias: Influences of Testing on Teaching and Learning." *American Psychologist, 19,* 193-202.

Fuchs, D., & Fuchs, L.S. 1989. "Effects of Examiner Familiarity on Black, Caucasian and Hispanic Children: A Meta-analysis." *Exceptional Children, 55(4),* 303-308.

> This paper presents a synthesis of 14 controlled studies of examiner familiarity effects that were coded in terms of methodological quality (high v. low) and race-ethnicity (Caucasian v. Black and Hispanic). The authors conclude that at the time of writing it was precipitous to assume a lack of testing bias toward minority children; more research is sorely needed.

Gaines, W.G., & Jongsma, E.A. April 1974. "The Effect of Training in Test-taking Skills on the Achievement Scores of Fifth Grade Pupils." Paper presented at the annual meeting of the National Council on Measurement in Education, Chicago, Illinois.

Gibb, B.G. 1964. "Test-wiseness as Secondary Cue Response." Doctoral dissertation, Stanford University. Ann Arbor, MI: University Microfilms, No. 64-7643.

Gillmore, G., & Dickerson, A.D. 1980. "The Relationship between Instruments Used for Identifying Children of Limited English Proficiency in Texas." *Bilingual Resources, 3(3),* 16-29.

Graziano, W.G., Varca, P.E., & Levy, J.C. 1982. "Race of Examiner Effects and the Validity of Intelligence Tests." *Review of Educational Research, 52(4),* 469-97.

Green, R. 1988. "Adaptive Testing by Computer." In R.B. Ekstrom (Ed.), *Measurement Technology and Individuality in Education: New Directions for Testing and Measurement* (p. 5-12). San Francisco, CA: Jossey-Bass.

Greenlee, M. 1981. "Specifying the Needs of a Bilingual Developmentally Disabled Population: Issues and Case Studies." *NABE Journal, 6(1)*, 55-75.

Hills, J.R. Winter 1989. "Screening for Potentially Biased Items in Testing Programs." *Educational Measurement: Issues and Practice, 4*, 5-11.

Hulin, C.L., Drasgow, F., & Parsons, C.K. 1983. *Item Response Theory: Applications to Psychological Measurement.* Homewood, IL: Dow Jones-Irwin.

Hyness, D. 1970. "Linguistic Aspects of Comparative Political Research." In R.T. Holt & J.E. Turner (Eds), *The Methodology of Comparative Research.* New Jersey: Free Press.

Jacobs, J.F., & DeGraaf, C.A. 1972. *Expectancy and Race: Their Influence upon the Scoring of Individual Intelligence Tests.* Dept. of Special Education, Southern Illinois University, Carbondale.

Jensen, A.R. 1974. "The Effect of Race of Examiner on the Mental Test Scores of White and Black Pupils." *Journal of Educational Measurement, 11*, 1-14.

Johnson, G.B. 1953. "Bilingualism as Measured by a Reaction-time Technique and the Relationship between a Language and a Non-language Intelligence Quotient." *Journal of Genetic Psychology, 82*, 3-9.

Joint Committee on Testing Practices. 1988. *Code of Fair Testing Practices in Education.* Washington D.C.: Author.

> This *Code of Fair Testing Practices in Education* describes the major obligations to test takers of professionals who develop or use educational tests. It considers separately the roles of test developers and of test users.

Jones, R.J. 1979. "Protection in Evaluation Procedures: Criteria and Recommendations." In *PEP: Developing Criteria for the Evaluation of*

160 Limited English Proficient Children

*Protection in Evaluation Procedures Provisions* (p. 15-84). Philadelphia,PA: Research for Better Schools.

Jones, R.L. (Ed.) 1988. *Psychoeducational Assessment of Minority Group Children: A Case Book.* Berkeley, CA: Cobb & Henry.

The author relies upon case studies to highlight practices designed to provide nondiscriminatory assessments of minority group children. This variety of assessment procedures should provide useful models for both educators and researchers.

Kaufman, A., & Kaufman, N. 1983. *Kaufman Assessment Battery for Children.* Circle Pines, MN: American Guidance Services.

Lam, T.C.M. 1987. "Testability: A Critical Issue in Testing Minority Students with Standardized Achievement Tests." Paper presented at the Minority Assessment Third Annual Conference, Tucson, Arizona.

This paper discusses issues related to exempting students with limited English proficiency from testing and modifying standardized tests for this population of students.

Lam, T.C.M. 1988. "Testing, Opportunity Allocation, and Asian and Pacific Americans." National Commission on Testing and Public Policy, Graduate School of Education, University of California, Berkeley.

Lam, T.C.M., Tonigan, S., & Panofsky, C. 1989. "State Policies for Testing Students of Limited English Proficiency." Paper presented at the annual meeting of the American Educational Research Association, San Francisco, CA.

A survey was conducted to examine state policies for exemptions and test modifications for students with limited English proficiency backgrounds.

Lange, D.C., & Clifford, R.T. 1980. *Language in Education: Theory and Practice,* 24. Arlington, VA: Center for Applied Linguistics.

Langer, G., Wark, D., & Johnson, S. 1973. "Test-wiseness in Objective Tests." In P.L. Nacke (Ed.), *Diversity in Mature Reading: Theory and Research, Vol. 1,* 22nd Yearbook of the National Reading Conference. National Reading Conference, Milwaukee, Wisconsin.

Laosa, L.M., & Oakland, T.D. April 1974. "Social Control in Mental Health: Psychological Assessment and the Schools." Paper presented at the 51st annual meeting of the American Orthopsychiatric Association, San Francisco.

Levin, H. 1985. "The Educationally Disadvantaged: A National Crisis (Working Paper No. 6)." Philadelphia, PA: Public/Private Ventures.

MacDonald, J.B. Spring 1975. "Some Moral Problems in Classroom Evaluation/Testing." *The Urban Review, 8(1),* 18-27.

Macias, R.F. 1977. "U.S. Hispanics in 2000 A.D.-Projecting the Number." *Agenda, 7(3),* 16-20.

Marston, D., & Magnusson, D. 1985. "Implementing Curriculum-based Measurement in Special and Regular Education Settings." *Exceptional Children, 52(3),* 266-276.

Mercer, J.R., & Lewis, J.F. 1977. *System of Multicultural Pluralistic Assessment.* New York: Psychological Corporation.

Mercer, J., & Ysseldyke, J. 1977. "Designing Diagnostic-intervention Programs." In T. Oakland (Ed.), *Psychological and Educational Assessment of Minority Children* (pp. 70-90). New York: Brunner/Mazel.

Millman, J., Bishop, C.H., & Ebel, R. 1965. "An Analysis of Test-wiseness." *Educational and Psychological Measurement, 25,* 707-726.

Millman, J., & Setijadi. February 1966. "A Comparison of American and Indonesian Students on Three Types of Test Items." *Journal of Educational Research, 59(6),* 273-275.

Mishra, S.P. 1980. "The Influence of Examiner's Ethnic Attributes on Intelligence Test Scores." *Psychology in the Schools, 17(1)*, 117-121.

Moore, J.C., Schutz, R.E., & Baker, R.L. 1966. "The Application of a Self-instructional Technique to Develop a Test-taking Strategy." *American Educational Research Journal, 3*, 13-17.

Mowder, B.A. 1980. "A Strategy for the Assessment of Bilingual Handicapped Children." Manuscript based on paper presented at the National Council on Measurement in Education, San Francisco, April 1979.

> A dual approach is needed to assess bilingual children with possible handicapping conditions. The author finds that pluralistic assessment techniques seem well-suited to sort out handicapped from nonhandicapped children. For determining educational needs, the criterion-referenced approach seems the most useful.

Natalicio, D.S. April 1976. "Sentence Repetition as a Language Assessment Technique: Some Issues and Applications." Paper presented at the annual meeting of the American Educational Research Association, San Francisco.

Neill, D.M., & Medina, N.J. 1989. "Standardized Testing: Harmful to Educational Health." *Phi Delta Kappan, 70(9)*, 688-697.

Nickerson, R.S. (Ed.) December 1989. Special Issue on Educational Assessment. *Educational Researcher, 18(9)*, 3-32.

Oakland, T. 1972. "The Effects of Test-wiseness Materials on Standardized Test Performance of Preschool Disadvantaged Children." *Journal of School Psychology, 10(4)*, 355-360.

> Test-wiseness, or familiarity with the format and language of test-taking situations, is here examined with regard to preschool and primary grade children. Specific abilities were identified as prerequisites for taking standardized readiness tests. Curricular materials were then designed to facilitate their

development. The paper focuses on evaluation of these materials.

Oakland, T. 1977. *Psychological and Educational Assessment of Minority Children.* (Ed.) New York: Brunner/Mazel.

The book contains an introduction and five papers from various authors that deal with different aspects of nondiscriminatory assessment, ranging from an historical account of the movement, legal issues, methods, and designing and operating diagnostic-intervention programs. The book also has eight appendices, including an annotated bibliography of language dominance measures.

Oller, J.W. 1979. *Language Tests at School.* London: Longman Group.

Two seriously underexamined issues are opened up in this book: (1) how language testing can relate to a pragmatic view of language as communication, and (2) how language testing can relate to educational measurement in general. In both areas the practical needs of the classroom teacher are of fundamental concern.

Olmedo, E.L. October 1981. "Testing Linguistic Minorities." *American Psychologist, 36(1),* 1078-1085.

The author describes such key conceptual issues as bilingualism, acculturation, and the "emictic" distinction as means of taking into account the diverse social, political, and economic realities that face linguistic minority groups. These issues, together with such operational ones as assessment of language dominance, test translation and development, and the examiner variable, should all be considered in the psychological and educational testing of members of linguistic minority groups.

Oxford, R., Poll, L., Lopez, D., Stupp, P., Gendell, M., & Peng, S. 1981. "Projections of Non-English Background Limited English

Proficient Persons in the United States to the Year 2000: Educational Planning in the Demographic Context." *NABE Journal, 5(3)*, 1-30.

Oxford-Carpenter, R., Pol, L., Lopez, D., Stupp, P., Gendell, M., & Peng, S. 1984. "Demographic Projections of Non-English-language Background and Limited-English-proficient Persons in the United States to the Year 2000 by State, Age, and Language Group." InterAmerica Research Associates, Inc.

Padilla, A.M. 1979. "Critical Factors in the Testing of Hispanic Americans: A Review and Some Suggestions for the Future." In R.W. Tyler & H. White (Eds.), *Testing, Teaching and Learning: Report of a Conference on Testing.* Washington, D.C.: National Institute of Education.

Pallas, A.M., Natriello, G., & McDill, E.L. June-July 1989. "The Changing Nature of the Disadvantaged Population: Current Dimensions and Future Trends." *Educational Researcher, 18(5)*, 16-22.

Pelavin, S.H. 1986. "Preliminary Report on the Title VII Student Entry and Exit Criteria Study." Paper presented at the annual meeting of the American Educational Research Association, Washington, D.C.

Pifer, A. 1979. *Bilingual Education and the Hispanic Challenge.* New York: Carnegie Corporation.

Pletcher, B.P., Locks, N.A., Reynolds, D.F., & Sisson, B.G. 1978. *A Guide to Assessment Instruments.* Northvale, NJ: Santillana.

Reynolds, C.R., Gutkin, T.B., Elliot, S.N., & Witt, J.C. 1984. *School Psychology: Essentials of Theory and Practice.* NY: John Wiley & Son.

Rosenfield, S. May 1982. "Some Problems and Solutions Concerning Psychoeducational Assessment of Bilingual-limited English Proficient-non-English Dominant Children." Paper presented at the Invitational Conference, Psychoeducational Evaluation of Pupils with Limited English Proficiency, New York State Education Dept.

Salvia, J., & Hughes, C. 1990. *Curriculum-based Assessment: Testing What is Taught.* New York: Macmillan.

Samuda, R.J. 1975. *Psychological Testing of American Minorities: Issues and Consequences.* New York: Dodd, Mead.

The author examines main controversies surrounding the use of standardized norm-referenced tests with American minorities. This book deals more with social justice than with psychometrics.

Sarnacki, R.E. 1979. "An Examination of Test-wiseness in the Cognitive Test Domain." *Review of Educational Research, 49,* 252-279.

Sattler, J.M. 1973. "Intelligence Testing of Minority Group and Culturally Disadvantaged Children." In L. Mann & D. Sabatino (Eds.), *The First Review of Special Education.* Philadelphia: Buttonwood Farms, Inc.

Sattler, J.M. 1988. *Assessment of Children.* San Diego, CA: Jerome M. Sattler, Publisher.

Scheuneman, J.D. 1987. "An Argument Opposing Jensen on Test Bias: The Psychological Aspects. In S. Modgil & C. Modgil (Eds.), *Arthur Jensen: Consensus and Controversy* (p. 177-190). NY: The Falmer Press.

Sechrest, L., Fay, T.L. & Zaidi, S.M.H. 1972. "Problems of Translation in Cross-cultural Research." *Journal of Cross-Cultural Psychology, 3(1),* 41-56.

The authors identify the translation problem of achieving equivalence in terms of experiences and concepts tapped as perhaps the most important in cross-cultural research. This survey of various types of translation problems suggests the pitfalls encountered in test translations for different subcultures. Direct translation, likely to be most inadequate when used for brief materials, is of particular significance here.

Shapiro, E.S. 1987. *Behavioral Assessment in School Psychology*. New York: Lawrence Erlbaum Associates, Inc.

> A developing concern with alternative strategies in the assessment process has resulted from school psychologists' increased involvement with intervention rather than diagnostic activities. Given this shift, behavioral assessment seems the most applicable methodology, as evidenced by current journal publications. This book discusses concepts and procedures of behavioral assessment in a manner useful to practicing school psychologists.

Shuey, A.M. 1966. *The Testing of Negro Intelligence (2nd Edition)*. NY: Social Science Press.

Slakter, M.J., Koehler, R.A., & Hampton, S.H. 1970. "Grade Level, Sex and Selected Aspects of Test-wiseness." *Journal of Educational Measurement, 7*, 119-123.

Stansfield, C. 1981. "The Assessment of Language Proficiency in Bilingual Children: An Analysis of Theories and Instrumentation." In R.V. Padilla (Ed.), *Ethnoperspectives in Bilingual Education Research: Bilingual Education Technology*, p. 233-248. Ypsilanti, MI. Dept. of Foreign Languages and Bilingual Studies.

Thorum, A.R. 1981. *Language Assessment Instruments: Infancy through Childhood*. Springfield, IL: Charles C. Thomas.

Ulibarri, D.M., Spencer, M.L., & Rivas, G.A. 1981. "Language Proficiency and Academic Achievement: A Study of Language Proficiency Tests and Their Relationship to School Ratings as Predictors of Academic Success." *NABE Journal, 5(3)*, 47-80.

Valdes, G., Barera, R., & Cardinas, M. Fall 1984. "Constructing Matching Texts in Two Languages: The Application of Propositional Analysis." *Journal of the National Association for Bilingual Education, 9(1)*, 3-19.

Wald, B. 1981. "On Assessing the Oral Language Ability of Limited English Proficient Students: The Linguistic Bases of the Non-comparability of Different Language Proficiency Assessment Measures." Presented at the Language Assessment Institute, National College of Education, Evanston, Illinois.

# TESTING IN JAPAN


## MIDORI YAMAGISHI


Taking tests is a major part of school life in Japan. One fourth grader wrote the following poem about tests:

Computation tests, vocabulary tests,
reading comprehension tests, achievement tests,
mid-term exams...
Tests, tests, tests,
Tests follow me all the time,
I have no time to rest.
Give me a break, Mr. Test.
I am tired.
(cited in Nakano, 1986, p.130)


Japanese children take tests every day at school. They are given 5-10 minute tests daily as drill in computation or vocabulary (ideographs or spelling), have weekly or monthly tests to review the materials covered in the class, and take several standardized achievement tests throughout the academic year. Fixed examination periods for mid-term and final exams are common from junior high level through college. From January through March when the "entrance examination season" hits the nation, some thousands of students who seek admission to high schools or colleges, or even to prestigious elementary schools and junior high schools, face the challenge of that once-a-year event of "the entrance examination." Applicants typically go through numerous trial or practice tests to improve their chances of success.

Testing continues throughout Japanese adult life. Personnel selection by large corporations and government agencies is based on performance on a general competency test, which often has an English language portion. More and more companies have adopted a series of exams as a basis for promotion of employees to middle level management. A prospective candidate is put into a comprehensive testing program which typically extends over several years as a part of training on the job. Professionals such as medical doctors and lawyers are required to take mandatory qualifying examinations to get a license to practice their profession. More than 600 varieties of vocational licenses and certificates are offered through national and prefectural government-run examinations (Cantor, 1987).

While extensive use of tests characterizes Japanese schools and the work place, empirical research on testing is weak in Japan. The Japanese literature on testing mostly consists either of the authors' impressionistic opinions of Japanese testing practices or of second-hand knowledge of the work of Western scholars. Much of the literature is concerned with general and ideological issues surrounding the use of tests in education, and little attention has been given to more specific issues such as the reliability and validity of published tests and entrance examinations. Japanese teachers, in general, are not well trained and prepared for testing and evaluation in classrooms, since a specialized course in measurement and evaluation is not required of students enrolled in teacher training programs. Beginning teachers' knowledge of testing is limited to what is provided by a brief overview section of a general educational psychology course.

As briefly described above, testing in Japan is characterized by its ubiquity coupled with a lack of academic interest in psychometrics. This apparent inconsistency between practice and research derives from unique circumstances of the Japanese educational system. To familiarize readers with the Japanese educational system, a brief description of the system is provided first. The remaining sections of this chapter provide an overview of the use of both standardized and teacher-made tests in Japanese schools, criticisms of testing and the resulting reform, and future directions of testing in Japan.

## THE JAPANESE EDUCATIONAL SYSTEM

Postwar education in Japan consists of elementary education for six years, secondary education composed of junior and high school education for three years, respectively, and college education for four years. Mandatory education starts at the age of six and finishes at fifteen; six years at the elementary school and three years at the junior high school are required (see National Institute for Educational Research, 1988 for details).

About 94% of junior high school graduates go on to high school. Then, about 36.3% of high school graduates enter various forms of higher education including junior colleges, which are predominantly female in enrollment (Monbusho, 1989). Very few college graduates continue to graduate school, though the numbers have increased in recent years.

Elementary schools and junior high schools are mostly publicly funded. The percentage of students enrolled in private schools is only 0.5% at the elementary school level, and 2.9% at the junior high school level. However, the ratio of private school enrollment increases to 28.1% at the high school level, 89.7% at the junior college level, and 72.7% at the university level (Gendai Kodomo DaiHyakka, 1988, p. 834).

The Japanese educational system is characterized by (1) strong central control by the national government, (2) egalitarian values in compulsory education, and (3) a highly competitive entrance examination system in higher education. First, the Ministry of Education determines the objectives[1] and contents to be taught at elementary through high school levels, and these objectives and contents are spelled out in detail in the "Ministry of Education Guidebook for Instruction." Textbooks to be used in any school, even a private school, must meet the requirements of the guidebook and must be approved by the Ministry of Education. Every effort is made by the national and local governments to provide education that meets this national standard throughout Japan. All students are taught using the same materials in elementary and junior high schools throughout Japan, at least in principle. Second, egalitarian values which are deeply rooted in the cultural values of Japanese society dictate educational policy and practice in compulsory education. In elementary and junior high schools, any attempt to use ability grouping or the tracking of students is strongly discouraged. Slow students are taught together with gifted students in the same classroom. The philosophy behind the single track system in compulsory education is that (1) everyone has an equal ability to learn and that (2) learning is determined by the learner's commitment and perseverance (Amagi, 1987). That is, in principle everyone is expected to learn, and failure to learn is attributed to lack of effort rather than to lack of ability.[2] Therefore, teachers pay a great deal of attention to the progress of below-average students and make a great effort to elevate the level of achievement of the class as a whole. Thus, the standardized curriculum and egalitarian-oriented teachers assure the government's effort to provide equal learning opportunities in compulsory education in Japan (Amagi, 1987).

While a strong egalitarian orientation dominates compulsory education, Japanese students are sorted and tracked into different achievement strata by means of entrance examinations. Japanese high schools and universities are implicitly ranked according to their prestige. A high school's prestige is based on its success in placing its graduates into prestigious universities, while a university's prestige is based on the number of students employed by prestigious and prosperous large companies. Thus, performance on the entrance examination determines not only the person's education but also his/her lifetime career opportunities. Admission into almost any Japanese university or high school is determined by the applicant's score on the entrance examination, which each school holds once a year, in January and March. Although more weight is given to junior high GPA in admission decisions for high schools, universities and colleges give little consideration to applicant's high school academic records. Thus, performance on a one-shot exam is the primary determinant in college/university admission.

These three characteristics of the Japanese educational system together create an environment in which evaluation and testing of students' mastery in the classroom receive little emphasis. One aspect of the Japanese education system often pointed out by educational researchers as well as teachers themselves is the lack of teachers' control over the content and method of instruction. Because classroom teaching must strictly follow government-set guidelines, teachers have little freedom in deciding what and how to teach. In addition, due to the strong egalitarian orientation, repeating a grade is greatly discouraged. Retention at the same grade level is considered morally wrong, at least in compulsory education, so that anyone who attends the required number of school days is automatically promoted to a higher grade, regardless of their mastery of classroom materials. Because the Japanese system guarantees students' automatic promotion, teachers need not be concerned with how successfully students have mastered the materials; what they are concerned with is only whether or not tasks assigned to a given grade level have been completed on time. Another factor making teachers less interested in evaluation and testing in the classroom is the impact of the entrance examination. The "ultimate goal" of secondary education for many students and their parents is their success in passing the entrance exam into a prestigious university. Performance at school, represented by GPA, is not as important as performance on the one-shot entrance examination. Both teachers and students place less emphasis on performance evaluation of coursework.[3]

## PREPARATION FOR MEASUREMENT AND EVALUATION

When teacher training programs were revised in 1949 as a part of a far-reaching educational reform following the defeat of Japan in World War II, educational psychology became a required subject for all prospective teachers. Students were to take one educational psychology course as well as either "child psychology" or "youth and adolescence," depending on the level of the certificate, as a partial requirement for a teacher's certificate. Courses beyond those two were not required. The content taught in the educational psychology course is largely borrowed from American textbooks and includes four major areas that give a balanced foundation for teaching. The four areas are learning, personality, development, and evaluation. Results of a survey conducted by the Japan Educational Psychology Association (Fujiwara, 1983) found that more emphasis was given to learning and development than evaluation. Only 28.3% of the responding teachers reported that their instructor covered testing and evaluation. Furthermore, the topics covered in the testing and evaluation section of the educational psychology course are often clinical tests. Theoretical and technical issues relevant to classroom evaluation are generally not covered. This suggests that Japanese teachers are generally poorly prepared in testing and evaluation.

## TYPES OF TESTS IN USE

The first Japanese examination system was established in 707 A.D., modeled after the famous Chinese examination system which selected elite talent for the imperial administrative bureaucracy. The Japanese examination system did not last long because Japan was governed mostly by a hereditary ruling class instead of bureaucrats. After Japan opened up to the West in 1868, a new civil service examination system was established in 1887, following the establishment of the modern education system in 1872.

Western intelligence tests were introduced to Japan early in this century. Binet's intelligence test was introduced in 1908 and its Japanese version was completed in 1919. During the 1920s and the 1930s when liberalism and innovation were dominant, various tests were developed. The first Japanese journal that specialized in testing, *Test Monitor*, was published in 1924. However, the testing movement halted after the outbreak of war on the Asian continent.

Modern theories and practices in measurement and evaluation were introduced with educational reform brought about by the American occupational force after World War II. Aptitude tests were used as a part of admission requirements for college entrance for a short period between 1946 and 1950. Despite support from psychologists, high school teachers and parents did not see greater merit in aptitude tests than in achievement tests that are developed by each institution every year to test the mastery of high school materials. For high school admission, achievement tests are developed every year by the local government. Entrance examinations consist of multiple-choice and short-answer type questions and stress "the mastery of facts, control over details, and practiced skill in the application of mathematical and scientific principles" (Rohlen, 1983, p.95).

Ito and Matsubara (1983) listed 490 psychological tests available in Japan and Asia, and classified them into four categories: 120 intelligence tests, 90 standardized achievement tests, 250 personality, aptitude, readiness, and diagnostic tests, and 10 individual tests. Ichitani (1987) reviewed several surveys conducted between 1960 to 1980 to identify patterns of test use in a clinical setting. He found Japanese versions of Binet's intelligence tests, WAIS, P-F Study, and Guilford Zimmerman Tests to be the most frequently used tests in clinical settings.

Information about test use in classrooms is very limited. The first national survey of classroom test use was conducted in 1977 (Kajita & Kuroi, 1977). The survey selected 2,281 elementary schools, 1,109 junior high schools, and 447 high schools based on hierarchical sampling. The response rates for elementary schools was 65.5%, 72.1% for junior high schools, and 71.1% for high schools. Each school was asked (1) if mid-term and final exam periods are set aside and (2) to name standardized tests in use, (3) to describe the form and contents of report cards, and (4) to provide opinions about educational evaluation.

Kajita and Kuroi found that almost all elementary and junior high schools used intelligence tests while 56.6% of the high schools used them. About 40% of elementary and junior high schools used standardized achievement tests. Those tests included nationally normed tests and regionally developed tests. The percentage varied greatly from region to region. The use of standardized achievement tests was much lower in high schools than in elementary schools and junior high schools; i.e., only 14.2% of high schools used standardized tests. The use of personality tests and aptitude tests revealed an opposite pattern. That is, very few elementary schools used personality tests, and the percentage increased to 36.9% among junior high schools, and to 52.8% among high schools. No elementary school used aptitude tests while 16.3% of junior high schools and 30.5% of high schools did.

In 1972, the Japan Teachers Union surveyed the use of mass produced ready-made tests in classrooms (Nippon Kyoshokuin Kumiai, 1972). The focus of the survey was to find out to what extent ready-made tests, in contrast to teacher-made tests, were actually used in classrooms. The sale of those tests created by publishers had

become a big business by the time of the survey. Because of the unique
nature of the market (those tests were ordered by teachers and financed
by parents), the widespread use of ready-made tests in the classroom
received attention from many concerned groups for two reasons. First,
there was an ethical concern about possible kickbacks or rebates to
teachers. The second issue concerned the educational implications of
such tests. The Japanese Teachers Union was particularly negative
about the implications of the use of such tests, saying: "There is no
education, but tests in Japanese schools" (p.18). They criticized the
ready-made tests for the following reasons: "First, the questions used
in those commercial tests force students to memorize trivial and
confusing fragments of knowledge that are irrelevant to the
understanding of scientific concepts and principles. . . . Second,
questions are often ambiguous. . . . Third, some questions do not have
the right answer or have several possible answers. . . . Fourth, some
questions are impossible to answer. . . . Fifth, some questions are too
difficult to answer for most students, so that such questions can be used
to distinguish 'able' students from 'poor' students. . . . Sixth, right
answers to some questions require certain ideological assumptions. . .
. And finally, figures and graphs are not of good quality" (pp.72-76).
Based on such criticisms, they called for a moratorium on the use of
commercial tests in classrooms.

The survey of schools in 10 regions found that 86.9% of the
schools used ready-made tests (Nippon Kyoshokuin Kumiai, 1974). The
tests were widely used in elementary schools. Those tests were used
mostly in classrooms, followed by homework assignments, and jishuu
(self-teaching hours). The most favored tests were those designed to
accompany textbooks used in the classroom. The most frequently cited
reasons why teachers use those tests was lack of time to construct their
own tests. After a detailed analysis of test items, they concluded that
(1) test items were poorly written, (2) emphasized route memory, (3)
and tested fragmented knowledge. The Union favored teacher-made
tests because of their greater perceived pedagogical value.

A more recent but less extensive survey was conducted by a
group of researchers at the National Institute for Education in 1984
(Kida, 1984). Data from junior high schools in three regions were
collected. The survey found that teacher-made tests were used by most
of the teachers during class hours. At the same time, ready-made tests
were used by 33% of the teachers during class hours and by 25-30% of

the teachers for homework assignments. Teacher-made tests were primarily used for feedback and end-of-the-quarter evaluation. All schools adopted trial tests developed and run by private companies to help students prepare for the high school entrance examination. Although those tests are technically not real "standardized" tests, they provide information to be used for estimating students' relative standing among possible high school applicants. The survey estimated that on the average, junior high school students take more than 100 tests yearly.

Three types of tests are widely used in Japanese schools, (1) standardized achievement and psychological tests (2) mass produced commercial tests, and (3) teacher-made tests, and this section focused on the first two types of tests. Unlike American schools, standardized achievement tests and aptitude tests are not extensively used but commercial tests are very popular in Japanese schools to supplement classroom instruction and to help students prepare for entrance examinations. Commercial tests are not standardized and their poor quality has been a focus of dispute. Most psychological tests are administered outside schools because school psychologists are not staffed in Japanese schools. The next section briefly discusses the nature of teacher-made tests which Japanese educators and parents consider more desirable than commercial tests, and then the following section introduces some of the major attempts for establishing a nation-wide testing program of academic achievement.

## CONTENTS OF TEACHER-MADE TESTS

The survey mentioned in the previous section (Kida, 1984) also examined the contents of teacher-made tests. Only 54% of schools surveyed turned in a set of mid-term and final examinations in the following five subject areas. The study analyzed 5,894 language arts items, and found that in language arts (i.e., Japanese), reading comprehension and vocabulary items dominated. Short answer or essay questions were rarely found. In social studies, 80% of the items were recall or recognition type items, and 90% of them were about facts and terms. In mathematics, items were classified using a simplified version of Bloom's taxonomy. The majority of the items were computation (68.9%) and understanding (22.7%), while only 5.1% were application and 3.3% analysis. The comparable figures for IEA (The International Association for the Evaluation of Educational Achievement) tests are 25.9% for computation, 33.3% for understanding, 37.5% for application and 4.2% for analysis. Science items were analyzed using the following five categories: knowledge, understanding, application, scientific thinking, and experiment and observation skills. Knowledge items were found to be dominant. In English, test items were classified into the following categories: knowledge, structure, usage of expression, writing, and comprehension. Mostly questions were knowledge-type questions.

## NATIONAL SURVEYS OF ACADEMIC ACHIEVEMENT

Nation-wide testing programs of academic achievement were a mixed success in Japan. Though Binet's intelligence test was standardized as early as 1910, there was little demand for developing a national testing program of academic achievement in the pre-war period. The highly centralized nationalistic education system substantiated a unified curriculum through government-mandated textbooks and frequent visitations by education officials to schools. The Ministry of Education initiated several attempts to establish national testing programs of academic achievement after the war, but none of them was successful due mainly to strong opposition from the Japan Teachers Union and a lack of support from the general public.

The first national achievement testing program in Japan was called "Sotei tests," and was used for screening 20 year-old males for military duties. The tests covered four subject areas (language arts, arithmetic, science, citizenship) and used a multiple-choice format. Tests were developed by local governments for the first two decades after the testing program started in 1905. Government involvement increased as the country became more nationalistic, and uniform tests were developed and administered by the Ministry of Education from

1931 to 1942. Some of the leading Japanese psychologists then were involved in designing the tests to assure their quality. The results of the "Sotei" tests provide valuable information on the levels of achievement among young Japanese males in the pre-war period. The data also help us to estimate the rate of decline in academic achievement after schooling (Ota, 1969).

During the post-war reform period there was a great concern about the possible decline in learning among students due to poor schooling during the war and confusion followed by American directed reforms. Research was conducted by several groups of concerned researchers to assess reading comprehension and other academic competencies in elementary and secondary schools from 1948 to 1955 (Nagano, 1984). The Ministry of Education also started a national testing program in 1956 to assess Japanese students' levels of academic attainment at the end of elementary school and at the end of junior high school. First, 5% of the total population of fifth and sixth graders and 10% of that of eleventh and twelfth graders were tested. Testing was later extended to include all students for those grade levels in 1961. The students were tested in four subject areas at the elementary school level and five subject areas at the junior high school level. Tests were developed every year by experts in the subjects using the framework of criterion-referenced testing. Once the test was mandated for every student, teachers were angry and frightened. The Japan Teachers Union campaigned strongly to stop the implementation of the government decision to test all students at four grade levels across the nation. They suspected that the test results would be used for teacher evaluation which was seen as having the potential to seriously threaten professional freedoms guaranteed to Japanese teachers. The government abandoned the testing program in 1966.

Other attempts to establish a unified national testing program are found in the government-led efforts for revising the entrance examination system. Japanese colleges educated a handful of elites before World War II and selected their students based on their performance on an achievement test that took the form of a lengthy written examination. Following World War II, Americans introduced aptitude tests for college entrance examinations. And then a newly developed uniform test was used for college admission along with achievement test score and High School GPA between 1948 and 1954. The test measured general ability, reading comprehension, and scientific thinking and was designed to differentiate science and engineering majors from humanities and social science majors. However, aptitude tests to measure general ability and potential for college education were unheard of by most Japanese in those days and evoked much controversy over the validity and usefulness of the newly developed uniform test. Although researchers argued that aptitude tests are better predictors of students' performance in upper-level college courses than content-oriented achievement tests, they did not seriously examine the validity of the content-oriented achievement tests.

The demise of aptitude tests is usually attributed to the Japanese perception of learning as accumulation of knowledge. That is, content-oriented achievement tests which were to assess the applicant's mastery of high school subjects were more congenial to this perception of learning than were aptitude tests measuring "unseen" potential for learning (Nishibori, 1978). Another attempt by the Ministry of Education to implement a national aptitude test called "Noken Test" (General Aptitude Test) was started in 1963, but it faced similar opposition from high school teachers and the general public. In addition, very few colleges and universities were willing to adopt the test for admission, and it was eventually abandoned in 1969.

Under the 1979 entrance examination reforms, a unified testing program called "Kyotsu Ichiji Test" (Unified National Achievement Test for College Admission) was finally implemented among national and public universities. Applicants to those universities now face a two-step procedure for admission. First, all applicants take the "Kyotsu Ichiji Test" in mid-January. The test is not an aptitude test but an objective, computer-scored achievement test that covers high school material. In March, applicants take the second-step admission tests, developed by each institution, that are more difficult and contain essay-type questions. Admission is based on combined scores on the two tests. The two-step procedure received heavy criticism because of its complexity and the lack of support from private institutions which make up about 75% of the total colleges/universities in Japan. In response to the criticisms of "Kyotsu Ichiji Tests," a new version of the test called "Shin Test" (New Test) is currently being implemented.

## CRITICISMS OF TESTING

Criticisms of testing in Japanese schools may be classified into the following four types: (1) negative consequences of testing, (2) the use of ready-made tests prepared by private publishers, (3) thinking skills required by multiple-choice tests, and (4) the current format of entrance examinations.

### Negative Consequences of Testing

It is often claimed that getting high scores on tests has become the goal of education. Teachers prepare students only for tests and, as a consequence, development of students' characters, creativity, potential, etc., is grossly underemphasized. In addition, repeated testing and constant teacher evaluation are believed to generate psychological and emotional problems and are harmful for establishing friendships. The effects discussed are not only the individual consequences of being labeled but also the collective consequences of promoting a competitive atmosphere in the classroom. Belief in those negative consequences of testing is so widely spread among the Japanese public and mass media that almost every problem with the Japanese youth is attributed to testing. News media blame tests for crimes, suicides, and all sorts of delinquent activities committed by stressed-out children who are forced to compete with classmates and suffer from failure.

### Ready-Made Tests

Since the curriculum is standardized throughout Japan on the basis of the "Ministry of Education Guidebook for Instruction," it is relatively easy to mass produce "ready-made" tests for teachers' use. By the early 1970s, publication of tests became a multi-million dollar business. Sales of those tests for elementary school pupils alone reached 300 million booklets by the early 1970s (Nippon Kyoshokuin Kumiai, 1972). The use of those tests was heavily criticized in the early 1970s for it was claimed to impersonalize the relationship between teachers and students.  The superiority of teacher-made tests over ready-made tests was blindly accepted by the general public as well as by teachers themselves, and the mass media joined the Japan Teachers Union's campaign against the use of ready-made tests in classrooms. A moratorium on the use of ready-made tests was won when a kick-back scandal among some teachers evoked public rage, but the moratorium did not last long.

## Multiple-Choice Tests

Social critics attack true-false and multiple-choice tests as the cause of a so-called "right-or-wrong way of thinking" that is often claimed to characterize young Japanese who are devoid of critical thinking and analytical skills.  True-false and multiple-choice tests are believed to test only pieces of knowledge, and thus the use of such tests is blamed for encouraging memorization of trivial knowledge and discouraging critical and creative thinking.  The use of true-false and multiple-choice tests is heavily criticized, especially when they are used in entrance examinations that are supposed to measure the applicant's "true" mastery of materials taught at school.

## Entrance Exam

Japan's "examination hell" phenomena is a constant target of criticism that has led to various reform attempts during the past 40 years.  Almost all criticism of testing in Japan is ultimately related to the importance of entrance examinations in the lives of many Japanese. The Japanese entrance examination system works as a social sorting device; fairness and validity of entrance exams are among the most serious and emotionally laden issues in post-World War II Japan.  The issues most often discussed in regard to the entrance examination are the one-shot administration and exam contents.   Generally, the admission decision is based on the result of one examination (covering several subject areas), so that luck can be an important factor.  Students can apply to several universities, but they have to wait another year to try again with the same university.[4]

The most serious issue concerning content is validity. Both content and predictive validity issues are raised. Entrance exams are often criticized since some questions require trivial knowledge and/or materials too difficult for most high school graduates. The issue of predictive validity has long been raised, but only recently have systematic studies of predictive validity of entrance exams been conducted.

The criticisms of testing in Japan briefly summarized above are characterized by their impressionistic nature. For example, essay exams are often recommended as an alternative to multiple choice tests, but those who recommend essay exams are not aware of the difficulties and problems of essay exams; attention has not been paid to a fundamental principle of testing--the validity of a test cannot exceed its reliability. It is only recently that empirical study of essay exams has begun (Watanabe et al., 1988). Another recommendation which is often found in those criticisms is to utilize criterion-referenced testing instead of norm-referenced testing. The recent shift in this direction is briefly described in the next section.


## SHIFT TOWARD CRITERION-REFERENCED TESTING


Since the late 1970s there has been a major change in testing practices in Japan. More and more emphasis is now being placed on criterion-referenced testing. While strong criticism against testing in the 1960s and the 1970s was based on moral grounds (i.e., screening and tracking students based on testing is morally wrong; tests used in classrooms should be constructed by teachers themselves with love and care; etc.) rather than technical grounds, this emerging movement toward criterion referenced testing at least assigns a positive role for testing.

The move toward criterion-referenced testing started with a series of reforms of the report cards handed to students and parents at the end of each quarter. The Japanese Teachers' Union and social critics strongly opposed the conventional format of report cards that report grades based on the student's relative standing in the class. This conventional grading practice was accused of failing to reflect the student's effort and progress during the quarter. In 1980, the newly revised "Ministry of Education Guidebook for Instructions" recommended that teachers use "totatsudo hyoka" (criterion-referenced) student evaluation techniques. This policy change has had a significant impact on teaching and evaluation practices in Japanese schools. Numerous projects were initiated to develop detailed instructional objectives and a framework for evaluation.


## FUTURE DIRECTIONS


Almost every aspect of testing in Japan has been affected, or I would say, distorted, by the dominant role of the entrance examination in the Japanese education system. The goal of education has become to prepare students for getting good scores on the entrance exams. Under high pressure to prepare students for entrance examinations, tests in schools have become practices for the entrance exams. In addition to tests in schools, students take trial tests, run by the extra-school educational industry, on weekends to evaluate their chances of success on the entrance examinations. Japanese children are thus over-tested, and seem to have negative images of tests. Negative feelings toward testing are frequently manifested in Japanese school children's writings and poems (see Nakano, 1986; Orihara, 1967, for examples). Many school children consider testing as the most unpleasant experience in school life (Kodomo Chosa Kenkyujo, 1974). Shibuya (1985) reported that ninth and twelfth graders perceived tests as "cold, dark and depressing," while sixth graders had rather neutral images of tests. He suspected that the frequent use of norm-referenced tests in higher grades caused the difference.

Japanese teachers also have negative feelings toward testing and, when asked, express their frustration with the role of entrance examinations in Japanese education. One survey found that 80% of the responding elementary and junior high school teachers were discontented with the current use of testing in their schools in terms of both frequency and the way in which results are used (Fukui Kyoiku Iinkai, 1984). However, only one-third of them openly supported the necessity of educational reform, while two-thirds of them felt that there is nothing they can do about it. Japanese teachers, especially those in compulsory education, generally consider testing as a burden or unnecessary task for their profession. Many of them say that they give tests to satisfy the demands made by administrators and parents. The two most frequently cited reasons for testing, the end-of-quarter grading and aiding in preparation for entrance examinations, are considered to be administrative responsibilities (Nihon Kyoiku Shinbunsha, 1980). Lastly, it is widely recognized that Japanese teachers do not feel comfortable in ranking and placing their students according to performance on tests (Cummings, 1980).

As described above, the Japanese school environment is not favorable to testing. And an interesting fact is that both students and teachers have negative attitudes toward testing. It seems that both groups feel helpless due to the dominant role of entrance examinations in Japanese society. To make the school environment more favorable to testing, major reforms such as the following are needed: (1) fundamental changes in the entrance examination system and (2) establishment of an evaluation system that is meaningful for both teachers and students.

A series of educational reforms implemented in the last decade brought about several important changes in testing practices in Japanese schools. Those changes may eventually promote a more favorable environment for testing in Japanese schools. The most significant change was the government's decision to adopt "totatsudo hyouka" (criterion-referenced evaluation) for the end-of-the-quarter grade report. Because criterion-referenced testing focuses on students' mastery of specific knowledge or skills, rather than on their relative standing in a group, teachers welcomed the change. They considered criterion-referenced testing as an effective method to reduce the problem of "ochikobore," an increase in the number of students who are "left behind." It is expected that the integration of teaching and evaluation through the use of criterion-referenced testing gives teachers more responsibility for evaluation and constant monitoring of students' progress (Murakoshi, 1978).

In addition to promoting meaningfulness and a sense of control in the evaluation task, the shift to criterion-referenced testing has facilitated empirical research and in-service teacher training in testing and evaluation. Since the implementation of criterion-referenced evaluation, technical training and publication of research on teacher-made tests have increased significantly, teachers are now participating in various research projects in which they develop a framework for analyzing instructional objectives and try out new testing techniques. Furthermore, with the emphasis of the "Shutokushugi" principle in Japanese schools, ability grouping has become a popular arrangement for accommodating the variability in students' mastery levels, especially at the high school level.[5] While the advantages of ability grouping are recognized, the technical as well as theoretical foundation for ability grouping has not been strong.

Lastly, the reform in the college entrance examination system in 1979 was also very important. Although the change affected only national universities which consist of 28% of the total number of Japanese universities, the new system clearly marked a significant milestone in postwar education history. Under the new system, a common achievement test is developed and administered by the National Center for University Entrance Examinations which was established in 1976. The unified testing program for college admission is the first of its kind since 1954 when the short-lived College Aptitude Test was abandoned, and thus it has had significant impact on methodological and technical development of the entrance examination. Another important change introduced by the new system is variability in the testing methods utilized in the second step test and the use of multiple criteria for arriving at the final admission decision. For instance, use of essays that can compensate for the weaknesses of multiple-choice tests is greatly encouraged at the second step in testing.

The changes described above are efforts to alter the pervasive effect of the entrance examination system on testing practices in Japanese schools. Much of the efforts to date have been directed to quantitative examination of the unified college admission test data and implementing criterion-referenced evaluation in elementary and secondary schools. That is, Japanese testing practices have begun to emphasize the use of tests for evaluation and pay more attention to their relevance to instruction and the learning processes. Although the idea of "evaluation" was introduced by Americans during the

Occupation period, it was not fully understood nor practiced until recently because of the prevalent use of tests for ranking and screening. Strong concern with the quality and content of tests rather than the results is replacing impressionistic evaluation of tests with empirically-oriented research.

While Japanese testing practices have undergone modernization in many respects, surprisingly little change was found in the content of entrance examinations over the last 40 years. There is no sign of movement from achievement tests to aptitude tests. Applicants for national universities are tested on at least five subject areas and test questions are heavily content-oriented. These tests are very similar to GRE Advanced Placement tests. The Japanese preference for achievement tests is so strong that none of the government attempts to introduce aptitude tests has been successful. The major objection to the use of aptitude tests was that aptitude tests do not directly relate to materials covered in high school, so that performance on such tests does not reflect the effort and energy spent on mastering the materials. That is, the Japanese generally consider that ability is a gift, it is pure luck and it has nothing to do with knowledge accumulated through students' efforts, so that screening applicants based on their ability is "discriminatory" and discourages students from trying to improve. This notion of ability may be the basis for egalitarian education and gives strong support to achievement testing. Fiske (1983) described the role of examinations in Japan as follows: "In Japan, examinations are designed in keeping with the Confucian tradition that education is essentially the conveying of factual knowledge" (p. A8). Unless the Japanese' belief of ability is challenged, fundamental change in the educational system and in testing practices will not occur.

## NOTES

[1]Educational objectives described by the Ministry of Education are not specific or behavioral. They are vague and only show the direction of desirable outcomes.

[2]The similarity between Japanese conceptions of learning and the mastery learning model (Bloom, 1976) was pointed out by Cummings (1980).

[3]Japanese educational researchers distinguish two principles for evaluating teaching activity: rishu-shugi and shutoku shugi (Horio et al., 1988; Kajita, 1975; Murakoshi, 1978). Shutoku-shugi means that teachers make sure that their objectives are accomplished by examining students' mastery level of classroom materials. In contrast, rishu-shugi does not pay attention to students' success in mastering classroom materials. It is only concerned with the fact that the required materials have been taught in the classroom in the manner specified by a guideline.

[4]Those who fail to enter the university of their choice, often spend a year as a ronin (masterless samurai) and try again in the following year. The Ministry of Education reported that ronin comprises 26.4% of the entering freshmen in 1989.

[5]A national survey of 1911 high schools found that some form of ability grouping was practiced by 45% of the schools surveyed (Amano et al., 1986).

# REFERENCES

Amagi, I. (Ed.) 1987. *Sogo ni mita nichibei kyoiku no kadai-nichibei kyoiku kyoryoku kenkyu hokoku* (Problems and issues of education in Japan and the United States: Report prepared by Research groups in the US and Japan). Tokyo: Daiichihoki. (United States version available)

Amano, I. 1983. *Shiken no shakaishi* (Social and historical analysis of examination system in Japan). Tokyo: University of Tokyo Press. Translated and published by Columbia University Press, 1989, as *Education and Examination in Modern Japan.*

> The first comprehensive book on the Japanese examination system published in Japan. After a brief introduction of the pre-modern Japanese examination system which dates back to 701 A.D., Amano, a sociologist, describes in detail the development of the modern Japanese examination system. He argues that the examination system played a significant role in facilitating Japan's rapid industrialization during the Meiji era.

Amano, I., Mimizuka, H., Hida, D., Kikuchi, E., & Sakai. A. 1986. "Kotogakko ni okeru gakushu shujukudobetsu-gakkyu hensei ni kansuru kenkyu" (An examination of "shujukudobetsu-gakkyu hensei" as a tracking system in Japanese high schools). (English Abstract) *School of Education Bulletin, 26,* 27-58, Tokyo University.

> The final report of the study conducted in Japan and the United States initiated in 1983 by President Reagan and Prime Minister Nakasone. Educational researchers from the two countries studied systems and problems of education in the two countries to enhance understanding of their own educational system.

Asai, K. April 1984. *Kyoiku Shinri kensa no genjo to kongo e no kitai* (Present and future of educational and psychological testing in Japan). *Shido to Hyoka.*

Describes three important questions that teachers should address before using tests: (1) whether the use of tests improves students' lives, (2) what actually is measured by the test, and (3) whether teachers can interpret the results adequately. Advocates the use of tailored testing in classrooms.

Beauchamp, E.R. 1978. *Shiken Jigoku* (The problem of entrance examination in Japan). *Asian Profile, 6,* 543-560.

Discusses causes and effects of "examination hell" in Japanese higher education and pre-university schooling.

Bloom, B. 1976. *Human Characteristics and School Learning.* New York: McGraw-Hill.

Cantor, L. 1986. "The Role of the Private Sector in Vocational Education and Training: The Case of Japan's Special Training Schools." *The Vocational Aspect of Education, 39(103),* 35-41.

Cummings, W.K. 1980. *Education and Equality in Japan.* Princeton: Princeton University Press.

An excellent book describing and analyzing egalitarian orientation at elementary level education in Japan.

Fiske, E.B. July 12, 1983. "Japan's Schools: Exam Ordeal Rules Each Student's Destiny." *New York Times,* A1, A8.

Fujiwara, K. 1983. *Kyoinyosei ni okeru kyoiku-shinrigaku no genjo* (The curriculum and role of educational psychology in teacher training programs in Japan). A report prepared for the Ministry of Education. (The Ministry of Education Research Grant No: A-57310017)

A report of a survey conducted in 1980 by the Japanese Association of Educational Psychology to examine the content and methods of instruction in educational psychology required of prospective teachers in Japan.

Fukui Kyoiku Iinkai (Fukui-prefecture Office of Education). 1984. *'84 Fukui no kyoiku hakusho* ('84 White paper on education in Fukui-prefecture).

*Gendai Kodomo DaiHyakka* (Encyclopedia of children in modern society). 1988. Tokyo, Chuohoki.

Horio, T., Fujita, H., Saeki, Y., Watanabe, H., & Shiomi, M. 1988. "Shiken to Hyoka" (Testing and Evaluation: Its purpose and social consequences). *Educational Research Bulletin, 28,* 126. Tokyo University.

Ichitani, T. 1987. "Wagakuni ni okeru shinrikensa riyo no genjo to kadai" (The Current and future use of psychological tests in Japan). *Bulletin of Teachers' College of Kyoto,* No. 71, 1-29. (Abstract in English)

> Reviewed major surveys conducted in 1960-1980 to illuminate the use of psychological tests in clinical settings in Japan. Based on a paper presented for the symposium at the 22nd International Congress of Applied Psychology in 1985.

Ikeda, H. 1978. *Tesuto de noryoku ga wakaruka?* (Do tests measure people's "real" ability?) Nikkei Book Series No. 287, Tokyo: Japan Economics Newspaper Company.

> Japan's leading psychometrician discusses some of the most important issues in educational testing and evaluation, and suggests various strategies for developing good objective tests. The last chapter compares the social environment of Japan and the United States surrounding testing.

Inoue, K. 1970. *Tesuto no hanashi* (A book on testing). Chuko Books, Chuokoronsha.

> A good introductory book on testing written for the general public.

Ito, R., & Matsubara, T. 1983. *Shinri Tesuto ho nyumon* (A Primer on psychological assessment). Nihon Kagakusha.

A manual for clinical training on 102 psychological tests published in Japan.

Kajita, K. 1975. *Kyoiku ni okeru hyoka no riron* (Theory of Educational Evaluation). Tokyo: Kaneko.

Kajita, K. 1980. *Gendai kyoiku hyokaron* (Modern theory of educational evaluation). Tokyo: Kaneko.

Outlines major models and methodology of educational evaluation including formative evaluation, criterion-referenced evaluation and curriculum evaluation, and emphasizes the importance of educational evaluation which is valid and meaningful for students.

Kajita, K., & Kuroi, K. March 1977. *Gakko ni okeru kyoka no genjo ni tsuite* (The current use of evaluation methods and instruments in Japanese compulsory education). Research Report, Division III, National Institute for Educational Research.

Kida, H. 1984. *Gakushi totatsudo ni kansuru sogoteki kenkyu* (A comprehensive study on academic achievement in secondary education). A report prepared for the Ministry of Education. (The Ministry of Education Research Grant No: A-56410002)

Consists of three studies: (1) academic achievement in language arts and sciences at the end of compulsory education, (2) evaluation of teacher-made tests in five subject areas at junior high schools, (3) assessment of mathematics and social knowledge of technical high school graduates in Japan in comparison with NAEP data.

Kodomo Chosa Kenkyujo (Research Institute on Children) 1974. *Kodomo chose shiryo shusei* (Data and statistics on children). Tokyo: Author.

Monbusho (Ministry of Education) 1989. *Nendo Gakko Kihonchosa* (1989 Education Statistics).

Murakoshi, K. 1978. *Kodomono tame no Kyoiku Hyoka* (Evaluation inspiring to children). Tokyo: Aoki Shoten.

> Criticizes the dominant use of norm-referenced evaluation in Japanese schools and proposes criterion-referenced evaluation to reduce the negative effect of evaluation on Japanese school children.

Murata, S. 1979. "Student Pressures in Japanese Education: The Problem of Entrance Examination Hell." *Viewpoints in Teaching and Learning, 55,* Fall, 41-48.

> Argues that the 1979 entrance examination reforms will not solve the problems of the Japanese Examination Hell. The solution of the problem requires fundamental changes in Japanese society.

Nagano, S. 1984. *Kyoiku hyokaron* (Educational Evaluation). Tokyo: Daiichihoki.

Nakano, M. 1986. "Children Followed by Tests." *Child Psychology, 40(10),* 129-136.

> Portrayed and explained over-tested Japanese children.

National Institute for Educational Research 1988. *Basic Facts and Figures About the Educational System in Japan.* Tokyo, Japan.

Nihon Kyoiku Shinbunsha (Ed.) 1980. *Kyoiku hyoka wa kore de iinoka?* (Is the current educational evaluation appropriate?) Tokyo: Kaneko.

> Based on a series of articles published in a newspaper which is widely circulated among educators and administrators. The first part discusses problems of current evaluation practices which dominate the use of commercial tests and grading on the curve.

The second part explores better ways of educational evaluation which help children fully develop their potential.

Nippon Kyoshokuin Kumiai (The Japan Teachers Union) 1972. *Shihan tesuto-Sono jittai to naiyo* (Commercial Tests: Their current use and quality). Tokyo: Author.

Nippon Kyoshokuin Kumiai (The Japan Teachers Union) 1974. *Hyoka to tesuto-shihan tesuto fushiyo undo no zenshin no tameni* (Evaluation and tests: Towards the moratorium of the use of commercial tests in schools). Tokyo: Author.

Nishibori, M. 1978. *Nyushi ni kansuru kyoiku-shinrigaku teki sho mondai* (Issues of entrance examination: From a view of educational psychology: part 1: college entrance). *Annual Report on Research in Educational Psychology, 17,* 117-126.

> Provided a brief history of the post-war college entrance examination system in Japan and discussed problems that need to be addressed by educational psychologists.

Orihara, H. 1967. " 'Test Hell' and Alienation: A Study of Tokyo University Freshmen." *Journal of Social and Political Ideas in Japan, 5,* 225-250.

> A sociologist teaching at Tokyo University critically analyzed the experience of test hell that his students had gone through to enter the most competitive university in Japan. His analysis of students' essays is mostly speculative but represents major themes of criticisms towards tests and examinations in Japan.

Ota, T. 1969. *Gakuryoku to ha naika* (What is academic competency?) Tokyo: Kokudosha.

Rohlen, T.P. Summer 1980. "The Juku Phenomenon: An Exploratory Essay." *The Journal of Japanese Studies, 6,* 207-242.

> Escalation of the "juku" phenomenon is well documented. Since the early seventies, the number of children attending some kind

of "social study" school has steadily increased (the percentages in large cities has reached over 40%). Rohlen points out the qualitative spread among "Juku" has grown, and ranking among "juku" is now intense and elaborate. He argues that "juku" differentiation is becoming an important ingredient of the ever-evolving system of Japanese social stratification.

Rohlen, T.P. 1983. *Japanese High Schools.* Berkeley: University of California Press.

An excellent study on Japanese high schools conducted from a cross-cultural perspective. Chapter 3, "University Entrance Exams: A National Obsession," describes the competitiveness, rewards, and content of the entrance examination, and special schools assisting them to prepare the examination.

Shibuya, K. 1985. "Tesuto to hihon no kyoiku fudo" (Testing and social climate of Japan: Theory and practice of teacher-made tests, No. 1). *Shido to Hyoka* (Teaching and evaluation), *3(1)*, 39-42.

Speculates that Japanese are very negative toward testing and unduly obsessed with test scores. He suggests teachers should know more about how to construct good objective tests.

Shimahara, N. 1978. "Socialization for College Entrance Examinations in Japan." *Comparative Education, 14(3),* 253-266.

Watanabe, H., Taira, Y., & Inoue, S. 1988. *Shoronbun hyoka deta no kaiseki* (An analysis of essays). *Educational Research Bulletin, 28,* 143-164. Tokyo University. (Abstract in English)

White, M. 1978. *The Japanese Educational Challenge: A Commitment to Children.*

Describes "the examinations" and "working with the exam-taker" (pp.140-145).

Yoshida, T. 1985. *Kyoiku hyoka no riron to jissen* (Theory and practice of educational evaluation). Fukumura Shuppan.

# TEACHERS AND STANDARDIZED TESTING OF STUDENTS

## KATHY E. GREEN

Many of the chapters in this volume refer to standardized tests of achievement, intelligence, or personality. This chapter deals exclusively with standardized achievement tests used with K-12 students. Since the 1970s, the public demand for accountability in education has increased and with it the demand for testing. This demand stemmed from groups who were unhappy with the status of education and dissatisfied with the performance of graduates of school systems. This led to new roles for testing with greater weight placed on test results. Linn (1989) cites competency testing, the testing of teachers, and public reporting of test results as three areas that underwent major expansion in recent years. In all three areas, objective (usually standardized) tests are the central indicators of performance. Objective testing seems socially acceptable in a country that needs to deal on an institutional basis with large numbers of individuals and so establishes bureaucratic systems, a country with an advanced level of technology, one which is technology conscious and number conscious (Haney, 1981), and one with an ethic of advancement by merit. Standardized tests are now given in most United States schools and are often required by state policy. Neill and Medina (1989) found that each child on the average takes 2 1/2 standardized tests per year with a national total of 105 million in the 1986-87 school year. With increased attention to minimal competency as a prerequisite to high school graduation and to promotion at elementary grade levels, this number may rise. With an increased demand by the public for information to compare states and districts, this number may rise. Standardized test use is extensive and costly and shows signs of becoming more so. Given a substantial investment of money and time, as well as legislative support of standardized testing, what are the potential and actual uses of standardized test results? In particular, how are standardized tests used by teachers? What issues central to the standardized testing debate are likely to have an impact on teachers? This chapter reviews the use of standardized test results by teachers and others and outlines issues that are the subject of debate regarding the use of standardized tests. The chapter concludes with speculations about future trends in standardized testing. Prior to discussing these issues, though, major characteristics of standardized tests are reviewed.

## CHARACTERISTICS OF STANDARDIZED TESTS

What distinguishes a standardized test from other tests? Standardized tests are characterized by a broader content focus than teacher-constructed tests, by the presence of standards or norms for interpretation of results, and by test administration and scoring directions to assure uniformity. Usually standardized tests are accompanied by technical information regarding psychometric characteristics. Published standardized tests should conform to the *Standards for Educational and Psychological Tests* (APA, AERA, NCME, 1985), a monograph that outlines criteria to be met by tests that are professionally constructed.

Standardized tests tend to address assessment of commonly accepted general objectives for instruction. Skills and information that would be taught in most school districts over a year or more form the basis for developing a standardized achievement test. Since standardized tests address general constructs (e.g., achievement in mathematics) more than particular skills, the test may have a greater or lesser match to a specific curriculum. Teacher-constructed tests have a much more restricted focus, typically reflecting the specific content or processes of a course or unit of instruction.

Norms provided for standardized tests allow objective comparisons with larger groups of students. Standardized criterion-referenced tests may or may not provide such norms and yield somewhat different information than norm-referenced tests. Norms are constructed in numerous ways. An individual's score may be compared to others (of a similar age or grade) and their percentile rank reported. Age or grade norms may be given. (See Chapter 2 for a review of the dangers of age and grade norms.) Quotient norms, normal curve standard scores, or scale scores may be provided. Chapter 2 presented a brief review of each of these types of scores. Norms may be given for national samples, district samples, or building samples. Local norms may be available for specified unique groups, such as different ethnic groups or socioeconomic groups.

Standardized tests are most often accompanied by an administration manual specifying how the test is to be given, when, and under what conditions. Administration of a standardized test is typically done under narrowly specified conditions. The setting, time allowed, materials, and directions must be controlled as much as possible so that comparisons across students (or states) will be meaningful. All test takers receive items drawn from a common set and take the test under similar physical conditions with the same time limits. Violation of standard administration conditions nullifies the usefulness of the test norms. The teacher's guide generally contains information about preparations for testing, directions for scoring, and tables of norms with information for interpreting test results. Some manuals also contain a section about how test results can be used in improving instruction. Prior to administration, the teacher's manual should be thoroughly examined and administration conditions clearly understood and followed.

Test users will also often receive a technical manual that includes information on test development, descriptions of the test, information on how norms were established, reliability and validity information, and information from the research literature on practice effects, coaching effects, sex differences, and correlations among subtests or different parts of the test battery. Such information is rarely available for teacher-constructed tests.

Standardized tests can be used in selection and placement, instructional planning, diagnosis, academic and vocational counseling, in program evaluation, student/school/district/state comparisons, and for feedback to students and parents regarding the student's standing in comparison with class, district, state, or national norms (Brown, 1983; Sax, 1989).

Increasingly test results are used by those who shape educational policy. Tests are used to report student achievement to the public and to enforce educational accountability. Tests are used to determine funding priorities and allocate compensatory monies, assess program and teacher effectiveness, and to certify successful student completion from preschool through high school.

The next section of this chapter reviews teachers' use of standardized tests and the use of test results by administrators and public agencies.

## USE OF STANDARDIZED TEST RESULTS

### Use and Lack of Use of Standardized
### Test Results by Teachers

A review of past practice suggests minimal use by teachers of the results of standardized tests in making instructional decisions (Fennessey, 1982; Green & Stager, 1987; Lazar-Morrison, Polin, Moy, & Burry, 1980; Ruddell, 1985). Stetz and Beck (1979) conducted a national study of over 3,000 teachers' opinions about standardized tests. They noted that 41% of the teachers reported making little use of test results. This finding is consistent with those of Goslin (1967) and Boyd, McKenna, Stake, and Yachinsky (1975). Little evidence was found of an influence of the standardized testing program upon the school curriculum. Tests were viewed as providing information that was supplemental to the wider variety of information the teacher already possessed (Airasian, 1979).

Two of the more recent studies of teachers' use of test results will be reviewed in greater detail here. Hall, Villeme, and Phillippy (1985) conducted a survey of 184 1981-1982 graduates of the College of Education at the University of South Florida. In Florida, high stakes state-wide testing has been in use since 1976 when the Florida Statewide Assessment Program began. Minimum competency tests in reading, writing, and mathematics are given to all students in grades 3, 5, 8, and 11. The study conducted by Hall et al. required beginning teachers to weight their use of teacher-constructed, district-wide, and state assessments in making seven different decisions. State assessments received the highest average weight in making decisions about students' academic progress, student promotion and retention, diagnosing of student weaknesses, adequacy of teaching, and adequacy of instructional materials. Teacher-constructed tests received the highest average weight in making decisions about student evaluation and in motivation of student learning. These results suggest that in a state with a required statewide testing program, beginning teachers rely on standardized tests more than might be suggested by previous research.

A second recent study (Green & Williams, 1989) sampled teachers from Wyoming (n=555) and from a metropolitan school district in Louisiana (n=253). Results were analyzed separately for these western and southern teachers. For these two samples, the percents of elementary teachers reporting test administration were 71.4% and 85.1%. Teachers at other levels reported less use of standardized tests. Results of this study suggest a greater use of test results, especially by the metropolitan southern teachers, than that suggested by previous research, although the use of test results for instructional planning seems to have remained at about 20%. Standardized test results were reported to be used primarily for individual diagnosis and because the district required testing. If states are mandating an increased use of tests, particularly high-stakes tests that may shape the curriculum, it would not be surprising to see an accompanying increase in the use of test results by teachers for some types of decisions. Instructional planning does not seem to be one of these types of decisions.

When test results are used by teachers, use seems to center around diagnosis of an individual's strengths and weaknesses (Goslin, 1967; Green & Williams, 1989; Hall et al., 1985). Other frequently reported purposes for testing are listed in Table 1 and include placement and test use due to a district or state requirement.

Reasons offered for why standardized tests are given but results not always used by teachers are a resistance to a perceived narrowing of the curriculum, resistance to management control, accountability avoidance (Darling-Hammond & Wise, 1985), failure of test publishers to report scores in a form useful to teachers (Lortie, 1975), the low quality of some standardized tests (Boyd et al., 1975), the vague purpose of some standardized tests (Whitehead & Santee, 1987), the delay between testing and receiving results (Stiggins, 1985), a limited understanding of score interpretation (Cramer & Slakter, 1968; Yeh et al., 1981) and inadequate preservice preparation, especially in statistics and standardized testing (Gullickson & Hopkins, 1987). The last of these barriers to use of test results will be examined in greater depth.

## Tests and Measurement Training

Marso and Pigge (1988) found teachers to perceive a lower need for standardized testing skills than for classroom testing skills. They also found that teachers reported lower proficiencies in standardized test score use and interpretation than in classroom test score use and interpretation. Gullickson (1986) found that teachers did not attach high importance to standardized tests and statistics. If limited understanding of tests and measurement is a factor in the lack of use of test results, increased training should result in increased use of test results. This relationship has, in fact, been found by two researchers (Tollefson, Tracy, Kaiser, Chen, & Kleinsasser, 1985; Yeh et al., 1981).

Training in measurement is not uniformly required in preservice programs. Although most institutions offer a course in tests and measurement, Schafer and Lissitz (1987) found that most programs in teacher education do not require the course. When offered as an optional course, professors report that less than 25% of students enroll (Gullickson & Hopkins, 1987). Estimates of the percent of teachers having at least one tests and measurement course range from 40% to 84% (Goslin, 1967; Green & Stager, 1987; Gullickson, 1982), with higher percentages reported by more recent studies. But even if most teachers have taken one preservice course in tests and measurement, is that sufficient for competency in understanding and using standardized test results? Two general standards for teacher competence in educational assessment hold that teachers "... be skilled in choosing assessment methods appropriate for instructional decisions" (including standardized tests) and that teachers be skilled in administering, scoring, and interpreting the results of standardized tests (American Association of Colleges for Teacher Education et al., 1989). While preservice training commonly incorporates a unit on standardized testing, it is often only 20% of the class. Newman and Stallings (1982) and Yeh (1980) found little evidence of change in competency since 1967 (Mayo). Hills (1977) polled district coordinators regarding the measurement competency of their teachers: 75% were judged as having incomplete, ineffective training. These authors conclude that training provided at the preservice level is inadequate with little inservice provided to strengthen teachers' knowledge. A general distaste for tests and statistics may impede knowledge acquisition in this arena.

Differential use of standardized tests across grade levels may indicate a need for differential emphases in preservice training of students preparing to teach at different levels. It has been suggested by several authors that college instruction in tests and measurement needs to be reoriented (Ebel, 1967; Fennessey, 1982; Gullickson, 1984, 1986; Newman & Stallings, 1982). Fennessey (1982) argued that college tests and measurement training should be focused on the curricular area of the student to be of most use. This requires a tailoring of coursework to curricular area--English, physical education, mathematics. Concurrent with this, tests and measurement courses could be (and sometimes are) structured for elementary, junior high, and senior high levels.

*Use of Standardized Test Results*
*by School Administrators and State Agencies*

Standardized test scores are used administratively for a number of purposes. Among them are the following. Test scores are used to report student achievement levels to the public; as indices of school and program effectiveness; to identify needs and allocate resources (to qualify schools for federal or state monies for special programs, to qualify students for entry into special programs); to reflect student growth, change, and progress over time; and to certify competency of students at any level (promotion and retention). Whereas classroom teachers may or may not be directly involved in test administration or the interpretation of test results, if standardized tests are used for any of these purposes there will be effects of testing on teachers.

A national concern for excellence in education is evident and has been for a number of years. This concern originated in the public perception that schools were ineffective. Some evidence for this came from standardized test scores (Scholastic Aptitude Test) that declined for several years, from test scores comparing United States students unfavorably with those of other nations, and from high school graduates who were unable to function effectively in society. This public perception of the ineffectiveness of the schools led to increased involvement in schools and school policy on the part of state legislatures and, more recently, business. While attributing unfavorable social changes to the schools and solely to the schools is overly simplistic, ignoring major societal influences such as increases in the technological knowledge needed to function well in society, serious international economic shifts, and shifts in population demographics and family structures, the schools are institutions that are perceived to be capable of playing a major role in shaping society. And, when the public asks about school effectiveness, standardized test scores are used as measures of effectiveness because they are thought to be informative and easily understood. Public reporting of test scores is likely to become more prevalent in the future. Schools judged to be ineffective may be subject to withdrawal of funds, reorganization, or even closure. Therefore, it is imperative that test scores be accurately reported and properly understood by policymakers. Concerns regarding reporting of test scores are presented in the succeeding section of this chapter.

Test scores used as indices of program effectiveness can directly impact teachers' professional lives. Programs may be funded or not, depending on indices of performance. Again, the indices of performance need to be accurate and clearly understood. Confusion between diagnosis/program improvement and accountability could result from the misunderstanding of assessment results by policymakers.

Use of test scores in student retention and promotion can also have a direct impact upon teachers' professional lives. One survey suggests that teachers feel the emphasis on standardized testing has affected their own (60%) and other teachers' (90%) behavior (Darling-Hammond & Wise, 1985). Specifically, teachers reported spending class time teaching students how to take the required test and how to take tests in general. Teachers may feel or in fact be compelled to adapt their curriculum to promote good performance on the standardized test used to make promotion and funding decisions.

Even though many uses of standardized test results are for administrative purposes, these uses will also, directly or indirectly, affect teachers.

## ISSUES IN STANDARDIZED TEST USE

Four areas of concern are reviewed here: issues in the use of standardized tests to make high-stakes decisions, issues regarding the evaluation of program effectiveness, issues concerning reporting test scores to the public, and issues in test quality.

### High-Stakes Testing

By high-stakes testing, I mean any test used for making decisions about promotion/retention, program evaluation, or school effectiveness--when the decision is primarily based on a test score.

Some of the perceived benefits of one form of high-stakes testing--minimum competency testing--include restoration of public confidence in the degrees or promotions granted, greater public involvement in education, improvement in the instructional process, motivation for students and teachers, diagnosis and remediation of students not achieving at minimal levels, and provision of an accountability mechanism. The major support for minimum competency testing comes from the public. Minimum competency tests are often constructed with representation from different constituencies such as teachers, educational organizations, parents, students, and business representatives and so promote public involvement in education. Since minimum competency testing may be subject to legal challenge, proponents view minimum competency testing as an incentive to carefully examine the curriculum and restructure it where basic skills instruction is lacking. Items on minimum competency tests must clearly stem from instruction for content validity to be supported. In some programs, a major goal of minimum competency testing is to identify students who need remediation prior to graduation and to identify where the educational process has failed these students. The utility of this purpose for testing assumes that schools will institute remedial programs or will be encouraged to do so by funding for remedial programs. While minimum competency and other high-stakes tests are perceived to have many benefits, there are continuing concerns and cautions in their use.

One issue of major concern in high-stakes testing is the power of the test to shape the curriculum; in particular, to narrow the teaching and learning process to what is demanded by the test. A second major issue is where the decision-making power resides when high-stakes tests are forced on a district by state mandate. "A resolution of the incompatibility of local specificity of instructional emphasis and state or nationally oriented tests is unlikely to be realized without either compromise on both sides or binding mandates from state boards or legislatures, as is the case with minimum competency testing programs." (Airasian & Madaus, 1983, p. 114) Whether tests are agreed upon or mandated, a narrowing of the curriculum can result in several ways. If the test is, for example, a statewide minimum competency test required of all high school seniors, the power to influence the curriculum is shifted from a local to a state locus. As more weight is placed on the test, the impact on instruction grows stronger. The local curriculum would adapt to emphasize the knowledge and skills assessed by the test. The curriculum would narrow, and greater control would go to the state. Greater emphasis on coverage of what will be tested may serve to increase scores on basic skills at the expense of other skills. Focus on narrower, more readily quantifiable skills comes at the expense of attention to abilities that are more difficult to assess such as critical thinking and problem solving. Other variables associated with learning such as positive attitudes and enthusiasm are ignored as well.

Test-driven instruction, it is argued (e.g., Cole, 1984; Madaus cited in McClellan, 1988) places a great burden on the test. Tests need to be of high technical quality and also need to reflect the important goals and processes of educational systems. For instance, most large-scale testing programs use multiple-choice tests. It is argued that multiple-choice tests do not adequately promote nor necessarily reflect the desired outcome itself (Madaus cited in McClellan, 1988). Wiggins (1989) uses the example of athletic performance--the outcome is clearly the performance itself. What are the desired outcomes of academic instruction? Valid tests of academic performance may need to be redesigned extensively to reflect the actual outcomes desired. At what real world behaviors is it intended that people excel?

Neill and Medina (1989) suggest that multiple-choice tests may not provide a valid format for assessing many skills or for assessing skills of certain groups. The stylized language in which questions are couched, the timed format, and removal from a broader context may adversely affect scores for groups such as some ethnic minorities, young children, or students who are less verbally proficient. While the major issue is corruption of the instructional process, whether by imposed high-stakes tests or by tests that do not measure what they need to measure, issues of form and bias are important as well.

*Evaluating Program Effectiveness*

Tests selected for local program evaluation may be very different in character from tests used for reporting educational achievement statewide or nationwide. Issues in the use of standardized test scores in evaluating program effectiveness include test selection which is in turn dependent upon program definition and a clear specification of program goals. The impact a program has on learning may be overlooked if goals and attendant assessment measures are not well defined. Kearney (1983) argues that test misuse stems from the failure to clarify what an assessment program can and cannot do. If a norm-referenced test is selected as an outcome measure, what is the overlap between the curriculum and the test? If a test is sensitive to instruction, overlap will be at a maximum. But, a program goal may be to influence a wider domain of content and so a test with less overlap would be preferred.

Phillips and Mehrens (1987, 1988) examined the issue of matching of instruction and textbook series to the test in an urban midwestern district. They found little effect of differences in test match to instruction on item performance. They suggest that differences within a district in test match to instruction may be small enough to lack practical significance. But differences may be greater if the test is customized for a local educational agency. If the norms for a standardized test are to be valid, content equivalence between the customized and the norm-referenced test is essential (Way, Forsyth, & Ansley, 1989; Yen, Green, & Burket, 1987).

## Reporting Test Scores

Frechtling (1989) discusses several issues involved when reporting test scores to the public. When scores are reported, the unit for reporting must be explicit. The range of scores may differ if reported by student, class, school, or district, or by subgroups (e.g., socioeconomic groups, ethnic groups). In addition, the metric used to report scores must be clear, with a definition and directions for appropriate interpretation of the accompanying scores. That is, the reporting format needs to be tailored to the relevant audience without dismissing complexities in interpretation.

When scores are used for comparative purposes, if the test and/or the group composition changes, results may be misleading. For example, the nature of the cohort may change due to shifts in economics and differences in the nature of people living in the area.

Such change can cause scores to increase or decrease regardless of school effectiveness. Frechtling suggests the use of longitudinal data to report change over time, with scores reported for the stable group, for newcomers, and for school-leavers. Tests given at different points in instruction, such as fall or spring, may perform differently as well.

Some of the difficulties in score interpretation were called to the public's attention by the Cannell report (Cannell, 1988). Also called the Lake Wobegon effect, the problem was that all 50 states and most districts reported themselves to be above average. Issues raised pursuant to this report were those of test use and also test design. Test scores are compared to norms, but the norms may be outdated or inaccurate. Large scale tests may be re-normed as infrequently as once every 10-15 years. Assuming some progress in education, a norm group from 10 years previous would be expected to have performed less well than today's students. Cannell suggested that, if tests are not actually rewritten from year to year, that norms can still be computed annually. Phillips and Finn (1988) suggest that the original norms may not have been accurate since districts and students in the original sample would have little motivation to do well. In subsequent years, schools may elect to participate or not, producing a self-selection bias in future years of test administration. Schools whose curriculum does not match the test well may opt for a different test. Schools that elect to use a particular test may do so year after year. In all of these instances, there may be distinct differences between the norming sample and the groups using the test thereafter.

A second issue raised by the Cannell report is that of test security and teaching to the test. Test publishers have little control over testing conditions, the selectivity of students who take the test, how data are synthesized, or whether the test is actually directly taught (Drahozal & Frisbic, 1988). If a standardized test is given under nonstandard conditions to groups of students different in composition from the norming sample and from each other, scores will not be comparable to the established norms. Cannell suggests that a test such as the National Assessment of Educational Progress (NAEP) be administered under strict security with results used solely for state and district comparisons and not for curriculum purposes. Such use would require clear designation of which students could be exempted from testing. Directly teaching to the test would, of course, invalidate test results.

A further concern in reporting test scores relates to the use of tests for atypical individuals or individuals in atypical settings. Children with handicapping conditions cannot reasonably be expected to take a standardized test under standard conditions, if at all. And children receiving instruction, for example, at home schools, are not reasonably assessed using a composite score on a standardized test interpreted according to national norms (Cizek, 1988). Norms are incorrectly interpreted as standards. Requiring any individual student to score above a specific percentile on a test to retain placement in a home school is inappropriate. Alternative ways of assessing the effectiveness of alternative educational programs would be preferable.

A final concern relates to the public's understanding (or misunderstanding) of test scores. As Cole (1984) notes: "Most test users have never studied proper test use as part of their own educational preparation. In many states beginning teachers are certified without any formal preparation in making or using tests. Most administrators, school board members, and state legislators have no such training." (p. 5) Training via books, workshops, or videotape might be possible.

## Test Quality

Neill and Medina (1989) suggest that existing tests are technically deficient and "hopelessly inadequate for promoting necessary school reform" (p. 695). Comments on technical inadequacy center around questions of test validity. Does the test truly measure what it promises? Can truthful statements about meaningful abilities be made using test scores? This is a perennial question in testing of any sort but of greater importance when sanctions are imposed using test scores. Haney and Madaus (1989) also point out that tests may give false information about the status of learning in schools and may actually be detrimental to the educational process. If test scores are inaccurate or predict little more than performance on another test, are tests truly useful?

Additional questions involve the adequacy of technical test reliability and validity studies. Assessment of stability may be as important as internal consistency but is less likely to be obtained since stability involves reassessment of a group of examinees. Two test administrations are involved and so this type of reliability is more awkward to find. Validation is often via factorial validity and correlation with like measures. If the previously existing measures lack validity, then invalidity is perpetuated.

Finally, more and more standardized tests are constructed and scores evaluated using item response theory. The use of item response theory in test design and analysis assumes assessment of a unitary attribute. Some attributes may be too complex to conform to a unidimensional linear scale, although item misfit statistics should be useful in identifying such attributes. Reporting of composite scores is inappropriate if multiple dimensions of attributes are found to exist.

Tests can provide valuable information--information that is in general objective; information that gives people a comparison against which to evaluate their own performance, that of a school, or a state. Such information is useful in many ways, including pointing out where change is needed and where improvements can be made. The concerns described in this section do not vitiate the need for standardized test information; they emphasize that great care must be taken in decisions about testing and in test design and validation. Haney commented in 1981 that standardized testing was on the upswing at the same time that tests were being viewed more and more critically. "That standardized testing has risen to public prominence so often over the last 70 [now 80] years is to some extent merely a reflection of its success as a social enterprise." (p. 1029) Standardized testing succeeds at its task in many ways. But, the task must be more clearly defined and the tests continually improved.

## FUTURE TRENDS IN STANDARDIZED TESTING

As a social enterprise, standardized testing seems to be criticized more and more, but is still on the upswing. Petrie (1987) says it is not "too much of an exaggeration to say that evaluation and testing have become *the* engine for implementing educational policy." (p. 175) Future change in testing will probably extend its scope beyond that enjoyed during the past decade.

As more tests are produced and used to make high-stakes decisions, concern with test security may increase (Fisher, 1988). Cheating on a standardized test is now a misdemeanor in Florida and South Carolina. Other states may follow suit and invoke penalties for cheating. Rudman (1987) sees a potential for a national test development and monitoring system.

Competency testing of students is likely to continue and to expand beyond basic skills testing to testing in subject areas such as history or geography. Statewide subject area tests would promote state-wide consistency in subject area instruction. Students who moved from city to city would be at less of a disadvantage; interested groups would have some assurance about what skills were considered important; university admissions officers would have more information to use in student placement. Subject area competency testing may promote not only close investigation of curricula but also continued debate regarding what the objectives of instruction truly are. With increased use of tests, testing should eventually be integrated more closely into the instructional process.

There is demand for effective measures of state-by-state comparisons for assessing progress that will *not* be directly used for classroom instruction. The NAEP is being adapted to meet this specific need for comparative data as called for by a Senate amendment to the bill to reauthorize federal elementary and secondary education programs (Linn, 1988).

Concurrent with national reporting, it is likely that greater attention will be given to developing a way to report and disseminate assessment results to policymakers in a more understandable fashion, one that is less open to misinterpretation. Reliance on a single composite score may yield to the reporting of multiple measures. In conjunction with an effort to make test scores more comprehensible still comes a need for greater expertise in test score interpretation and practical (in contrast to theoretical) measurement techniques. To promote appropriate test use, users need to be more sophisticated, test results easier to understand, and more effort devoted to translating measurement techniques into methods useful to laypersons. Kearney

(1983) also suggested a national clearinghouse providing information and examples of test reporting.

Rudman (1987) sees a future demand for tests tailored to local objectives, although he points out that it is questionable whether local curricula differ that much. Item banking combined with computer adaptive testing, with norms calibrated via item response theory methods will be emphasized in locally tailored tests. Developments in cognitive science show promise for helping to understand how people solve problems. Research on misconceptions and why people make errors may eventually provide guidance in how to correct errors. Tests that result from such work would be intimately tied to instruction and would be diagnostic in nature rather than normative. With future widespread availability of computer-adaptive testing software and greater expertise in its use, the benefits of the microcomputer may be realized. Testing would be timely and frequently available and would be one essential element of a wider diagnostic-prescriptive learning system. Standardized testing in this setting would bear strong similarity to teacher-constructed testing. In fact, tests used in this manner would merely supplement teacher-constructed tests. The future will probably see greater use of testing as a form of teaching. With more attention given to what skills we wish students to acquire, innovation in types of test formats and items will be required.

With greater attention given to early childhood education, alternative approaches to assessment at young ages will be investigated. Forty-three states report some use of academic readiness tests prior to first grade (Schultz, 1989). Concerns are the validity of tests used with young children, the stress testing places on children and teachers, and representative sampling of the age group.

The future will probably see a continuation of the debate regarding whether two of standardized testing's disparate purposes (provision of comparative data and local, diagnostic use) can harmoniously coexist. Can the instructional process benefit from testing on a national basis? If not, will local educational agencies be resistant to the pressure to conform their curricula to promote test performance?

A continued concern for excellence in education predicts continued requirements for better tests and for a view of testing as an integral part of learning. Tests are more useful if they correct and direct than if they merely describe. The future requires greater facility in using tests to learn how to promote better achievement and more care in using tests for comparison and accountability.

## REFERENCES

Airasian, P.W. 1979. "A Perspective on the Uses and Misuses of Standardized Achievement Tests." *NCME Measurement in Education, 10(3)*, 1-12.

Airasian, P.W., & Madaus, G. 1983. "Linking Testing and Instruction: Policy Issues." *Journal of Educational Measurement, 20*, 103-118.

American Association of Colleges for Teacher Education, American Federation of Teachers, National Council on Measurement in Education, & National Education Association. March 1989. "Draft: Standards for Teacher Competence in Educational Assessment of Students." Paper presented at the American Educational Research Association annual meeting, San Francisco.

American Psychological Association, American Educational Research Association, & National Council on Measurement in Education. 1985. *Standards for Educational and Psychological Tests.* Washington, DC: American Psychological Association.

> Lists and describes standards to which tests should conform including test uses, selection, reliability, validity, score interpretation, and ethical issues.

Boyd, J., McKenna, B.H., Stake, R.E., & Yachinsky, J. 1975. *A Study of Testing Practices in the Royal Oak (Michigan) Public Schools.* Royal Oak, MI: Royal Oak City School District. (ERIC Document Reproduction Service No. ED 117 161).

Brown, F.G. 1983. *Principles of Educational and Psychological Testing (3rd edition)* New York: Holt, Rinehart & Winston.

Cannell, J.J. 1988. "Nationally Normed Elementary Achievement Testing in America's Public Schools: How All 50 States are Above the National Average." *Educational Measurement: Issues and Practice, 7(2)*, 5-9.

Describes data suggesting all states to be above average in academic achievement, presents potential explanations of this, and suggests improvements in testing for the future.

Cizek, G.J. 1988. "Applying Standardized Testing to Home-based Education Programs: Reasonable or Customary?" *Educational Measurement: Issues and Practice, 7(3),* 12-19.

Discusses the use and misuse of standardized test results in evaluating the progress of children schooled at home.

Cole, N.S. 1984. "Testing and the 'Crisis' in Education." *Educational Measurement: Issues and Practice, 3(3),* 4-8.

Cramer, S., & Slakter, M. 1968. "A Scale to Assess Attitudes toward Aptitude Testing." *Measurement and Evaluation in Guidance, 1(2),* 96-102.

Darling-Hammond, L., & Wise, A.E. 1985. "Beyond Standardization: State Standards and School Improvement." *Elementary School Journal, 85,* 315-336.

Drahozal, E.C., & Frisbie, D.A. 1988. "Riverside Comments on the Friends for Education Report." *Educational Measurement: Issues and Practice, 7(2),* 12-16.

As one of several reactors to the Cannell report in this issue, the authors present potential explanations of the Cannell data and give suggestions for future test design and interpretation.

Ebel, R.L. 1967. "Improving the Competence of Teachers in Educational Measurement." In J. Flynn & H. Garber (Eds.), *Assessing Behavior: Readings in Educational and Psychological Measurement.* Reading, Ma.: Addison-Wesley.

Fennessey, D. 1982. "Primary Teachers' Assessment Practices: Some Implications for Teacher Training." Paper presented at the annual conference of the South Pacific Assn. for Teacher Education, Frankston, Victoria, Australia. (ERIC ED 229 346)

> Responses to a mail survey of 129 teachers regarding test use are reported.

Fisher, T.H. 1988. "Testing the Basic Skills in the High School--What's in the Future?" *Applied Measurement in Education, 1(2)*, 157-170.

> Fisher projects future trends in competency testing, basic skills testing in subject areas, concerns about test security, the impact of technology on testing, and the advent of state-by-state comparisons.

Frechtling, J.A. 1989. "Administrative Uses of School Testing Programs." In R.L. Linn (Ed.), *Educational Measurement (3rd edition)*. New York: Macmillan.

Goslin, D.A. 1967. *Teachers and Testing.* New York: Russell Sage Foundation.

> Goslin studied the use of standardized tests at the elementary and secondary levels. Teachers use standardized tests primarily in diagnosis and for feedback but make little use of standardized test results in general.

Green, K.E., & Stager, S.F. 1987. "Differences in Teacher Test and Item Use with Subject, Grade Level Taught, and Measurement Coursework." *Teacher Education and Practice, 4(1)*, 55-61.

> Types of tests and types of test items user are examined for a sample of 555 Wyoming teachers. Significant differences in test and item use were found for subject, grade level, and extent of training in tests and measurement.

Green, K.E., & Williams, E.J. March 1989. "Standardized Test Use by Classroom Teachers: Effects of Training and Grade Level Taught."

Paper presented at the annual meeting of the National Council on Measurement in Education, San Francisco.

> Reports use of standardized tests for Wyoming and Louisiana samples for elementary, middle level, and secondary teachers with and without tests and measurement training. While test use differed across grade levels, attitudes did not.

Gullickson, A.R. 1982. "The Practice of Testing in Elementary and Secondary Schools." Paper presented at the Rural Education Conference, Kansas State University, Manhattan, Kansas, ERIC ED 229391.

> Responses to a survey of 336 South Dakota teachers regarding test use were analyzed by grade and curricular level.

Gullickson, A.R. 1984. "Teacher Perspectives of Their Instructional Use of Tests." *Journal of Educational Research, 77,* 244-248.

> Teacher attitudes toward testing and the classroom use of tests were assessed. Results indicate that teachers use tests heavily but have limited testing expertise.

Gullickson, A.R. 1986. "Teacher Education and Teacher-perceived Needs in Educational Measurement and Evaluation." *Journal of Educational Measurement, 23,* 347-354.

> Compares the views of professors and teachers about preservice educational measurement. In five of eight content areas, the emphases given by professors differed from those recommended by teachers. Major differences and their implications are discussed.

Gullickson, A.R., & Hopkins, K.D. 1987. "The Context of Educational Measurement Instruction for Preservice Teachers: Professor Perspectives." *Educational Measurement: Issues and Practice, 6(3),* 12-16.

Professors from 28 midwestern colleges expressed their views regarding measurement course activities, course content, and their own preparation.

Hall, B.W., Villeme, M.G., & Phillippy, S.W. 1985. "How Beginning Teachers Use Test Results in Critical Education Decisions." *Educational Research Quarterly, 9,* 12-18.

Weights were assigned to teacher-made, district, and statewide tests by first year teachers. Results suggest that greater weight is placed on statewide assessments for making educational decisions.

Haney, W. 1981. "Validity, Vaudeville and Values: A Short History of Social Concerns over Standardized Testing." *American Psychologist, 36,* 1021-1034.

Haney reviews the place of standardized testing in society from the early 1900s, provides examples of appropriate and inappropriate use, and projects future issues.

Haney, W., & Madaus, G. May 1989. "Searching for Alternatives to Standardized Testing: Whys, Whats, and Whithers." *Phi Delta Kappan, 70(9),* 683-687.

Describes alternatives to standardized tests that may develop due to cognitive science and computer assisted testing; criticisms of standardized tests are discussed.

Hills, J.R. 1977. "Coordinators of Accountability View Teachers' Measurement Competence." *Florida Journal of Education Research, 19,* 34-44.

Kearney, C.P. 1983. "Uses and Abuses of Assessment and Evaluation Data by Policymakers." *Educational Measurement: Issues and Practice, 2(3),* 9-12,17.

Kearney identifies three basic purposes of large-scale assessment (public reporting, identifying needs and allocating resources, and making judgments about promotion and graduation) and gives examples of test use and misuse by policymakers and by assessment program designers for the first two categories.

Lazar-Morrison, C., Polin, L., Moy, R., & Burry, J. 1980. *A Review of the Literature on Test Use.* Los Angeles: Center for the Study of Evaluation, California State University, ERIC ED 204411.

Linn, R.L. 1988. "State-by-State Comparisons of Achievement: Suggestions for Enhancing Validity." *Educational Researcher, 17(3),* 6-9.

Subsequent to a Senate call for achievement data representative on a national, regional, and state basis, Linn presents the background of the NAEP and validity and content issues.

Linn, R.L. 1989. "Current Perspectives and Future Directions." In R.L. Linn (Ed.), *Educational Measurement (3rd edition)* New York: Macmillan.

This chapter prefaces the latest edition of this volume. Linn describes current developments and controversies in educational measurement.

Lortie, D.C. 1975. *School-teacher: A Sociological Study.* Chicago: The University of Chicago Press.

Marso, R.N., & Pigge, F.L. 1988. "Ohio Secondary Teachers' Testing Needs and Proficiencies: Assessments by Teachers, Supervisors, and Principals." *American Secondary Education, 17,* 2-9.

Mayo, S.T. 1967. " Preservice Preparation of Teachers in Educational Measurement." Chicago: Loyola University.

McClellan, M.C. 1988. "Testing and Reform." *Phi Delta Kappan, 69(10),* 768-771.

McClellan reports the responses of a panel of well-known educational researchers to questions about the implications of testing of teachers and the effects of testing on the instructional process.

Neill, D.M., & Medina, N.J.    May 1989.    "Standardized Testing: Harmful to Educational Health."    *Phi Delta Kappan, 70(9),* 688-697.

This article, written by FairTest employees and associates, argues against the use of tests in educational reform.    Tests are criticized on a number of bases.

Newman, D.C., & Stallings, W.M.    1982.    "Teacher Competency in Classroom Testing, Measurement Preparation, and Classroom Testing Practices."    Paper presented at the American Educational Research Association annual conference, New York.    (ERIC ED 220 491)

Teachers in Alabama, Florida, and Georgia were surveyed to establish the extent of preparation, testing practices, and knowledge.  Results suggest no change in competency since that reported in 1967.

Petrie, H.G.    1987.    "Introduction to 'evaluation and testing.'"    *Educational Policy, 1,* 175-180.

Phillips, G.W., & Finn, C.E., Jr.    1988. " The Lake Wobegon Effect: A Skeleton in the Testing Closet?"    *Educational Measurement: Issues and Practice, 7(2),* 10-12.

As reactors to the Cannell report and officials of the U.S. Department of Education, these authors delineate factors that contribute to Cannell's findings and describe the Department's response.

Phillips, S.E., & Mehrens, W.A.    1987.    "Curricular Differences and Unidimensionality of Achievement Test Data: An Exploratory Analysis."    *Journal of Educational Measurement, 24(1),* 1-16.

Phillips, S.E., & Mehrens, W.A.    1988.    "Effects of Curricular Differences on Achievement Test Data at Item and Objective Levels."    *Applied Measurement in Education, 1(1),* 33-51.

This study and a 1987 study by the same authors examined the impact of different curricula within a school district on standardized achievement test scores at item and objective levels. The purpose was to determine if different curricula generate different patterns of item factor loadings. No curricular effects on major factors were found.

Ruddell, R.B. 1985. "Knowledge and Attitudes toward Testing: Field Educators and Legislators." *Reading Teacher, 38,* 538-543.

Rudman, H.C. 1987. "The Future of Testing is Now." *Educational Measurement: Issues and Practice, 6(3),* 5-11.

Rudman points out that current test development will probably determine testing in the year 2000. He describes forces within testing companies and from external sources and projects a possible future.

Sax, G. 1989. *Principles of Educational and Psychological Measurement and Evaluation (3rd edition)* Belmont, CA: Wadsworth Pub. Co.

As a tests and measurement textbook, this volume presents basic information in a clear, comprehensive form. It contains several chapters on standardized testing and is recommended for any teacher without tests and measurement coursework or who wants a thorough, up-to-date review.

Schafer, W.D., & Lissitz, R.W. 1987. "Measurement Training for School Personnel: Recommendations and Reality." *Journal of Teacher Education, 38(3),* 57-63.

Results of a national study of teacher preparation in measurement are reported. The authors conclude that recommendations from professional groups are not being met and suggest that curricular changes be undertaken to ensure that teachers have adequate assessment skills.

Schultz, T. October 1989. "Testing and Retention of Young Children: Moving from Controversy to Reform." *Phi Delta Kappan, 71(2)*, 125-129.

Schultz reviews the use of tests with young children, its historical origins, the effects of testing, and suggests reforms and alternatives policymakers and practitioners should consider.

Stetz, F.P., & Beck, M.D. 1979. "Comments from the Classroom: Teachers' and Students Opinions of Achievement Tests." Paper presented at the annual meeting of the National Council on Measurement in Education, San Francisco.

The results of a national study of teachers' opinions of the usefulness of standardized tests are reported.

Stiggins, R.J. 1985. "Improving Assessment Where It Means the Most: In the Classroom." *Educational Leadership, 43,* 69-74.

Tollefson, N., Tracy, D.B., Kaiser, J., Chen, J.S., & Kleinsasser, A. 1985. "Teachers' Attitudes toward Tests." Paper presented at the American Educational Research Association annual conference, Chicago.

Way, W.D., Forsyth, R.A., & Ansley, T.N. 1989. "IRT Ability Estimates from Customized Achievement Tests Without Representative Content Sampling." *Applied Measurement in Education, 2(1),* 15-35.

Subsets of ITBS items were selected from four subtests and were customized or were representative of the total item content. For the customized tests in three of the four tests, ability estimates were systematically higher than those based on the full tests. The authors conclude that for content-customized tests, ability estimates cannot be expected to be equivalent to those based on full-length tests.

Whitehead, B., & Santee, P. 1987. "Using Standardized Test Results as an Instructional Guide." *Clearinghouse, 61,* 57-59.

Wiggins, G. May 1989. "A True Test: Toward More Authentic and Equitable Assessment." *Phi Delta Kappan, 70(9)*, 703-713.

> This paper presents criticisms of standardized testing and several examples of what preferable types of tests could be.

Yeh, J.P. 1980. "A Re-analysis of Test Use Data." Los Angeles: Center for the Study of Evaluation, California University ERIC ED 205590.

> Teacher training, knowledge, and test use are analyzed.

Yeh, J.P., Herman, J.L., & Rudner, L.M. 1981. "Teachers and Testing: A Survey of Test Use." Center for the Study of Evaluation, California University, Los Angeles. (ERIC Document 218 336)

> California elementary school teachers were surveyed regarding their use of tests and competency in contemporary measurement practices.

Yen, W.M., Green, D.R., & Burket, G.R. 1987. "Valid Normative Information from Customized Achievement Tests." *Educational Measurement: Issues and Practice, 6(1)*, 7-13.

> This paper provides an illustration of the effects of customizing a test to meet local needs on normative interpretations. The authors emphasize the importance of matching the content of the customized test to that of the normed test if accurate norm interpretation is needed.

# LEGAL ISSUES IN STANDARDIZED ACHIEVEMENT TESTING

## DEBRA J. MADSEN

This chapter discusses the legal principles and court decisions which impact how teachers and school districts may use standardized tests as measurement tools. A review of the various legal principles used to challenge testing is discussed in the context of court decisions. The discussion also focuses on the legal challenges in relationship to the type and purpose of testing: minimum competency as a graduation requirement and achievement and intelligence for purposes of ability grouping. The chapter concludes with a summary of the current state of the law and trends for the future.

## LEGAL CHALLENGES TO TESTING

Generally, educators are given extreme freedom in determining the proper instructional methods to be employed in the schools. The courts are in unanimous agreement that a school district has a legitimate state interest in maintaining and upgrading the quality of education provided to its students (Horner, 1985). Why, then, are tests subject to litigation and review by the courts? The courts have interfered with state educational systems only when necessary to protect freedoms and privileges guaranteed to the individual by the United

States Constitution (e.g., *Debra P. v. Turlington,* 1981). Therefore, whenever a particular instructional method used in the schools, i.e., testing, has a deleterious impact upon a student, the courts are more likely to undertake a review of that method to determine if it meets constitutional requirements.

There are two constitutional theories which have been used to challenge the use of tests: (1) the Equal Protection Clause of the Fourteenth Amendment; and, (2) the Due Process Clause of the Fourteenth Amendment. With respect to handicapped students, the statutory challenges are based on The Education for All Handicapped Children Act and Section 504 of the Rehabilitation Act of 1973. Each of these theories will be discussed within the context of a court decision and the type of testing being challenged.

## COMPETENCY TESTS AS A DIPLOMA REQUIREMENT

*Constitutional Challenges - Debra P. V. Turlington*

In 1976, the Florida legislature passed comprehensive legislation, known as the "Educational Accountability Act of 1976." This legislation established three requirements for graduation from a Florida public school: (1) a minimum number of credits; (2) mastery of basic skills; and, (3) satisfactory performance in functional literacy. In 1978, additional legislation was implemented requiring that all students pass a functional literacy examination, the "SSAT II" as evidence of the third graduation requirement. Students who met these three requirements received a high school diploma. Students who failed the SSAT II exam received a certificate of completion. Provisions were also made for remediation of students who failed the test.

The objectives of the SSAT II were to ensure that students had the ability to successfully apply basic communications and mathematics skills to everyday life situations (564 F. Supp. 179, 1983). The test covered twenty-four skills: eleven reading and writing eleventh grade basic skills and thirteen mathematics eleventh grade basic skills. The

SSAT II was administered on three separate occasions prior to the litigation arising from the test: fall 1977, fall 1978 and spring 1979. In the fall of 1977 the test was administered to eleventh graders in the public schools. Thirty-six percent of all test-takers failed one or both sections of the test. When evaluating these numbers along racial lines, 78% of the black students failed one or both sections, compared to 25% of the white students. The second administration, in the fall of 1978, followed a similar pattern with 74% of the black students retaking the test, now as high school seniors, failing one or both sections, compared to 25% of the white students. By May of 1979, 20% of all black high school seniors had failed the test compared to 1.9% of the white students. The overall failure rate was 5.8% (474 F. Supp 244, 1979).

In evaluating this information for purposes of a legal challenge, it is important to remember that those students failing the SSAT II received a certificate of completion, not a high school diploma. The failure to receive a high school diploma "triggers a number of economic and academic deprivations" (474 F. Supp. 249). Economically, students without high school diplomas were limited in their future job opportunities. Testimony was introduced which showed that only 10% of the Florida state government jobs were available to individuals without a high school diploma. Academically, the students would have reduced opportunities to study at a Florida university since all but one of the nine Florida universities required a high school diploma for admission (Hollander, 1982). One expert testified that based on the number of students failing the SSAT II for the second time this would result in a 20% decline in black students' college attendance (474 F. Supp. 249, n.6).

In 1979, a lawsuit challenging the use of the SSAT II was filed on behalf of all present and future senior high school students who have failed or will fail the SSAT II, and, more specifically, all present and future senior high school black students who have failed or will fail the SSAT II. The plaintiffs argued that the test violated the equal protection and due process clauses of the Fourteenth Amendment.

### Equal Protection

The Fourteenth Amendment of the United States Constitution provides that "no State shall make or enforce any law which shall . . . deny to any person within its jurisdiction the equal protection of the laws." The equal protection clause has become the single most important provision in the Constitution for the protection of individual rights (Nowak, Rotunda, & Young, 1983). The clause, as interpreted by the courts, provides that all persons similarly situated will be treated in a similar manner. It does not prohibit the government from classifying individuals. Nowak et al. (1983) summarize equal protection as requiring that the classifications

> not be based on impermissible criteria or arbitrarily used to burden a group of individuals. If the government classification relates to a proper governmental purpose, then the classification will be upheld. Such a classification does not violate the guarantee when it distinguishes persons as 'dissimilar' upon some permissible basis in order to advance the legitimate interests of society. Those who are treated less favorably by the legislation are not denied equal protection of the law because they are not similarly situated to those who receive the benefit of the legislative classification. (p. 525)

In determining whether the requirement that all students pass the SSAT II in order to receive a high school diploma violated the equal protection clause, the court first looked at whether the legislation advanced a legitimate societal interest. The court determined that the legislation was intended to enhance the education offered in the Florida schools and that the SSAT was a legitimate means by which to obtain that goal. Jaeger (1989) notes that the use of competency tests, for an appropriate use such as a condition of graduation, has been upheld in all relevant court cases.

*The Test*

The second portion of the equal protection analysis focused on the *subject matter* of the test. In order to pass a Constitutional challenge, the court determined that a test must be a fair test of that which was in fact taught. Should the test not cover material taught in the classroom it is not rationally related to a state interest, i.e., enhancement of the educational process, and would violate the equal protection clause (644 F.2d 406). Since the state had not proven the instructional validity of the SSAT II, the case was remanded back to the District Court for further findings on the issue (644 F.2d 400).

What evidence must the state or school districts provide in order to prove instructional validity? In *Debra P.*, the District Court on remand found that what is required is evidence that the skills are included in the official curriculum and that the majority of teachers recognize them as being something they should teach (564 F. Supp. 186). The State of Florida met this burden by introducing into evidence the results of a study it conducted to determine whether the material tested was being provided to the students. The survey focused on: (1) whether junior and high school principals had incorporated the skills measured by the tests into their curriculum, (2) whether teachers in grades 2 through 12 were teaching the skills assessed, and (3) methods used by school districts to provide instruction in the skills assessed. Students were also surveyed as to whether they felt that they had received instruction in the skills assessed. In addition, on-site visits were conducted to verify the accuracy of the surveys. The on-site inspectors, an employee of the Florida Department of Education and two educators from the school district, interviewed administrators and teachers and compared the instructional materials used in the district with those listed in the survey (564 F. Supp. 180-81). The validity of the survey was the subject of extensive debate by the expert witnesses testifying for each side. The plaintiffs challenged the survey on grounds that it was flawed because it was not a reliable indicator of what actually went on in the classroom, nor did the survey follow students throughout their entire careers (564 F. Supp. 182-83). The court in rejecting this argument emphasized that it is impossible to determine the education received by each student. Therefore, it found that the survey provided adequate proof that the skills tested are included in the curriculum and that a substantial number of public school teachers adhere to this curriculum by including these skills in their classes (564 F. Supp. 177).

Other courts have faced the issue of determining the instructional validity of a standardized test, and it is clear that they do not seek to dictate what subjects are to be taught or in what manner (644 F.2d 406). The decision to require instructional validity simply comports with constitutional requirements in that you do not deprive a student of a high school diploma on the basis of a test which does not test what they have had the "opportunity to learn." That is, states requiring passage of a competency test must show that students were given the opportunity to learn the material that is tested.

This requirement may seem to put a heavy burden on school districts when challenged as to the instructional validity of a competency test. In *Anderson v. Banks* (1982), the court stressed the importance of the judicial policy of providing great deference to educators in academic decision-making.

> To require school officials to produce testimony that every teacher finished every lesson and assigned every problem in the curriculum would impose a paralyzing burden on school authorities and hamper them in constructing an academic program which they believe effectively meets the needs of their students (540 F. Supp. 765-66).

The Anderson court found that the school district had met its burden of proof by demonstrating via the testimony of an expert witness, school officials and teachers that the content of the test was included in the curriculum and that the material was actually taught.

*Racial Discrimination*

A second equal protection argument advanced by the plaintiffs focused on the discriminatory impact the test had on black students. It was the plaintiffs' contention that the SSAT II perpetuated the effects of past purposeful discrimination since blacks failed in a disproportionate number as compared to white students. In analyzing this claim, the court looked at the "dual school system" which was in place in Florida when the affected students began school in the 1967-68 term.   The court found that almost all of the black plaintiffs attended segregated schools which were inferior in all respects to white schools during this time period (474 F. Supp. 251).   Although Florida schools had completed their physical integration by the 1971-72 term the "vestiges of the inferior elementary education they received are still present [and] . . . the effects of past purposeful segregation have not been erased or overcome" (474 F. Supp. 252).   The trial court did not find a *present* intent to discriminate; it found, however, that the past purposeful discrimination was perpetuated by the test and diploma sanction.   The court concluded that "punishing the victims of past discrimination for deficits created by an inferior educational environment neither constitutes a remedy nor creates better educational opportunities" (474 F. Supp. 257).   Therefore, the use of the SSAT II as a diploma sanction violated the equal protection clause on these grounds.   To remedy this, the court prohibited the school district from using the SSAT II as a graduation requirement until the 1982-83 school term when the vestiges of past discrimination had been removed.

*Remediation Purposes*

The third issue raised by the plaintiffs was whether the use of the SSAT II for purposes of placing students in remedial classes was a violation of the equal protection clause.   Since a disproportionate number of black students were placed in the remedial classes, the plaintiffs argued that this perpetuated the effects of past purposeful discrimination and resegregated the students (474 F. Supp. 268).   The court found that the remediation program was designed to "remedy the present effects of past discrimination through better educational opportunity," and therefore, did not violate the equal protection clause (474 F. Supp. 268).

## Due Process

The Fourteenth Amendment also provides a safeguard that states shall not "deprive any person of life, liberty, or property, without due process of law." This concept is referred to as "procedural due process." Due process rights are not guaranteed by the Fourteenth Amendment unless the state action deprives the individual of their life, liberty or property. In *Debra P.*, the court determined that a property interest existed since the state had created an expectation that a diploma would be conferred if a student attends school during the required years, and takes and passes the required courses. In addition, the denial of a diploma injures a student's reputation and has an adverse impact on their future employment opportunities.

Once a property interest has been found to exist, the issue then becomes whether adequate notice was provided prior to the deprivation of that interest. More specifically, in *Debra P.* the issue was whether the implementation schedule for the SSAT II was a violation of the students' procedural due process rights. The additional requirement of the SSAT II was imposed first on the 1979 graduating class. Since the test was administered for the first time in 1977, the court found that these graduating students were advised "in the eleventh hour and with virtually no warning" that the requirements for graduation had been changed (644 F.2d 404). Such a schedule did not provide the students with adequate notice so that they could prepare for the test. In order to provide an adequate notice period, the court prohibited the state from using the SSAT II as a graduation requirement until the 1983 graduating class.

The issue of what is an adequate notice period is not strictly defined. The *Debra P.* court is on the conservative end of the scale by imposing a six-year period. One court found that a year to eighteen months was not adequate notice (*Brookhart v. Illinois State Board of Education* 1983), while another court found that twenty-four months was an adequate notice period (*Anderson v. Banks* 1981). In evaluating the year to eighteen months notice period the Brookhart court commented that the notice period in this set of circumstances is incapable of a precise definition in terms of a specific number of years. It determined, however, that one indicator of an adequate notice period is it ensures that the students are sufficiently exposed to most of the material on the test (Brookhart, 697 F.2d 187).

## Competency Tests and the Handicapped Student - Brookhart v. Illinois State Board of Education

The issue of whether competency tests may be used to deny diplomas to handicapped students has generated a great deal of litigation. Plaintiffs generally argue, in addition to the Constitutional protections of the Fourteenth Amendment discussed above, that The Education for All Handicapped Children Act and Section 504 of the Rehabilitation Act of 1973 prohibit the use of competency tests as a diploma sanction when applied to handicapped students.

The courts have repeatedly affirmed the right of states and local school systems to apply the same competency requirements to handicapped and nonhandicapped students (Jaeger, 1989). In *Brookhart v. Illinois State Board of Education* (1983), handicapped students in the Peoria School District challenged a school district policy which required *all* students to pass a minimum competency test as a graduation requirement. Students who did not pass received a Certificate of Program Completion and were allowed to retake the competency test until they reached the age of twenty-one. The handicapping conditions of the plaintiffs ranged from physically handicapped, to educable mentally handicapped and learning disabled (697 F.2d 181).

## Education for All Handicapped Children Act

The plaintiffs argued that the denial of a diploma was a violation of the Education for All Handicapped Children Act ("EAHCA"). The EAHCA provides that all handicapped children in elementary and secondary schools be afforded a "free and appropriate education." The United States Supreme Court in 1982 determined that a "free and appropriate education" means that handicapped students are to be provided with a public education which is appropriate to their needs. The legislation does not, however, guarantee any particular level of education (*Board of Education v. Rowley,* 1982). Based on this decision, the Brookhart court concluded that although the EAHCA mandates access to specialized and individualized educational services, it does not mandate a specific result, i.e., a high school diploma. Therefore, the denial of a diploma to a handicapped student for failure to pass the minimum competency test is not a denial of a "free and appropriate education" (697 F.2d 183).

## Rehabilitation Act of 1973

The second argument advanced by the plaintiffs was that the minimum competency test requirement was discriminatory under Section 504 of the Rehabilitation Act of 1973. This statute states:

> No *otherwise qualified handicapped individual* in the
> United States . . . shall, solely by reason of his handicap,
> be excluded from the participation in, be denied the
> benefits of, or be subjected to discrimination under any
> program or activity receiving Federal financial assistance
> . . . . (29 U.S.C. 794).

This provision has been interpreted by the United States Supreme Court as meaning that an "otherwise qualified handicapped individual" is one who is able to meet all of a program's requirements in spite of his handicap (*Southeastern Community College v. Davis,* 1979). This statute requires that handicapped and nonhandicapped students receive even-handed treatment. The handicapped student must not be excluded solely on the basis of his handicap, nor must the school district provide extraordinary treatment which favors the handicapped. Therefore, the Brookhart court found that "denial of diplomas to handicapped [students] who been receiving the special education and related services required by the Act, but are unable to achieve the educational level necessary to pass the minimum competency test, is not a denial of a 'free appropriate public education'" (697 F.2d 183). Horner (1985) emphasizes the point by concluding that Section 504 guarantees only an education, not a passing score on a competency test.

Do handicapped students have any alternatives when required to pass a minimum competency test in order to receive a diploma? The Brookhart court stated that a handicapped student would be the victim of discrimination if he is unable to demonstrate his abilities because of the test format or environment. Therefore, a test must be modified to minimize the effects of the student's handicap (697 F. 2d 184). The type of modification does not apply to content, but rather to the way in which the test is administered. For example, a blind student must be given the test orally or in braille, or a recorder must be provided to record the responses of students who are physically unable to do so (Jaeger, 1989).

## ACHIEVEMENT AND INTELLIGENCE TESTS --ABILITY GROUPING

The use of intelligence tests for purposes of placing students in educable mentally retarded ("EMR") classes has been the subject of extensive litigation since the late 1970s. Two early decisions highlight the disagreement among the courts in determining whether these tests are permissible for purposes of placing students in EMR classes. *Larry P. v. Riles* (1984), decided in a California federal court, held that intelligence tests which were culturally biased, may not be used in assessing black children for purposes of placement in special education classes. Another case, decided a year later, but in a different jurisdiction, held that the intelligence tests were minimally culturally biased and did not discriminate against black children. Therefore, the use of the tests was permissible (*Parents in Action on Special Education ("PASE") v. Hannon*, 1980). However, before an appeal was heard in PASE the school district agreed to discontinue its use of standardized tests for placement of black children in EMR classes (Pope, 1983). A conflict among courts, such as this, is not uncommon. It leads, however, to inconsistent results across the nation as states must ensure that their policies conform to the court decisions within their jurisdiction.

It appears that today the prevailing rule is to allow school districts to use some form of achievement and intelligence tests for purposes of ability grouping. In *Georgia State Conference of Branches of the NAACP v. State of Georgia* (1985), the Georgia NAACP and individual plaintiffs filed suit against the state and thirteen school districts, claiming that ability grouping in Georgia public schools is intended to achieve or results in intraschool racial segregation and is therefore unconstitutional as a violation of the equal protection clause of the Fourteenth Amendment (775 F.2d 1408). The school districts involved in this suit used various standardized achievement and intelligence tests, in addition to other methods such as oral performances and teacher evaluations, for determining the appropriate academic placement of elementary school students. The plaintiffs in this case challenged the placement procedures for the educable mentally retarded alleging that minority students were assigned to these classes on the basis of race. The plaintiffs did not, however, specifically challenge the *use of the tests* for placement purposes.

In analyzing the plaintiffs claim that the ability grouping violated the equal protection clause, the court stated, "[i]t is established in this [court's jurisdiction] that ability grouping is not *per se* unconstitutional even when it results in racial discrimination in the classroom" (775 F.2d 1413). However, a school district may not implement an ability grouping program until the district has operated a unitary school system for a period of years. A school district which has not been declared fully unitary may implement an ability grouping program so long as the school district can "demonstrate that its assignment method is not based on the present results of past segregation *or* will remedy such results through better educational opportunities" (775 F.2d 1414). The court upheld the ability grouping scheme in this case on the grounds that the placement will remedy the consequences of prior segregation through better educational opportunities. It was also influenced by the expert witness testimony that ability grouping is a sound educational practice and that the students placed in the EMR classes had made significant academic progress since the program began. With respect to the issue of the tests themselves, the court commented that although the lower court did not specifically state that the tests used by the school districts adequately measure the student's ability, this finding was implicit in the decision (775 F.2d 1420).

A 1989 decision also demonstrates the courts approval of using standardized test scores for purposes of ability group. In *Quarles v. Oxford Municipal Separate School District* (1989), the court upheld an ability grouping system which was based on the use of Stanford Achievement Test scores in language arts and mathematics. The school district also provided that students may be moved into another achievement level after the initial placement if the teachers agree that a student would benefit from another placement. As in the Georgia NAACP case, the court did not specifically address whether the use of the tests was permissible. They simply acknowledge the use of the tests in upholding the ability grouping system.

The challenges to ability grouping are not limited to the placement of students in EMR classes. Recent cases have challenged the placement (perhaps more accurately stated as failure to place) of students in academically gifted classes. In *Student Doe v. Commonwealth of Pennsylvania* (1984), a high school student brought suit against the State of Pennsylvania Department of Education and the local school district challenging a state regulation which provided that students with an IQ score of 130 or above were eligible for the gifted program. The court in concluding that the use of the IQ test score was valid stated, "this method [use of a minimum cut-off score on the IQ test] may not be perfect, indeed it may not be the best method available, but the Court is unable to conclude that it is a method that cannot reasonably be used" (593 F. Supp. 57).

## CONCLUSIONS

The use of standardized tests for the purposes described herein were the focus of much litigation in the 1970s and early 1980s. The extent of the litigation surrounding testing appears to be on the decline as test developers and school districts put into place the principles enunciated in these earlier opinions. Future litigation may focus on the use of tests for placement in gifted programs, although it is doubtful that these challenges will be successful.

The use of a minimum competency test for purposes of conferring a high school diploma is permissible so long as the test being used is measuring what the student has had the opportunity to learn. In addition, students must be provided with adequate notice that the test has become a graduation requirement before the implementation of the testing process. Although adequate notice is not strictly defined, it is generally viewed as the length of time necessary to ensure that the students are sufficiently exposed to the material on the test. Before imposing such a requirement school districts should evaluate their curriculum and determine if its content adequately prepares students for the test being used as a diploma requirement. Once confident that the students have had the opportunity to learn the material the school district can then proceed to implement the requirement, with a recommended minimum eighteen months waiting period before the requirement becomes effective.

The use of tests for purposes of ability grouping appears to be permissible so long as the test adequately measures a student's ability and is not culturally biased. When the ability grouping has a disproportionate impact on minority students the grouping practices are permissible if they are not based on the present results of past discrimination or the grouping will result in better educational opportunities and aid in removing the past effects of discrimination. It is also important that the school district adopt other methods of assessing a student's ability, such as teacher evaluations, which will ensure that the placement is accurate and provides for movement into other levels.

Whenever extensive legislation exists legal challenges are more likely since the attack can be based on specific statutory language rather than general constitutional principles. This is the case with regard to the testing of handicapped students and the two major acts discussed herein. Since the United States Supreme Court has interpreted the general thrust of this legislation as ensuring that handicapped children are treated equally to nonhandicapped children the courts are not going to require that school districts modify the test's content. What is required is that handicapped children have the opportunity to demonstrate their ability and knowledge. This means that school districts must be prepared to provide and modify testing procedures so that the handicapped students have an adequate opportunity to demonstrate their ability.

An understanding of the legal principles described in this chapter is not limited to state department of education personnel or school district officials. Teachers should have a basic understanding of these principles in order to better assist the school district in fulfilling its educational policies and goals within the confines of these legal principles. Teachers involved in placement decisions need to be aware of the Constitutional principles that prohibit placements which achieve or result in intraschool racial segregation. Additionally, teachers need to recognize that the use of minimum competency tests is permissible so long as the students have had an opportunity to learn the material that is being tested. Teachers should have knowledge of these tests and their content and provide the students with this opportunity. This, of course, raises the issue of whether teachers are now structuring their classroom instruction simply for these tests. That issue is left by this author to educators.

# REFERENCES

## *Cases*

*Anderson v. Banks*, 520 F. Supp. 472 (S.D. Ga. 1981), appeal dismissed, 730 F. 2d 644 (11th Cir. 1984).

> Court held that the two-year notice period for implementing the competency test was adequate.

*Anderson v. Banks*, 540 F. Supp. 761 (S.D. Ga. 1982), appeal dismissed, 730 F. 2d 644 (11th Cir. 1984).

> Court held that the California Achievement Test used as a graduation requirement was a fair test of the material actually taught.

*Board of Education v. Rowley*, 458 U.S. 176 (1982).

> The United States Supreme Court interpreted the "free appropriate public education" language of the Education for All Handicapped Children Act to mean that handicapped students are to be provided with a public education on appropriate terms. The Act does not guarantee any level of education.

*Brookhart v. Illinois State Board of Education*, 697 F.2d 179 (7th Cir. 1983).

> Court held that the use of competency tests as applied to handicapped students did not violate either the Education for All Handicapped Children Act or Section 504 of the Rehabilitation Act of 1973. The Court also held that the students procedural due process rights were violated when they were given only one and one-half years' notice that a competency test would be used as a graduation requirement.

*Debra P. v. Turlington* is a series of four different opinions beginning in 1979 and ending in 1984. The first district court opinion, 474 F. Supp. 244 (M.D. Fla. 1979) held that the test discriminated against black students in violation of the equal protection clause and the implementation schedule of the test violated the due process clause. The court of appeals decision, 644 F.2d 397 (5th Cir. 1981) reviewed the district court opinion and held that the test must cover material actually taught in order to be constitutionally permissible. The case was remanded back to the district court for a finding as to the instructional validity of the test. On remand, the district court found that the material covered on the test was being taught in the schools. 564 F. Supp. 177 (M.D. Fla. 1983). The final appellate decision, 730 F.2d 1405 (11th Cir. 1984) upheld the findings of the district court that the test was instructionally valid.

*Georgia State Conference of Branches of the NAACP v. State of Georgia*, 775 F.2d 1403 (11th Cir. 1985).

> Court held that ability grouping was not per se unconstitutional. Although black students were disproportionately represented in educable mentally retarded classes the placement would remedy the results of past segregation through better educational opportunities.

*Larry P. v. Riles*, 495 F. Supp. 926 (N.D. Cal. 1979), aff'd in part, rev'd in part 793 F.2d 969 (9th Cir. 1984).

> Court held that intelligence tests were culturally biased and could not be given to black students for purposes of placement in special education classes.

*Parents in Action on Special Education v. Hannon*, 506 F. Supp. 831 (N.D. Ill. 1980).

> Court held that intelligence tests were not culturally biased and did not violate the equal protection clause.

*Quarles v. Oxford Municipal Separate School District*, 868 F.2d 750 (5th Cir. 1989).

Court upheld the use of ability grouping.

*Student Doe v. Commonwealth of Pennsylvania*, 593 F. Supp. 54 (E.D. Pa. 1984).

Court upheld the use of IQ tests for placement in gifted program.

*Southeastern Community College v. Davis*, 442 U.S. 397 (1979).

The United States Supreme Court interpreted the "otherwise qualified handicapped individual" language of the Rehabilitation Act of 1973 to mean an individual who is able to meet all of a program's requirements in spite of the handicap.

*Articles*

Cannell, J.E. 1983. "Brookhart et al. v. Illinois State Board et al.: Court Upholds Minimum Competency Program but Awards Diplomas to Eleven Handicapped Students." *Education Law Reporter*, 8, 549-53. St. Paul: West Publishing Co.

Review of Brookhart decision.

Hollander, P. 1982. "Legal Context of Educational Testing." In A.K. Wigdor & W.R. Garner (Eds.), *Ability Testing: Uses, Consequences, and Controversies*. Washington, D.C.: National Academy Press.

Summarizes the cases challenging all forms of educational testing.

Horner, J.J. 1985. "A Review of the Development of and Legal Challenges to Student Competency Testing Programs." *Education Law Reporter*, 2,3 1-10. St. Paul: West Publishing Co.

Discusses the legal theories used to attack competency tests.

Jaeger, R.M. 1989. "Certification of Student Competence." In R.L. Linn (Ed.), *Educational Measurement (3rd edition)*. NY: Macmillan.

Discusses legal challenges to competency testing.

Lufler, H.S. 1987. " Pupils." In S.B. Thomas (Ed.), *The Yearbook of School Law*. Topeka: NOLPE.

Annual text devoted to developments in school law.

McCarthy, M.M. 1984. "Minimum Competency Testing on Trial." *Education Law Reporter, 13,* 191-97. St. Paul: West Publishing Co.

Review of *Debra P.* case before final appellate court opinion.

Nowak, J.E., Rotunda, R.D. & Young, J.N. 1983. *Constitutional Law.* St. Paul: West Publishing Co.

One-volume treatise devoted to Constitutional Law.

Pope, L.M. 1983. "Judicial Testing of IQ Tests." *Education Law Reporter, 6,* 875-87. St. Paul: West Publishing Co.

Review of Larry P. and PASE decisions.

Zirkel, P.A. & Stevens, P.L. 1987. "The Law Concerning Public Education of Gifted Students." *Education Law Reporter, 34,* 353-67. St. Paul: West Publishing Co.

Review of decisions relating to gifted student programs.

# COMPUTER USE IN CLASSROOM TESTING

## SUSAN F. STAGER AND DANIEL MUELLER

The myth that computers have revolutionized the educational system is alive and well. Many teachers, especially at the postsecondary level, do use microcomputers on a daily basis. But their primary computing activity is word processing--preparing course syllabi, worksheets, and administrative reports. Some teachers do give computer assignments, but few give assignments which are facilitated by the computer. Few teachers have integrated the computer into the curriculum. And few teachers use computers to enhance the student assessment process.

Policymakers, the American public and many classroom teachers at all levels of the educational system are convinced that computing technology will revolutionize teaching and learning. This statement is supported by our discussions with parents, administrators, and teachers. This statement is also supported by observations about the number of journal articles, books, and conferences devoted to the topic of computing technology in education and knowledge of the amount of funds supporting computing in the nation's classrooms. Finally, this statement is supported by knowledge of the curriculum of many teacher education programs, curricula designed to provide preservice and inservice teachers with the skills necessary to implement computing technology in the classroom. Teacher education programs are under pressure to incorporate computer technology training. For example, twenty-three states and the District of Columbia require some or all new teachers to show proficiency in computer use. Eleven states require teachers in public schools to take a computer course to be certified (*Chronicle of Higher Education,* July 1989).

This generalized support for computing technology has been backed with financial commitments, through funding of computing equipment for both classroom teachers and students. The National Educational Association has called on school districts to provide computer systems for every elementary and high-school teacher by 1991, and school districts have responded. Nonetheless, computer technology thus far has not changed the way that most teaching, learning, and assessment of learning is done in the nation's classrooms. Schank and Farrell (1988) wryly note that children are 'trooping' down to the computer room in neighborhood schools because their parents and teachers want students to be computer literate, and because kids enjoy playing computer games. The authors also note that children are subjected to unimaginative educational software that provides nothing more than automated worksheets.

The potential for computer technology to revolutionize education does exist. Part of the reason that computing technology has yet to revolutionize daily classroom activities at the elementary, secondary, and post secondary education levels is that computing technology is slowly *evolving* rather than changing rapidly as manufacturers and the media would like us to believe. At the present level of development of this technology, hardware and software in many cases simply automate tasks that teachers have always done or they automate teaching strategies that teachers have always used instead of revolutionizing educational practice.

Another reason computers have not revolutionized education is that training programs for teachers tend to focus on computer literacy, the use of computers for personal productivity and the mechanics of computing, rather than on integrating computing into the curriculum as a problem-solving tool. Hence teachers have only a limited number of models for effectively using computer technology in the classroom. Once their training is complete, teachers go out into the field and focus on computer literacy rather than on computers as a tool for personal productivity, instruction, research, and student assessment. Teachers teach as they were taught and teachers test as they were tested. Without preservice and inservice experiences with computerized testing, the number of teachers will be using computers to enhance the teaching/learning process or the student assessment process will remain small.

What are the potential benefits of computerized testing in the classroom? What criticisms have been leveled at computerized tests? What is the future of computerized tests in the classroom? This chapter explores these questions.

## WHAT IS COMPUTERIZED TESTING?

If asked, preservice or inservice teachers can readily list advantages of computerized testing and define the term "computerized testing." The available literature can be confusing, however, because different authors use different terms (adaptive testing, computer assisted testing, computer-based testing, computer-managed testing, response contingent testing, sequential testing, and tailored testing) for what is globally referred to in this chapter as "computerized testing."

Many teachers equate computerized testing with drill and practice exercises that are part of computer assisted instruction (CAI) software packages. Others equate computerized testing with machine scoring of preprinted answer sheets on which students indicate the correct answer by blackening a circle with a number two pencil. Machine scoring has been the mainstay of districtwide testing programs for years, reducing turnaround on both individual test results and summaries of student performance by class, building, and district. Teachers are not alone in equating computerized testing with machine scoring. Many administrators and the public also share this narrow view of computerized testing, since their only personal experience with computerized testing may have been with machine scoring and preprinted answer sheets. This narrow conception of computerized testing will be widened as computerized testing is incorporated in the teacher training curriculum.

By equating computerized testing only with automated scoring functions or drill and practice exercises, teachers may be missing the true potential of computerized testing systems. Computerized testing also means that the testing experience can be individualized, that detailed information can be provided about the student's strengths and weaknesses (computerized diagnostic testing), and that the testing situation can more closely resemble real life situations (computerized simulations). These concepts and the potential of computerized testing are detailed in the next section.

## CAPABILITIES OF COMPUTERIZED TESTING

Why bother with computerized testing?  The merits of computerized testing are listed here and explained in the following pages.  A computerized testing system:
*    automates the process of creating tests
*    automates the process of scoring tests
*    facilitates the creation of equivalent versions of the same exam
*    provides access to existing test banks
*    can be used to train preservice or inservice teachers to administer tests
*    standardizes test administration procedures
*    provides more detailed feedback to the student
*    enables placement testing
*    minimizes data entry problems
*    enables teachers to become classroom researchers
*    provides students with information about strengths and weaknesses, not just a summary test score
*    provides analyses of the errors in strategies students are using

## Computerized Testing Automates
### the Process of Creating Tests

Teachers report spending from 10% to 15% of their time in test construction, test administration, scoring, and returning tests (Carlberg, 1981; Fennessey, 1982; Gullickson, 1982; Newman & Stallings, 1982; Stager & Green, 1984). All of these tasks can be automated with current computerized testing software. With computerized tests, teachers are relieved of the tedious tasks of grading papers and recording scores in grade books and of the time-consuming task of calculating test item statistics.

Today, many major publishers of introductory textbooks provide teachers with test generation software. In sociology, for example, by 1986 nine introductory college texts included test generation software (Sturtevant & Johnson, 1988). This software typically prompts the teacher to pick and choose among test questions created by the publisher. Test questions typically are displayed on the computer screen one at a time, and the teacher is prompted to indicate whether the question should be included on the exam. The teacher can also add additional test questions, reword questions, and correct spelling errors. Some of the more versatile software allows the instructor to prepare a file that can be used with standard word processing packages, saving the instructor from learning yet another software package. Finally, after the teacher is prompted for an exam title, course name, instructor's name, and date, the test can be printed, along with an answer key and answer sheets. As in the case of other software, test generation software is very easy to use once you have installed it and read the documentation describing how to use it. Unfortunately, getting the software installed and running can try the patience of even computer enthusiasts.

With computerized testing, students can take tests on their own time with minimal teacher intervention and administrative staff can handle many testing-related tasks. The only skills required of the administrative staff are starting the computer, responding to questions about the administration procedures, checking identification if the student is unknown to the administrator, and collecting any copies of the results from the printer. As a result, teachers are free to spend time producing higher quality tests or to interact with students for instructional purposes.

*Computerized Testing Facilitates the Creation*
*of Equivalent Versions of the Same Exam*

Another attractive aspect of computerized testing is that teachers can enter (type) questions and answers into a data file using test generation software, thus creating a test item bank. Once a test item bank has been constructed, this same computer software can be used to generate equivalent versions of the test. By definition, equivalent tests have equal length, the same content subsets, and equal item difficulty.

Equivalent versions of the same exam are frequently required at both the secondary and post-secondary education levels where there are multiple sections of the same course. Multiple sections of the same course necessitate equivalent versions of the same exam to offset the effects of the student grapevine that guarantees that sections meeting later in the day will know what questions are on the test before taking the test. Equivalent versions of the same exam are also used in testing of large numbers of students in close proximity, since cheating is more likely to occur when students are tested in close proximity.

To create equivalent versions of the same exam, it is not enough simply to randomly select two sets of questions from the same item bank. Computerized testing software which creates more than one version of a test by random selection of different subsets of test items from the test item bank, creates "multiple" versions of the same test, not "equivalent" versions of the same test, just as the classroom teacher who manually selects random subsets of test items from a test bank does not create equivalent versions of the same test. Computerized testing software is available that will help teachers create equivalent versions of the same exam, but extra work is required of the teacher. The teacher must include information in the test bank about which test item(s) measures which instructional objective and about the difficulty level of test items, if known. Thus, testing software can be programmed to ensure that each version of a test includes items that assess mastery of all instructional objectives and that each version assesses the same instructional objectives. However, the teacher must take the time to label each item as measuring one or more objectives. Needless to say, computers still have not solved the problem of students in the first and third period classes telling students in the sixth and seventh period classes what questions to expect on the exam.

Equivalent versions of tests also require a rather large test item bank. Creating a large test item bank is not as difficult as one might think. Teachers create new tests every year or at least some new items, so by the end of the third year, a large bank of items has been created and probably buried in a file drawer. It might be easier to obtain multiple versions of textbooks and use the multiple teacher guides to create one large test item bank. For example, there must be at least six good textbooks for high school American history courses. If history teachers took the best questions about the American Revolution contained in the six teacher manuals, edited the items, and created a test bank using testing software, they could generate multiple, equivalent tests on the American Revolution. This is probably a good time to emphasize that the phrase, "create a test bank," means typing (or having an assistant type) the test questions when prompted to do so by the testing software. The software will then prompt the user to indicate which instructional objective is assessed by this item. Once one recovers from the embarrassment of not having thought about instructional objectives prior to this moment, one can proceed. Most teacher guides contain a list of instructional objectives at the beginning of each unit.

*Computerized Testing Provides Access to Existing Test Banks*

Computer technology is helping some teachers access existing test item banks. For example, teachers in Florida can access a data bank of science test questions stored on Florida State University's mainframe. George Dawson (1987) from Florida State University received a grant to re-edit a large science test bank developed cooperatively by Florida and Georgia universities in the 1970s and to place the test bank on FSU's mainframe computer for general use. To access the database, a teacher logs onto the FSU mainframe using long distance phone lines and an FSU computer account. (Computer accounts are obtained from FSU and account holders outside the state of Florida are charged for the time they are using the FSU mainframe.)

Once logged on, the teacher sees a series of menus on the screen. For example, the first menu requires teachers to indicate whether they are interested in elementary, middle school, or high school science test items. Additional menu selections lead the teacher to test items from the specific science area of interest (anatomy, bacteriology, behavior, biochemistry, etc.) and from the specific process that the teacher wishes to evaluate (communicating, using space-time relationships, measuring, observing, classifying, etc.). Teachers can elect to have both instructional objectives and test items printed to a file that can be used to construct a test or can elect to print only the test items, producing a ready-made exam.

## Computerized Testing Can Be Used to Train Preservice or Inservice Teachers to Administer Tests

Using computerized tests to train individuals with assessment responsibilities to administer tests is not a new idea. In optometry, computer technology has been used to assess student's ability to assess patient eye problems (Hanlon & Ryan, 1986). The "Patient Management Problem," or "PMP," computer simulation duplicates the classic eye examination, requiring optometry students to make the same decisions that they would in a clinical setting. Test takers must complete the examination in the appropriate amount of time, the average time allotted for an eye exam at most clinics, or be forced to formulate a final diagnosis with limited data. This concept could be extended to enhance the testing practices of classroom teachers.

## Computers Can Standardize Test Administration Procedures

One of the greatest advantages of using computers to administer tests in the classroom is the potential for reducing several types of assessment errors. One type of error occurs when the teacher accidentally alters the test instructions or otherwise misdirects the pupil. These errors occur most commonly when a teacher is dealing with more than one section of a course. Ironically, the same teacher who is fanatical about controlling conditions in his or her high school or college campus laboratory is sometimes lax about controlling testing conditions across different sections of a multiple-section course.

Perhaps the greatest inequity in testing conditions results when students are given different directions for the same exam. For example, a seventh grade math teacher probably presents first period students with a different set of directions than he/she presents to the eighth period class. The instructions provided during the eighth period may be more concise or more detailed than those provided during the first period, depending upon the response to the exam taken by students earlier in the day. Similarly, the test directions provided by different graduate student assistants in a multiple-section college course may vary considerably. Test scores of the students may be affected by modifications in the instructions.

Modifications to directions for routine, teacher-made tests, such as the seventh grade math test mentioned above, have little impact on decisions about children. Altering instructions becomes a serious problem with standardized tests administered at the elementary school level and at higher educational levels where test scores may determine honors, scholarships, admission to other educational programs, and generally have important, direct consequences for the individual student. If a teacher or a test administrator elaborates upon the published test administration instructions for a nationally normed achievement test, pupils may be given an unfair advantage. In fact, test administration manuals for standardized achievement tests caution that deviations from the printed administration instructions produce error. With computerized testing, all students can receive the same test instructions, thus reducing this form of testing error.

### Computerized Testing Can Provide More Detailed
### Feedback to Both the Student and Parent

Most parents receive computer-generated feedback about the test performance of their children several weeks after their children complete standardized, nationally normed tests. The feedback typically comes in the form of percentiles, stanines, grade-equivalents, or normalized test scores and is generated during the process of machine scoring the exams. In addition to scores the feedback may include interpretive information about the test scores and about educational practices appropriate for the child. For example, one statewide testing program provided parents with interpretations of language arts score from a national exam such as the following:

> Your daughter scored higher than 99% of all
> 2nd grade students in the nation in total
> language. Language mechanics was higher than
> 99%; language expression was higher than 94%.
> She has mastered all of the skills measured
> by the language arts test. You may want to
> discuss with the teacher a direction for
> additional challenges for her in this area.

Computerized tests also make it possible for students to receive detailed feedback about their strengths and weaknesses during or after the test. A description of feedback during testing appears in an article by Gwinn and Beal (1988) about a computerized testing program for anatomy and physiology undergraduates:

> After sign-on, the student selects the desired test. The
> management control permits the student to request only
> tests for which she/he is eligible. A multiple\choice
> question is presented with five alternatives and the
> student's response is followed by immediate knowledge
> of the results plus corrective feedback. If the answer is
> correct, another sentence is presented to reinforce that
> answer, but an incorrect response is explained and a
> second chance at the same question is offered. If this

corrective feedback enables the student to choose correctly the second time, he receives half credit for that item. (p. 241)

Anatomy and physiology students using the computerized testing system reported that the system was advantageous in that it tested only one week's material at a time, enabled the student to take the test whenever desired, provided immediate feedback to the student, gave students a second attempt to answer a test question, and enabled students to retest to raise a score. Of course all of these reported advantages could be achieved with traditional paper-and-pencil tests, but computers make such testing easier. The major problems with computerized testing, as reported by these same university students, are hardware or software problems, long response time, noise and distraction at the computer clusters, vague or unclear questions, long waits for use of a terminal, and errors in test scoring. But all these are problems which can be remedied.

*Computerized Testing Enables Placement Testing*

At all levels of schooling, teachers make judgments about their students' levels of proficiency and their mastery of basic material. First grade school teachers may assume that their pupils can recite the alphabet, recognize all 26 letters, and count to 20 as a result of their kindergarten or preschool experience. Calculus teachers may assume that students have mastered the concepts of algebra and geometry as a result of their previous coursework. Teachers of Spanish 201 may assume that students have mastered the vocabulary and grammatical skills of Spanish 101.

One of the frustrations of teaching is that such assumptions prove incorrect for some students. All students do not have the level of proficiency necessary to benefit from the next level of instruction, yet these students are enrolled at the next level of instruction. The teacher must work with non-proficient students to bring them up to speed while simultaneously presenting new material to the rest of the class. This is particularly problematic at the higher education level where a passing grade from one high school seldom means an equivalent level of knowledge as a passing grade in the same course from a different high school.    Consequently, high school transcripts are an imperfect indicator of proficiency.   Courses are not equivalent even within the same university.   Although many college courses have prerequisites, multiple factors enable students to enroll in a course with inadequate mastery of the prerequisite skills.   Computerized tests can be used for preplacement testing of hundreds of students simultaneously with little effort.   Or, once the student has matriculated, college instructors can allow students to take computerized competency tests until mastery is achieved with minimal effort on the part of the instructor.

At Brigham Young University, placement exams for most language courses are computerized (Larson, 1987).   The College of Humanities operates the computer laboratory responsible for language placement testing.   During the first week of classes, students are instructed to go to the laboratory for the placement exams which are accessed from the computer network.   Monitors check student identification cards to verify that the test taker is the appropriate person.   The language program at Brigham Young also relies heavily on a computerized diagnostic homework system.   Students of Spanish, French, German, Swedish, French, English and English as a second language, as well as algebra students, are often assigned to complete exercises with an on-line testing component.

The College Board has developed Computerized Placement Tests (CPTs) covering reading comprehension, sentence skills, arithmetic, and algebra (College Entrance Examination Board, 1987). These tests are designed to access entry-level skills of college students. The tests are adaptive, meaning the software selects successive test items based on the student's performance as the test proceeds.   The software can generate individual report forms and group report forms and can run on an IBM PC or compatibles.   The College Board anticipates that CPTs will revolutionize college placement testing. Complementary software is available to enable administrators to evaluate students' academic preparations, place students in appropriate course sections, and maintain student records.

### Computerized Testing Can Minimize Data Entry Problems

All record keeping can be automated with extant computerized testing software. Testing software virtually eliminates calculation errors and data entry errors by automatically calculating test scores and directly entering scores in electronic grade books. In addition computerized testing reduces error by minimizing the likelihood that a student will record an answer in the wrong space on the answer sheet or record an answer that is outside the range of the possible answers. For example, if the student is answering question 26, the software will record the student's answer as a response to question 26 and only question 26 (unless the software has a bug!). This is particularly helpful at the elementary school level where young children are prone to skipping test questions accidentally or losing their place on the answer sheet. By placing the right answer in the wrong place on the answer sheet, the child produces a test score that doesn't accurately reflect her knowledge. Even college students can benefit from the error checking capability of computerized testing. If a multiple choice test item has four possible answers (a, b, c, and d), the testing software can be structured so that an answer of "e" will not be accepted, and a student making this response will be asked to type in a different answer. Teachers can also benefit from this feature of testing software. Teachers are often frustrated when students provide more than one answer to the same question or provide an illegible or ambiguous answer (for example, an "a" that looks like a "d"). Testing software will force students to enter only one answer, and the answer is always legible. All these error detection features of computerized testing software increase the likelihood that the test performance is an accurate measure of the student's knowledge.

### Computerized Tests Enable Teachers to Become Classroom Researchers

If computerized testing is limited only to test scoring functions, much of the enormous potential of existing software remains untapped.

An often overlooked benefit of computerized testing may be in the area of classroom research. The methodology of computerized testing closely parallels that of educational researchers. Data are collected about learners, data are entered into the computer, data are analyzed, data are interpreted. Classroom teachers, with a little encouragement, may become more interested in carrying out experiments in the classroom, especially since the results of the experiment are easily and quickly determined.

*Computerized Tests Provide Students with*
*Information About Strengths and Weaknesses,*
*Not Just a Summary Test Score*

For testing to aid learning, several steps must be followed. The student must receive specific feedback about strengths and weaknesses and must be directed to learning activities that will lead to remediation of the material (Feuer, 1986). Computerized testing can enable teachers to provide diagnostic information about strengths and weaknesses by structuring the testing experience so that students navigate through the material on an "as-needed" basis rather than on a "linear" path. This navigational feature of computer software is often referred to as "branching."

Branching may occur in the following situation. If a student is taking a basic English skills exam, there is no reason for that student to complete all questions on verb usage if he demonstrates mastery of verb usage during the course of the exam. Logistically the software is programmed so that if a student correctly answers certain test items, other questions assessing this same skill area will not be administered. The student will be directed down another branch of the test. The student will be required to answer a predetermined number of questions in this area to demonstrate mastery.

Some computerized testing software is programmed in such a way that students receive information about which topics they have or have not mastered. Students are then given another opportunity to answer test items correctly. Obviously this type of testing experience leads to enhanced learning but compounds the difficulty of the teacher's task of assigning grades. Does the student who answers all questions the first time receive the same exam grade as the student who had multiple opportunities to answer correctly the same test items or different test items on the same topic?

Major development of computerized diagnostic testing is being carried out by the College Board and the Educational Testing Services (Forehand, 1987). Pilot studies have shown that students prefer computer tests to paper-and-pencil tests and report no difficulty using the computer.

*Computerized Testing Provides Analyses of the Error Strategies Students are Using*

Educators have long acknowledged that too much time is spent analyzing "how many questions" a student answers incorrectly on a test instead of analyzing why a question was missed. Unless a student is just guessing wildly, there usually is a specific reason why a test item is missed. Software has been developed that identifies the incorrect strategies used in solving elementary mathematics problems. McDonald, Beal and Ayers (1988) developed the Diagnostic Test of Computational Skills for this purpose. The software includes a bank of addition test items where each possible answer could be derived in one and only one way. Thus, if a student answers the question "34 + 4 =" with "30," we assume he subtracted instead of added (operational error). If a student answers "83" we assume he/she inverted the correct answer. If a student answers "11," we assume he/she added all the digits. This information could be obtained by manual examination of each test paper. But the computerized testing software automates the process and summarizes the data for ease of use. Similar systems have been developed by Attisha and Yazdani (1983, 1984) for addition, multiplication and subtraction; by Janke and Pilkey (1985) for whole number operations; and Travis (1984) for multiplication. These systems for identifying students' error strategies are another example of ways in which computerized testing can improve upon traditional testing methods.

## WHY HAVE WE NOT PROGRESSED?

The merits of computerized testing have been reported for nearly 20 years. Still we have not found wide-spread use of computerized testing methodologies in the elementary, secondary or higher education classroom. Why not?

One reason that computerized testing has not been generally adopted may be that innovation and change is met with resistance by many people. Classroom teachers, like professionals in every other field, sometimes throw up defenses in the face of pressure for innovation and change. They may fear a usurpation of their role or simply resent a secondary role in the innovation. Some education professionals do not resist change but firmly believe that computerized testing is inferior to traditional paper-and-pencil techniques. The professional literature about computerized testing for elementary, secondary, and higher education has focused on concerns that computerized testing is inferior to existing paper-and-pencil testing methods in terms of student achievement, student attitudes, and administration time. Some professionals argue that, when compared with equivalent paper-and-pencil tests, students perform less well on computerized versions of tests, feel negative about the testing experience when computers are used as a testing medium, and test administration time is actually increased with computers because of student's greater facility with computers. The following criticisms are discussed in this section:

Computerized testing
* is expensive
* produces lower student achievement
* is limited to assessing information recall and recognition
* separates the student evaluation process from instruction
* increases student anxiety about the testing process
* removes the teacher from the evaluation process
* places assessment decisions in the hands of the noncredentialed
* is psychometrically faulty

## Computerized Testing is Expensive

Some earlier financial obstacles to the widespread use of computerized testing in education, including the high cost of computing, insufficient numbers of publicly-available microcomputers or terminals, lack of networking of these microcomputers or terminals, and lack of trained personnel, have been overcome in many schools. The introduction of low-cost, low maintenance, relatively user friendly, high performance microcomputers in the 1980s was an "educational milestone." In many respects, computing is part of the educational process today not because of the advances in software and hardware, but because microcomputer technology is affordable by the typical school district or college.

But most teachers have not gravitated toward computerized testing in spite of the presence of computer hardware in their classroom and the availability of testing software. At the elementary and secondary school level obstacles to computerized testing methodologies requiring one computer per student may still exist, but almost every school contains one or more computers that can be used for testing purposes. Of course, there is another expense, the expense of implementing the testing program. The start-up costs for computerized testing, including modifying classroom procedures, modifying the curriculum, modifying the software, setting up the testing system, cannot be trivialized. As with any educational innovation, time spent implementing one innovation usually means that another innovation cannot be implemented. Computerized testing is competing with other educational innovations for the teacher's time and resources.

## Computerized Testing Produces Lower Student Achievement

It might be hypothesized that students will perform less well on computerized versions of tests than on paper-and-pencil versions of the same test because of the anxiety induced by "technology." The content of items on paper and pencil and computerized tests can be the same, but the presentation and mode of entering answers differ. Students have years of experience taking exams with paper-and-pencil and therefore may be more adept in that medium than with computers. This may lead to some anxiety. The bulk of the research suggests that there are no differences in achievement for college-aged students between the two testing methods although some earlier studies suggest that computer phobia results in increased anxiety levels for students using computerized testing systems. (See Roid, 1986, for a summary of early research in this area.)    With the increased acceptance of computers as primary tools for learning, it would be expected that students will be less anxious about using computers for testing. At the university level we have noticed an increased comfort level with computing with each successive freshmen class.    More and more college students have access to computers both in the school and home prior to entering college.

Hypothetically, students may also score lower on computerized versions of tests because they are forced to approach problem solving in a different way. Ronau and Battista (1988) state that eighth grade students both do mathematics differently when working with computers, and they obtain lower scores on the computerized version of math tests than on the paper-and-pencil version. The burden on researchers in this area is to demonstrate that computerized and paper-and-pencil versions of tests are equivalent. Ronau and Battista note, for example, that students are unable to return to items that they had previously skipped or wished to change on the computerized version of the mathematics test in their study. Additional research is certainly needed in this area.

Finally, we hypothesize that students may score lower on computerized tests than on paper-and-pencil test for ergonomic reasons. Research shows that tables and chairs must be at the proper height, monitor glare must be reduced, and lighting must be adequate, among other things. Reading a test from a computer monitor and responding with a keyboard may be more physically demanding than taking the exam via traditional testing methods (Heppner, Anderson, Farstrup, & Weiderman, 1985). More research is needed in this area.

## Computerized Testing Is Limited to Assessing
## Information Recall or Recognition

Some critics claim that computerized testing systems restrict teachers to assessing the lower levels of Bloom's taxonomy. This claim is false and stems in part from some erroneous assumptions about test items. It is commonly assumed that only essay questions assess higher order learning. The only generalization that can be made about essay tests is that they assess writing in the discipline, which is certainly worthy of assessment. The literature shows that 80% of tests written by teachers using any testing medium, and any test item type are written at the lower levels of thinking. Many teachers simply are not writing tests that assess critical thinking and evaluation skills. Computer software should not be blamed for this problem.

Although test generation software is programmed to produce all test item types, it is true that test scoring software typically handles only true/false and multiple-choice questions. Some software will score short answer responses. It is possible, though, to write true-false and especially multiple choice test items that assess the upper levels of the taxonomy. It is also possible to develop software that simulates scenarios which require demonstration of critical thinking and problem solving skills, such as software being developed by medical educators (Norman, Muzzin, Williams, & Swanson, 1985). The problem is teacher training and testing practices, not the computer software. Teachers can learn to write multiple choice questions that can be scored by testing software while assessing higher order learning. In the future, expert systems may be available enabling teachers to computerize essay tests as well.

## Computerized Testing Increases Student Anxiety
## About the Testing Process

Another frequently discussed concern is that students will become extremely anxious taking computerized tests due to a generalized anxiety about computer technology. As stated above, computers are a part of everyday life for students today. In a survey of college students participating in a pilot computerized testing program at Santa Fe Community College, 97% reported that they "liked it a lot" and 93% were "comfortable using the computer." In the same pilot study, 68% of the participating students at Miami Dade stated they preferred to take a computer-administered test to a paper-and-pencil test while 17% preferred a paper-and-pencil test and 15% had no preference (League for Innovation in Community Colleges, 1988). Computer anxiety is greatest for those of us who grew up without a computer in their classroom and home. In some cases, critics may be projecting their fear of computers upon the students rather than observing actual anxiety about computerized testing.

### Computerized Testing Separates the Student Assessment Process from Instruction

Some educational professionals maintain that computerized testing provides no link between instruction and evaluation. Of course, this criticism can be leveled at all testing methodologies.

We argue here that computerized testing methods may be the testing method most capable of making the link between instruction and evaluation. Computerized testing software exists that provides students with a discussion of each incorrect answer. Of course, the computer does not provide this discussion. The classroom teacher is required to prepare a text of explanations to parallel each question and the computer software links test items to these explanations. This method insures that the examination process will be a learning experience. When a student misses a question on the computerized exam, the correct answer will appear on the screen along with information about why other answers are incorrect.

Realistically, classroom teachers do not have the time to prepare a text of explanations to parallel each test question and to enter these explanations into a database. But publishers may be able to provide this feature in a cost-effective way, as part of the testing software distributed with textbooks. We would expect to find more and more future testing software that provides feedback about *why* a student's response is wrong.

### Computerized Testing Removes the Teacher
### From the Evaluation Process

One legitimate concern about any automated educational innovation is that teachers will detach themselves from the educational process to the degree that they are unaware of student performance and will only interact with students on a limited basis. Computerized testing may provide an opportunity to detach themselves from the evaluation process, but it is unlikely that teachers will take advantage of this opportunity. Teachers feel most confident about their understanding of student mastery or nonmastery when personally grading each and every exam. But there are trade-offs here. Teachers can still scan the work of low scoring students for clues to learning problems, but there is really no need to grade personally the tests of everyone in the class, regardless of the size of the class. Computerized testing helps increase scoring efficiency but does not reduce the extent to which student assessment information is used to guide the curriculum. Without manually grading exams themselves, teachers can access students' exams from the computer storage medium, scan them online or with printed hardcopy, and use this information to tailor instruction to individual needs.

### Computerized Testing May Place Assessment Decisions
### in the Hands of the Noncredentialed

One professional group readily embracing computerized testing, psychologists, has already become concerned about potential abuse by those who fail to understand that computers are only a tool, and are an ineffective tool without the guidance of an experienced professional. Psychologists fear that sophisticated assessment procedures, which are the exclusive domain of certified psychologists and psychometricians, could be placed in the hands of noncertified personnel. The Committee on Professional Standards and the Committee on Psychological Tests and Assessment of the American Psychological

Association already has developed guidelines for the use of computerized tests (APA, 1986).

Some educational professionals also fear that computerized testing, in the guise of a 'user-friendly tool,' will provide test item analysis information to persons with little or no training in the proper use of this information, such as teachers' aides. There is also the potential for teachers to misuse item analysis information if they have not received sufficient inservice or preservice training. Measurement courses are not uniformly required as part of the preservice teacher education curriculum (Green & Stager, 1987). It is true that the classroom teacher no longer needs to be able to calculate manually the standard deviation or the mean or other descriptive statistics. Today's testing software can provide not only descriptive statistics, item difficulties, and discrimination indices taught in most introductory measurement courses but also complex generalizability analyses and item response theory analyses (Luecht, 1987). It is possible, therefore, that teachers could generate information about student performance that is misused simply because the teacher has not had the proper measurement training. The ready availability of computerized testing software for classroom use may accelerate the need for educational professionals to receive both preservice and inservice measurement training.

Computer technology can do many things to enhance testing practices at the elementary, secondary, and postsecondary educational levels but computer technology cannot create valid tests. The classroom teacher ultimately is responsible for the validity of testing instruments used in his or her classroom, whether the test is homemade or purchased from a major publisher. In order to be valid, a test must provide results that are representative of the subject matter and instructional objectives. Computers cannot create such tests. Computers *can* be used to help teachers readily calculate what percent of pre-determined categories of questions compose the final test. It is the classroom teacher who classifies each test item as assessing instructional objective A rather than instructional objective B. Preservice and inservice training programs must continue to provide teachers with the skills to do this. Computers can be used to determine what percent of the highest scoring class members answered a certain question correctly, and subsequently calculate difficulty indices. But only the classroom teacher can decide what the correct answer is.

Again, the burden is upon preservice and inservice training programs to provide classroom teachers with the skills to use computerized testing. With continued emphasis on tests and measurement in the preservice and inservice curriculum, teachers and computers can work together to optimize student assessment.

## *Computerized Testing is Psychometrically Faulty*

Sarvela and Noonan (1988) have described several measurement problems associated with computerized testing systems. These authors caution that from a psychometric point of view, it is undesirable to provide students with feedback about their test performance during the testing session. To understand this psychometric problem, let's use the analogy of a classroom test as a stimulus presented during an experiment. Given what we know about the effects of positive and negative feedback on performance, it would be inappropriate to provide some members of the same experimental group with positive feedback and others with negative feedback. But this is exactly what happens during a computerized test when feedback is provided during the test rather than immediately following the test. Low achieving students will receive negative feedback during the test and be negatively motivated on subsequent test questions. High achieving students will receive positive feedback during the same test and be positively motivated.

Sarvela and Noonan also caution that psychometric problems may result from using the same computer test item bank for practice tests and for retesting failing students. In both cases, the testing "experiment" is contaminated. Of course, this type of contamination can be produced without aid of computers. It is not unknown for teachers to provide hardcopy sample tests as study guides for exams or to use the same hardcopy test as a retest for failing students. Finally, Sarvela and Noonan note that psychometric problems may result when tailored testing is used. In tailored testing, students receive different test items and different numbers of test items depending upon their mastery of the material as determined during the testing session. One student may have to answer only three questions to demonstrate mastery of the concept of mitosis while another may have to answer ten questions.  In essence each student is participating in a different experiment.


# THE FUTURE


Although the benefits of computerized testing have been available for more than 20 years, only a minority of elementary, secondary, and postsecondary classroom teachers use computers for testing.  As more inservice and preservice tests and measurement training programs incorporate computerized testing into the curriculum, this will change.  Without incorporation into the majority of preservice and inservice training programs, we anticipate that computerized testing will remain the invaluable tool of only a few innovative classroom teachers.

It is predicted that the way in which computerized testing currently is taught in preservice and inservice training programs will also change.  To date, much of the emphasis of these programs has been upon understanding the bits and bytes of computers rather than integrating computing technology into the teaching and evaluating learning, but at least it is a beginning.  In the future, teacher training programs will use computerized testing techniques rather than study computerized testing techniques as an isolated curriculum unit.

Coupled with changes in inservice and preservice training programs will be changes in the classroom teacher's desire to learn more about computerized testing.  Classroom teachers will be more active in their efforts to receive information and instruction about computerized testing as their computing skills increase and their anxieties about computers are reduced.  The past failure of teachers to seek out information about computerized testing, learn computerized testing techniques, and subsequently adopt computerized testing practices in some cases may be attributed to a fear of computers.  Some teachers remain computer phobic long after one or more computers are placed in their classroom just as some professionals in other fields remain computer phobic long after a computer is placed on their office desktop. Any attempt by school districts or college training programs to promote computerized testing practices must deal with fears, apprehension and opposition to computers (Jay, 1981).

It is predicted that computerized testing also will receive a boost from the current national emphasis on assessment. Most state boards of education have either established or plan to establish assessment programs. The accountability movement that resulted in competency testing for elementary and secondary students has now permeated higher education. It is predicted that educational institutions will explore computerized-testing systems. State and federal officials will seek assessment methods that individualize the process yet are efficient and less expensive than other assessment methods. Computerized testing systems may fill the bill.

Another trend may be greater involvement of classroom teachers in the development of computerized testing software, both at the K-12 and university levels. University faculty have produced hundreds of instructional software packages and will probably move into the testing software development area over time. The drawback of these enterprises is known. In today's university structure there is little reward for software development. Software development is incredibly time consuming. Even if the actual computer programming is contracted out, decisions must be made about routing procedures, instructions to test takers, item types, security, screen display conventions, type fonts, response capturing and scoring (Mizokawa & Hamlin, 1984; Sarvela & Noonan, 1988). Faculty caution their brethren not to get involved in software development until they achieve tenure. Although software development is time consuming, it seldom carries the same weight as a scholarly publication.

It is predicted that different modes will be developed for informing classroom teachers about existing testing software to reduce redundancy in development efforts, as has been the case with instructional software development. In addition to the danger of having software development become totally consuming, there is the danger that teachers will reinvent the wheel. Countless software programs exist to teach introductory biology concepts, and there is no limit to the number of programs that could be developed to test knowledge of these concepts. Mechanisms must be developed to acquaint educators with existing software products and to bring teachers into the development process as consultants rather than programmers. As more sophisticated testing software and more item banks are made available to teachers, it will become easier for teachers to participate in the development process. As more information about testing software is made available, innovative classroom teachers will be able to concentrate on truly innovative testing projects rather than reinventing existing products.

It is predicted that the nature of testing software will change. Artificial intelligence capability will enable automated scoring of complex test questions, with greater scoring accuracy resulting. It is intuitive that computer scoring of a test is more accurate than human scoring for true/false, matching, and multiple choice questions. As artificial intelligence is added to computerized testing systems, the accuracy of scoring short answer questions will also increase. Accuracy will be improved in several ways. First, the software can be set up by the teacher or developer so that more than one answer is accepted as correct. For example, for the test item, "Who discovered America?" credit may be given for an answer of either "Columbus" or "Vikings." Computerized testing software also can reduce inter- and intra-scoring error by clarifying scoring criteria. With some computerized testing software, the person(s) grading the tests can press the "Help" key on the computer and review scoring criteria displayed on the computer screen. Alternatively, another key can be pressed to reveal examples of correct answers. This type of software is particularly helpful when multiple graders are used because it helps ensure that the same criteria are used for scoring by each grader.

Finally, as computerized testing becomes more pervasive, the trend will be for educational professionals to begin monitoring computerized testing practices in their profession. As stated above, psychologists are already monitoring computerized testing in their profession. School-based professionals such as school counselors and school psychologists are also struggling to find the proper role of computerization in complex and time-consuming assessment tasks. They have been especially vigilant about the use of such software by inexperienced or unqualified individuals. Just as professional counseling organizations have become involved in the development and evaluation of computerized counseling systems (Lindsay, 1988) and monitoring the use of such systems, professional organizations for classroom teachers will become increasingly involved in the development and monitoring of computerized testing systems.

In summary, we predict that more and more preservice and inservice teacher training programs will incorporate computerized testing into the curriculum. The emphasis of the curriculum will be less on the mechanics of the computerized systems and more on how to incorporate computerized testing into daily classroom activities. We predict that teachers will become more and more interested in computerized testing and will become an integral part of software development efforts. Finally, we predict that all of these events will be fueled by the greater interest in accountability and testing by policymakers and the public.

# REFERENCES

American Psychological Association. April 1986. "Guidelines for Computer-based Tests and Interpretations." Paper presented at the annual meeting of the American Educational Research Association, San Francisco.

Attisha, M., & Yazdani, M. 1983. " A Micro-computer Based Tutor for Teaching Arithmetic Skills." *Instructional Science, 12,* 333-342.

Attisha, M. & Yazdani, M. 1984. "An Expert System for Diagnosing Children's Multiple Errors." *Instructional Science, 13,* 79-92.

Carlberg, C. 1981. *South Dakota Study Report.* Denver, Co.: Midcontinent Regional Educational Laboratory.

College Entrance Examination Board. 1987. *Computerized Placement Tests.* New York: College Entrance Examination Board.

Collins, M. 1984. "Improving Learning with Computerized Testing." *American Biology Teacher, 46(3),* 188-191.

> This paper describes a computerized testing software package (Learning Systems) developed for use in an introductory biology course at the university level. Students who used the computerized testing system outscored students using traditional testing methods.

Dawson, G. 1987. "10000 Science Questions by Modem." *The Science Teacher, 54(3),* 41-44.

> Describes the Florida Department of Education's "Florida Catalog of Objectives" project and the test item database developed at Florida State University. The database is accessible from the FSU mainframe.

Eaves, R., & Smith, E. 1986. "The Effect of Media and Amount of Microcomputer Experience on Examination Scores." *Journal of Experimental Education, 55(1),* 23-26.

> This study compared university students with and without microcomputer experience using two different testing mediums: the traditional paper-and-pencil and microcomputers. No difference in performance was found.

Fennessey, D. July 1982. "Primary Teachers' Assessment Practices: Some Implications for Teacher Training." Paper presented at the annual conference of the South Pacific Association for Teacher Education, Frankston, Victoria.

Feuer, D. 1986. "Computerized Testing: A Revolution in the Making." *Training, 23(5),* 80-86.

> Discusses the major issues of computerized testing including the advantages of immediate feedback, storage, reporting capabilities, and simulation.

Forehand, G. 1987. "Development of a Computerized Diagnostic Testing Program." *Collegiate Microcomputer, 5(1),* 55-59.

Green, K.E., & Stager, S.F. 1987. " Differences in Teacher Test and Item Use with Subject, Grade Level Taught, and Measurement Coursework." *Teacher Education and Practice, 4(1),* 55-61.

Gullickson, A.R. 1982. "The Practice of Testing in Elementary and Secondary Schools." Paper presented at the Rural education conference, Kansas State University, Manhattan, Kansas.

Gwinn, J.F., & Beal, L.F. 1988. "On-line Computer Testing: Implementation and Endorsement." *Journal of Educational Technology Systems, 16(3),* 239-252.

> This paper describes how an interactive computer testing and record keeping system was implemented at the university level for an anatomy and physiology course.

Hanlon, S., & Ryan, J.  1986.  "A Pilot Study of a Computer-based PMP (Patient Management Problem)."  *Journal of Optometric Education, 11(3),* 20-25.

> Clinical scores on a computer-simulation module developed by the National Board of Medical examiners were compared with three other measures of clinical ability of optometry students. Subjects were second and third year optometry students. A moderate correlation was found between the PMP and the other three measures.

Heppner, F.H., Anderson, J.G.T., Farstrup, A.E., & Weiderman, N.H. 1985.  "Reading Performance on a Standardized Test is Better from Print Than from Computer Display."  *Journal of Reading, 28(4),* 321-325.

Janke, R., & Pilkey, P.  1985.  "Microcomputer Diagnosis of Whole Number Computational Errors."  *Journal of Computers in Mathematics and Science Teaching, 5,* 45-51.

Jay, T.B.  1981.  "Computer Phobia: What To Do about It."  *Educational Technology, 21(1),* 47-48.

> The author discusses symptoms, causes, and remedies of computerphobia based on the author's discussions with administrators, teachers, students, and educational technologists.

Larson, J.W.  1987.  "Computer-assisted Language Testing: Is It Profitable?"  *Association of Departments of Foreign Languages Bulletin, 18(2),* 20-24.

League for Innovation in Community Colleges.  1988.  "Computerized Adaptive Testing: The State of the Art in Assessment at Three Community Colleges."  Laguna Hills, California: League for Innovation.

Lindsay, G.  1988.  "Strengthening the Counseling Profession via Computer Use: Responding to the Issues."  *The School Counselor, 35(5),* 325-330.

The author discusses ten major issues affecting computer use in the school counseling profession and suggests how computers can be used to strengthen the profession.

Luecht, R.M. 1987. "Test Pac: A Program for Comprehensive Item and Reliability Analysis." *Educational and Psychological Measurement, 47(3),* 623-626.

Describes public-domain software "Test Pac," developed by the author. This menu-oriented software enables classroom teachers not only to perform standard item analyses but also advanced analyses such as generalizability theory and item response theory.

McDonald, J., Beal, J., & Ayers, F. 1988. "Computer-administered Testing: Diagnosis of Addition Computational Skills in Children." *Journal of Computers in Mathematics and Science Teaching, 7(1),* 38-43.

Mizokawa, D.T., & Hamlin, M.D. 1984. "Guidelines for Computer-managed Testing." *Educational Technology, 24(12),* 12-17.

The authors review major design decisions for computer-managed testing (CMT) and identify major errors of software developers.

Newman, D.C., & Stallings, W.M. March 1982. "Teacher Competency in Classroom Testing, Measurement Preparation, and Classroom Testing Practices." Paper presented at the annual meeting of the National Council on Measurement in Education.

Norman, G.R., Muzzin, L.J., Williams, R.G., & Swanson, D.B. 1985. "Simulation in Health Sciences Education." *Journal of Instructional Development, 8,* 11-17.

Rocklin, T.O., & O'Donnell, A.M. 1987. "Self-adapted Testing: A Performance-improving Variant of Computerized Adaptive Testing." *Journal of Educational Psychology, 79(3),* 315-319.

Computerized adaptive testing, self-adaptive testing, and traditional testing were experimentally compared. Analyses of variance using Rasch estimates ability suggested that self-adaptive testing procedures led to higher estimates of ability and minimized anxiety.

Roid, G.H. 1984. "Generating Test Items." In R.A. Berk (Ed.), *A Guide to Criterion-Referenced Testing.* Baltimore, MD: Johns Hopkins University Press.

Roid, G.H. 1986. "Computer Technology in Testing." In Plake, B.B., Witt, J.C., & Mitchell, J.V., Jr. (Eds.), *The Future of Testing.* Hillsdale, NJ: Lawrence Erlbaum Associates.

This review discusses some broad themes in the future of computing technology as applied to testing. Contains a very complete review of the technical literature.

Ronau, R., & Battista, M. 1988. "Microcomputer versus Paper-and-Pencil Testing of Student Errors in Ratio and Proportion." *Journal of Computers in Mathematics and Science Teaching, 7(3),* 33-38.

An attempt was made to construct alternate versions, paper and pencil and computer, of an eighth grade mathematics test diagnosing ratio and proportion errors. Students exhibited different patterns of errors on the two tests.

Sarvela, P., & Noonan, J. 1988. "Testing and Computer-based Instruction: Psychometric Considerations." *Educational Technology, 28(5),* 17-20.

Psychometric problems of computer-based testing are discussed. There are psychometric implications to the computer software's inability to recognize all correct short answer responses. Contamination also occurs when students are administered a different number of items, different items, a different item order, and items at different times during the course.

Shank, R.C., & Farrell, R. 1988. "Creativity in Education: A Standard for Computer-Based Teaching." *Machine-Mediated Learning,* 2(3), 175-194.

> Intelligent simulation programs are discussed which can support an experiential learning environment. The authors propose that these programs should become the new standard for computer-based teaching.

Stager, S.F., & Green, K.E. 1984. "Wyoming Teachers' Use of Tests and Attitudes towards Classroom and Standardized Tests." Report to the Wyoming State Department of Education, Department of Educational Foundations and Instructional Technology, University of Wyoming.

Sturtevant, V., & Johnson, B. 1988. "Micro-computer Test-generation Systems: A Software Review." *Teaching Sociology,* 16, 49-54.

Travis, B. 1984. "Computer Diagnosis of Algorithmic Errors." In V. Hansen & M. Zweng (Eds.), *Computers in Mathematics Education (1984 Yearbook)* (pp. 211-216).

Turner, J.A. July 19 1989. "Teacher-training: Colleges' Slow Move to Computers Blamed for Schools' Lag in Integrating Technology." *Chronicle of Higher Education,* 11-12A.

# COGNITIVE PSYCHOLOGY AND TESTING

## CHARLOTTE WEBB FARR

In the same way that a director's presence is felt but unseen on the stage, the work of cognitive scientists is making its presence felt in education. The infusion of concepts from cognitive science into the classroom, in the form of new methodologies, innovative curricular materials, renewed interest in teaching critical thinking, fledgling attempts to accommodate differences in learning styles, and divergent conceptions of the role of testing, is often so subtle that some of these changes have not been explicitly attributed to cognitive science. While credit *per se* may be unimportant, it is important to know their source in order to understand the changes taking place.

In the present chapter we are going to look at cognitive science and examine the ways in which it has influenced educational tests and measurement. In order to do that I will begin by defining what is meant by cognitive science, we will then look at its development and compare it with its predecessor and contemporary in educational measurement, psychometrics. Because cognitive science is such a broad field and because the literature in this field is so profuse, we will narrow the discussion from cognitive science to cognitive psychology and even then will discuss cognitive psychology only in a general way, citing some examples which are neither exhaustive nor totally representative but which nevertheless exemplify the concepts important to understanding the implications of cognitive psychology for educational testing and measurement. As an example of an application, further in the chapter we will examine one exemplary theory of the construct of intelligence spawned by research in cognitive psychology. We will contrast this with psychometric theories of intelligence. While cognitive psychology bears implications for the assessment of many traits, skills, and aptitudes, intelligence was selected as an example because of its implicit interest to educators. Finally, we will look at pertinent issues in cognitive psychology, articulate the most common research methodologies, and consider the possibilities for the future of a testing model that integrates the results of cognitive research with psychometric theory.

## THE DEFINITION AND DEVELOPMENT
## OF COGNITIVE SCIENCE

Cognitive science is the study of cognition, the study of the act or process of knowing. As such it is concerned with the processes inferred to be operating in the brain when learning is taking place. Typically cognitive science is concerned with everything from the initial input (sensations) to the final output (behavior) of the human mind. Snow and Lohman (1989) have included sensation, perception, pattern recognition, memory, attention, reasoning, thinking, language comprehension, knowledge representation, and problem solving all as appropriate areas of study in cognitive science. Others would include decision making (Sternberg, 1981), emotion, belief systems, consciousness, development, interaction, learning, performance, skill, and thought (Norman, 1980). Still others would include topics from computer, linguistic, and neurophysiological sciences (Snow & Lohman, 1989). For the purposes of this chapter we will ignore the last three and confine our discussion to the topics which are more commonly a part of cognitive psychology only.

## Historical Development

The history of cognitive psychology is mirrored in its present state. That is, it is neither linearly nor chronologically well ordered. Just as it had its roots in many sources and in many disciplines, it still encompasses many areas of research and many branches of knowledge. Cognitive psychology is not a unified entity. It is a body of knowledge whose central focus is the cognitive processes and contents involved in any mental activity informing complex behavior but which has no set methodology and no set research agenda. In some ways it is defined more by what it is not than what it is. For instance, it is not psychometrics (Hunt, 1987) although it shares its history with early educational measurement, and there are those who recognize that the two disciplines overlap and/or converge (e.g., Sternberg, 1984). It is also not behaviorism. In fact, it has its modern origins in the reaction to behaviorism by Gestaltists and linguists, both of whom objected to the contention that only observable behavior was worthy of scientific examination.

The exact origin of cognitive psychology is difficult to specify since it did not so much originate as aggregate. Many different factors had to be in place. But many texts (e.g., Anderson, 1980) point to the studies in perception and attention of Donald Broadbent at the Applied Psychology Research Unit in Cambridge, England, to the studies in memory by Miller at Harvard, and later to the work of Newell and Simon in artificial intelligence. Broadbent expanded on research conducted during World War II on human skills and performance, combined this with information theory regarding the way knowledge is processed to develop the information-processing approach (Anderson, 1980). Similarly, Miller's seminal publication in 1956, "The Magical Number Seven Plus or Minus Two: Some Limits on Our Capacity for Processing Information," built upon information theory by integrating empirical support for internal processes. Later, in his work with Galanter and Pribram (Sternberg, 1985), he delineated what he thought those processes were. Newell and Simon's work on artificial intelligence had an indirect effect on cognitive psychology by affording psychologists a model for the processes which purportedly operate in the brain during learning. The aggregation of these and other contributions into a legitimate science was accomplished in 1967 with the publication of Ulric Neisser's book *Cognitive Psychology*.

If one is to understand the impact of cognitive psychology on educational measurement, one needs to understand the relationship between it and psychometrics, particularly what it is that distinguishes the two and how these distinctions resulted from their respective developments.

## The Psychometric Approach

The psychometric approach evolved from the work of Alfred Binet, an early pioneer in intelligence assessment (Anastasi, 1988). Binet was commissioned to develop tests to predict the school success of retarded children. These tests consisted of items thought to measure judgment, comprehension, and reasoning regarded by Binet as the basic elements of intelligence. Scales were empirically developed for his tests by administering the tests to normal children and establishing levels based on their performance. He selected items for the tests according to their supposed level of difficulty, then tested the items on normal children. On the basis of the pretesting, he then categorized the items according to age levels. For example, included in the three-year level were items passed by 80 to 90% of all three-year-olds, in the four-year level were items passed by 80 to 90% of all four-year-olds, similarly on up to age thirteen. Unfortunately, this empirical approach led to classification of individuals according to mental level, then mental age, and finally intelligence quotient (mental age divided by chronological age), giving the impression that intelligence was an entity within the individual which could be represented and described by one single number.

Those who followed Binet agreed in principle with his empirical approach to establishing scales. However, in an attempt to more clearly define what intelligence was they began to analyze the tests to determine what underlying factors might account for performance on the tests. The method they used to determine this was factor analysis, a statistical technique for analyzing the correlations between items or tests. Depending on the way factor analysis was conducted, one or more factors were identified and intelligence was then viewed as a product of those factors. While there was disagreement over the number of factors in intelligence, there was agreement that what was measured was a static structure which was the basis for, and predictive of, intelligent behavior.

*Distinctions Between Psychometrics*
*and Cognitive Psychology*

What distinguishes psychometrics from cognitive psychology is this emphasis of psychometrics on products, or factors, rather than processes and its emphasis on correlation and description as methodologies rather than on experimentation. Additionally, psychometric models of intelligence and other constructs are generally less theory driven than empirically driven. That is, the justification for tests is in the applicability of their results not in the psychological theory behind them (Snow & Lohman, 1989).

Snow and Lohman (1989) argue that such an empirical approach overlooks the fact that no test serves the same function for all people, that in reality "A score reflects a complex combination of processing skills, strategies and knowledge components..., some of which are variant and some invariant across persons, or tasks, or stages of practice, in any given sample of persons or tasks" (p. 268). In other words, an item is difficult, not because an individual does not possess *n* amount of intelligence, but because the individual has had limited experience with such items, because the individual did not allow enough time to solve the problem, because the individual used the wrong strategy to solve the problem, or because of a variety of other causes. To a cognitive psychologist item difficulty is not a function of one source but of many sources. This argument was not initially posited by psychometricians, perhaps because focusing on products obscured the complexity of the issue.

*The Computer as a Model for Human Intelligence*

It was the advent of the computer, and with it the ability to conceptualize "artificial" intelligence, that brought about the idea that intelligence might be comprised of processes.  A central premise of cognitive psychology is that comprehension is a constructive process involving information from the environment and from semantic memory (Doyle, 1983).  Humans respond to an external stimulus based on the stimulus itself and upon past experience retrieved from long-term memory which is relevant to the stimulus.  Like computers, humans are seen as symbol-manipulating entities (Norman, 1980).

The basic model for explaining complex human behavior used by cognitive psychologists is based on the metaphor of the computer and envisions humans as information-processing mechanisms.  A generic model (adapted from Gage & Berliner, 1984) looks like this:

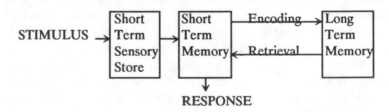

In applying the concepts of information-processing to research on human problem-solving, researchers often began with computer simulations of human problems (e.g., Larkin, McDermott, Simon, & Simon, 1980).  The programs were designed to reproduce the human processes purportedly necessary to solve a specific problem.  Information of what these processes were was derived from analysis of the task itself, analysis of researchers' problem-solving methods, thoughts reflected by other problem solvers, and observations of persons solving problems.  The programs simulated the performance of persons at different levels of skill, making it possible to predict the number and types of errors made and the time required for different responses.  By comparing the results of different problem-solvers (e.g., adults and children; experts and novices) it was possible to speculate about the processes involved, the knowledge base necessary for accurate solution of the problem, even the form in which this knowledge is stored in memory and how it is retrieved (Anastasi, 1988).

Research based on the information-processing model has been very productive. Emerging from this work is a picture of intelligent behavior much more complex and detailed than formerly imagined. So, while these research studies have answered many questions, they have raised new questions. There are many unresolved issues which remain to be reckoned with. These include among others: the issue of knowledge as product and process; the reciprocal roles of automaticity and ability to deal with novelty; the representation and organization of knowledge; and the function of metacognition. We will discuss these issues throughout this chapter. An understanding of these issues is important to understanding how constructs can be measured.

## BASIC APPROACHES TO STUDYING INTELLIGENCE USING INFORMATION-PROCESSING TECHNIQUES

Sternberg (1981) outlined four basic approaches to studying intelligence based on an information-processing paradigm: correlation, components, training, and content. They are briefly described below.

Correlation--subjects are measured in their ability to perform a specified task presumed by the researcher to measure a basic human information-processing ability such as attention allocation. Usually the subject is to perform this task as quickly as possible and thus equipment, such as a tachistoscope or a computer terminal, is necessary to measure response time. An example of such a task is a memory-scanning task used by S. Sternberg (1969) in which subjects were asked to state whether a target digit, such as 3, appeared in a previously memorized set of digits, such as 1 4 3 7. Characteristic performance on this task was compared across individuals and across tasks. That is, subjects' performances on the memory-scanning task were compared to each other, and their performances on this task were compared with their performance on other measures of intelligence (e.g., numerical subscale of Stanford-Binet). The central focus of this type of research is generally perception, learning, and memory tasks.

Component--subjects are measured in their ability to perform tasks that are taken directly from IQ tests. Again, equipment is necessary because accuracy is not the only variable considered. Response time is usually one of the primary variables considered, as is error pattern. Obviously, correlation with IQ test score is not the object in this kind of research. Rather the researcher is interested in identifying key components which contribute to performance from a theoretical viewpoint. Usually performance is compared to a formal model of performance which might be based on either a mathematical model or a computer simulation. The central focus of this type of research is generally reasoning and problem-solving tasks.

Training--less able subjects are measured in their ability to perform tasks after receiving training in aspects of the task hypothesized to account for their weaknesses. For example, it might be assumed that the ability to compute, to set up problems, and to identify relevant information is necessary in order to solve mathematics word problems. If there is reason to believe that less able students do poorly because they are unable to identify the relevant information in the problems, the researcher might train the students in identifying relevant information and then retest the trained subjects on mathematics word problems. If performance improves, it is possible to draw some conclusions about the relative importance of the ability to identify information relevant to solving word problems. This technique may be used with individual tasks like memory scanning or more complex tasks like problem solving. One significant finding from this line of research is the necessity of training both at the metacognitive and performance levels.

Contents--compares the performance of experts and novices in complex tasks in a variety of content domains, notably physics and chess. Results of this research point out the importance of the way information is represented and organized in long-term memory. For example, it is known that experts link new knowledge with old knowledge in more complex, substantive ways than novices.

Snow and Lohman (1989) categorize the various approaches to studying intellectual processes according to the specific techniques used: protocol analysis, computer modeling, chronometric analysis, mathematical modeling, analysis of reasons, analysis of eye movements, and analysis of systematic errors.

During protocol analysis subjects are asked to think aloud while performing a task or to relate retrospectively what they did to accomplish the task. Their remarks are then analyzed for patterns in procedures. Protocol analysis may be utilized in its own right, or it may serve as a basis for computer modeling. Computer modeling tries to identify and represent the actual procedures encountered in human performance and to match this model with observed performance. Chronometric analysis measures response times, or the time it takes for a subject to react to various stimuli. On the basis of the time it takes to respond, inferences are made about the differing processing loads of different tasks (e.g., encoding, inferring, and mapping processes used in solving analogies). Mathematical modeling uses response time, accuracy, and error rate in the development of probability models which are then used to predict correct responses based on underlying processes. Analysis of reasons requires subjects to provide a rationale for answering a question a certain way or for choosing one response over another. Analysis of eye movements monitors the direction and duration of visual attention during task performance. Analysis of systematic errors examines subjects' errors for misconceptions, inaccurate procedures, inappropriate representations, or distorted conceptual models.

*Expanded View of Intelligence*

All of these techniques expand on the psychometric approach to understanding intelligence and in turn have expanded our conceptualization of what intelligence is. One result of using the above techniques has been the realization that different individuals might perform the same task in different ways or that the same individual might perform similar tasks in different ways across items or across situations (Snow & Lohman, 1989; Wagner & Sternberg, 1984). This realization has led to a stress on studying the role of strategies and styles in assessing cognitive ability. This realization also means we can no longer defend the notion that a single score represents cognitive ability nor that such ability is fixed since performance is dependent on context (Martin, 1989).

*Sternberg's Triarchic Theory of Intelligence*

As an example of how the conceptualization of intelligence has changed, we are going to look now at one particular theory. Sternberg's (1985) triarchic theory was chosen primarily because it is so comprehensive and because it incorporates potential explanations of many of the issues raised as a result of cognitive research. For a more thorough accounting of his theory, the reader is referred to his book, *Beyond IQ: A Triarchic Theory of Human Intelligence.*

Sternberg's theory is comprised of three subtheories, the contextual, the experiential, and the componential, each delineating different aspects of intelligence. The contextual aspect of intelligent behavior refers to the concept that individuals act within a sociocultural context (i.e., they are born into a specific societal environment). In responding to the societal environment in which they find themselves, individuals may choose to adapt to the environment in which they find themselves, to select another more desirable environment, or try to shape the present environment to better meet their needs. The experiential aspect of intelligent behavior refers to the concept that intelligent behavior, in part, is a matter of experience. Both the ability to accommodate novelty and to automatize familiar tasks are related to the amount of experience an individual has with the tasks. Lastly, the componential aspect of intelligent behavior refers to the fact that the sources of individual differences in intelligence may be attributed to one of three information processing components or to a combination of these: metacomponents, performance components, and knowledge-acquisition components.

"Metacomponents are higher-order executive processes used in planning, monitoring, and decision making in task performance" (Sternberg, 1986a, p.99). Metacomponents are responsible for deciding what to do, how to do it, and if it is done well. In solving analogies, for instance, metacomponents are responsible for the overall strategy, including how much time should be spent on the processes of encoding, mapping, inferring, and applying.

"Performance components are processes used in the execution of a task" (Sternberg, 1986a, p.99). Performance components are responsible for doing what the metacomponents indicate should be done. Since many behaviors are possible, the number of performance components is quite large, but with regard to measuring intelligence, a few components are more important than others. This is so because these components are general across many tasks found on intelligence tests. For example, one such set of components is inductive reasoning, classification, problem solving, and reading comprehension. Since many different performance components are possible, which components are used to solve a given task depends upon the individual's experience and the context of the task.

"Knowledge-acquisition components are processes used in learning new information" (Sternberg, 1986a, p.99). These knowledge-acquisition processes consist of selective encoding, selective combination, and selective comparison. Selective encoding pertains to the ability to separate relevant from irrelevant information in a task. Selective combination involves combining the relevant information in some meaningful and appropriate way. Selective comparison entails relating old to new information.

According to Sternberg (1985) the componential aspect of intelligence is most closely related to what is currently measured by psychometric tests. Verbal tests, particularly, measure knowledge-acquisition components explicitly. They also measure performance components explicitly and metacomponents implicitly. For this reason, there is a high correlation between psychometric tests and the type of cognitive tasks measured in the laboratory.

However, there is little correlation between psychometric tests and some measures of real world success (Wagner & Sternberg, 1984). This is the case because the other aspects of intelligence postulated by Sternberg are not currently measured by psychometric tests. Insight, creativity, tacit knowledge, the ability to adapt to one's environment, being more closely tied to context and to an individual's experience, are not easily measured. Precisely because different individuals and different groups have different experiential backgrounds, it is difficult to find tasks which measure these qualities fairly. This emphasis on sociocultural and experiential factors is one quality that distinguishes cognitive theory from psychometric theory.

## CONTRIBUTIONS OF COGNITIVE PSYCHOLOGY TO TESTING

Because the field of cognitive psychology is so diverse, it is impossible to include all who have made significant contributions or to discuss all relevant theories and methods. Collectively, however, the field has the potential to make significant contributions to testing and it is these which will be summarized now. Again, this will be done from two perspectives (Snow & Lohman, 1989; Sternberg, 1981) which are neither all inclusive nor independent. Both of these perspectives reflect syntheses of the literature. Examples from the literature are included to elaborate on and support these authors' contentions.

### *How Cognitive Psychology Might Improve Educational Measurement*

Snow and Lohman (1989) list three ways in which cognitive psychology can contribute to the improvement of educational measurement. "Cognitive analyses of existing measures can help improve understanding of the constructs represented by them.... Cognitive study might suggest alternative measurement strategies and refinements of existing instruments.... Cognitive study might lead to new and improved theories of aptitude, learning and achievement in education" (p. 266).

Considering these one at a time, it is apparent that cognitive research can contribute evidence in support of construct validity (Embretson, 1985; Messick, 1989). In addition to the usual correlational approach to establishing construct validity, cognitive psychology has now made it possible to identify the theoretical processes underlying constructs. By decomposing tasks into the components required to accomplish the tasks, it is possible to develop a model of the task, a "construct representation." For example, Sternberg (1985) decomposed performance on analogical reasoning tasks into the following subset of tasks: encoding, inference, mapping, application, comparison, justification, and response. While Butterfield,

Nielson, Tangen, and Richardson (1985) identified level of knowledge and number of operations as the cognitive variables in performance on letter series tasks.

The ability to establish a construct representation is useful in a variety of ways. It enables researchers to identify processes which are task specific, common to several tasks, or generalizable over many tasks. The ability to regroup numbers in subtraction is an example of a process which is task specific. The ability to perform multiple operations in mathematics problem solving is an example of a process common to several tasks. By extension, the ability to perform multiple operations in any problem solving situation is an example of a process that is generalizable over many tasks. By designing tests with different configurations of processes, it is possible to learn more about the processes themselves and about how those processes are used by individuals. It is also possible to see how different processes are related and the relative importance of particular processes to different tasks. Understanding the theoretical mechanisms underlying tasks makes it possible to design tests which more clearly describe individual performance by providing an understanding of what makes items difficult for different individuals. Returning to the letter series task of Butterfield et al. (1989), it is possible to design tests using only elementary knowledge and multiple operations, tests using higher levels of knowledge but only singular operations, and tests using different levels of knowledge and multiple operations. In so doing it is possible to determine if an individual is having trouble because he/she cannot perform multiple operations, because he/she has insufficient prior knowledge, or both. In conjunction with item response theory (see Chapter 2 of this book) it may soon be possible to design tests to precisely measure specific cognitive skills (Hambleton, 1989). Ultimately this would lead to tests that are diagnostic as well as predictive.

Finally, the above changes will contribute to further theory building. Assuming that new or revised tests are built upon some theory regarding human behavior, information gleaned from using the tests will either support or refute such theories. As tentative explanations for observed phenomena, it is important to subject theories to empirical testing. This is accomplished by deducing, or making predictions of, logical consequences of the theory and gathering data to see if the predictions are borne out. In addition to lending credibility to theory, linking tests to psychological theories in this way contributes to the validity of tests. Two excellent examples of the synergetic relationship between measurement and theory are Flavell's (1977) theory of metacognition and Anderson's (1980) theory of automaticity. These theories led to attempts to measure metacognition and automaticity respectively and those attempts spawned further theorizing about the roles of metacognition and automaticity in intelligence.

## HOW COGNITIVE RESEARCH WILL CHANGE TESTING

Sternberg (1986b) outlined 12 ways in which testing could change due to ongoing research in cognitive psychology. These ways are listed below.

1. Increased use of psychological theories.
2. Increased breadth in intelligence measurement.
3. Increased emphasis on measuring the processes underlying intelligence.
4. Increased emphasis on the practical side of intelligence.
5. Increased emphasis on ability to cope with novelty.
6. Increased emphasis on synthetic and insightful thinking.
7. Merging of testing and learning functions.
8. Enhanced assessment of learning styles.
9. Increased measurement of learning potential.
10. Computerized adaptive testing.
11. Increased use of dynamic computerized testing.
12. Reduced longevity of tests.

Some of these predictions may appear obvious from the previous discussion in this chapter. However, several of the items bear further clarification. Items 2-6 all pertain to the new conception of intelligence. Nowhere is this new conceptualization more visible than in the attitude of cognitive psychologists regarding real world intelligence. There is growing awareness that success outside of formal education is reflective of intellectual activity and that there is a relationship between real world intelligence and formal learning (Vygotsky, 1986). Increasingly we will see attempts to relate test performance to real world correlates.

Item 7 may prove to be one of the most significant areas of change. The merging of testing and learning functions stemming from our ability to refine tests and to design tests to measure particular variables will make diagnosis of individual deficiencies possible on a level never before imagined. There are two ways to accomplish this: the error classification approach and the componential approach (Nitko, 1989). One emphasizes the identification and classification of students' incorrect responses. The other decomposes complex performance into two or more components. In both cases, this information is then used to prescribe appropriate remediation procedures. Prototypes, such as DEBUGGY (Burton, 1982), for such diagnostic testing currently exist. DEBUGGY is "an off-line diagnostic computer program that includes a means of measuring the error diagnostic properties of subtraction tests and of helping to create better tests" (Nitko, 1989, p. 460). Using this approach it is possible to create a 12-20 item test of subtraction which elicits nearly all possible errors and which allows the diagnostician to distinguish all of the error types.

Psychometric measures tell us if students master designated instructional objectives by indicating whether students get an item right or wrong. Assessment procedures congruent with cognitive psychology may shed light on why learners are able (or unable) to master the designated instructional objectives. These assessment procedures go beyond the surface level of knowledge and assess how "deeply" learners have organized knowledge, or to what extent the students have linked concepts with other concepts.

Of course, these procedures are dependent on technical assistance provided by computers, which accounts in part for items 10-11. Technology has enhanced the possibility of helping individuals gain the most from instruction by reducing the labor involved in making the kinds of decisions necessary to tailor instruction to individual needs (Linn, 1989). The possibility of aptitude treatment interaction (ATI) was recognized years ago (see Cronbach & Snow, 1981) but was unrealistic then because of the time required to diagnose deficiencies and prescribe remediation. Computers may change that.

Items 8 and 9 require entire chapters to adequately explain. Certainly, cognitive psychologists have called our attention to many factors which have an impact on learning previously overlooked by the traditional approaches of behaviorism and psychometrics. Since these are beyond the purview of this chapter, they will not be discussed here except to point out that they affect educational measurement. The notion that learning is context specific (Brown, Collins, and Duguid, 1989; Perkins and Salomon, 1989) has implications for testing and for instruction. For instance, instruction may be patterned after apprentice learning whereby students learn incidentally by interacting with fellow students and experts in addition to receiving explicit instruction. Likewise, tests may need to have local, as well as national norms, in order to take into account the various contexts in which learning takes place. Tests may need to be redesigned to measure not only facts and procedures but the relationships between them. Tests may need to reflect a broader notion of what is meant by learning outcomes, a notion that encompasses thinking (Schoenfeld, 1988). Many of these implications will generate renewed interest in the way we assess culturally diverse students (Sewell, 1979).

Many of these implications also apply directly to the classroom teacher, particularly the framework within which classroom teachers construct tests. Recognizing that the classroom teacher is most acutely aware of the learning context, the classroom teacher is in a unique position to see that assessment appropriately matches the learning environment and that measurement is well integrated with instruction. Therefore, there is likely to be increased demand for teachers to construct tests which accurately reflect course content and goals, which are designed to measure not only facts and procedures but the relationships between them, and which incorporates the broader notion of learning that includes thinking.

Consequently, classroom teachers will need to become more sophisticated about measurement and the role of measurement in education. They will need to be informed as to how they can take advantage of the existing technology to access pools of test items, to evaluate the reliability of their test results, to individualize testing, and to utilize the diagnostic capabilities of measurement. Because the impact of teacher-made tests is greater by far than the impact of standardized tests (Crooks, 1988), it is imperative that classroom teachers embrace the changes generated by research in cognitive psychology.

## SUMMARY

Cognitive psychology is of interest to educators in that it is concerned with the processes which underlay learning. If "Education is primarily an aptitude development program....(and) Intelligence is both a primary aptitude for learning in education and a primary product of learning in education " (Snow, 1982, p. 29), then the work of cognitive psychologists is of immense concern to educators. The variety of techniques and methods employed by cognitive psychologists simply underscores the fact that new perspectives on learning are appropriate. The implication of this for educational measurement is that we need to develop new ways to evaluate learning. Research in cognitive psychology has generated interest in issues regarding knowledge as process or product, the relationship between insight and automaticity, the role of tacit and formal knowledge, the importance of strategies in complex behavior, and metacognition. In the process of developing new methodologies for studying cognitive processes, cognitive psychology has afforded educators the opportunity to try to enhance individuals' ability to learn. Tests no longer just predict who will succeed but enable us to help students benefit from instruction. As Sternberg (1986b) said: "Cognitive research can inform testing practices. The question is whether it will."

# REFERENCES

Anderson, J.R. 1980. *Cognitive Psychology and Its Implications.* San Francisco: W.H. Freeman.

Anastasi, A. 1988. *Psychological Testing (6th edition).* New York: Macmillan Publishers.

> Comprehensive text. Appropriate for general understanding of psychological tests and measurement.

Brown, J.S., Collins, A., & Duguid, P. 1989. "Situated Cognition and the Culture of Learning." *Educational Researcher, 18(1),* 32-42.

> Posits logical argument for belief that all learning is situational. Suggests how apprentice type instruction can address this issue.

Burton, R.R. 1982. "Diagnosing Bugs in a Simple Procedural Skill." In D. Sleeman & J.S. Brown (Eds.), *Intelligent Tutoring Systems* (pp.157-183), New York: Academic Press.

Butterfield, E.C., Nielsen, D., Tangen, K.L., & Richardson, M.B. 1985. "Theoretically Based Psychometric Measures of Inductive Reasoning." In S.E. Embretson (Ed.), *Test Design: Developments in Psychology and Psychometrics.* New York: Academic Press.

Cronbach, L.J., & Snow, R.E. 1981. *Aptitudes and Instructional Methods: A Handbook for Research on Interactions.* New York: Irvington Publishers.

> Probably the most definitive work detailing the relationship between student aptitude and instructional methods.

Crooks, T.J. 1988. "The Impact of Classroom Evaluation Practices on Students." *Review of Educational Research, 58(4),* 438-481.

Doyle, W. 1983. "Academic Work." *Review of Educational Research,* *53(2),* 159-199.

Embretson, S.E. (Ed.). 1985. *Test Design: Developments in Psychology and Psychometrics.* New York: Academic Press.
> Comprehensive introduction into the concept of test design as it has been affected by cognitive psychology. Particularly useful for insights into the issue of construct validity.

Flavell, J.H. 1977. *Cognitive Development.* Englewood Cliffs, NJ: Prentice-Hall.

> Details the development of cognition in children from a Piagetian perspective. Introduces the concept of metacognition and examines its role of in learning.

Gage, N.L., & Berliner, D.C. 1984. *Educational Psychology (3rd edition).* Boston: Houghton Mifflin Company.

> Solid text which discusses the implications of research in psychology for education. Appropriate for graduate students.

Hambleton, R.K. 1989. "Principles and Selected Applications of Item Response Theory." In R.L. Linn (Ed.), *Educational Measurement (3rd edition)* (pp. 147-200), New York: American Council on Education/Macmillan Series on Higher Education.

> Very technical article dealing with the topic of item response theory.

Hunt, E. 1987. "The Cognitive-Psychometric Connection." In R.R. Ronning, J.A. Glover, J.C. Conoley, & J.C. Witt (Eds.). *The Influence of Cognitive Psychology on Testing, Volume 3* (pp. 11-40). Hillsdale, NJ: Lawrence Erlbaum.

> Compilation of a variety of papers on the influence of cognitive psychology on testing.

Larkin, J.H., McDermott, J., Simon, D.F., & Simon, H.A. 1980. "Models of Competence in Solving Physics Problems." *Cognitive Science, 4,* 317-345.

Linn, R.L. 1989. "Current Perspectives and Future Directions." In R.L. Linn (Ed.), *Educational Measurement (3rd edition)* (pp. 1-12), New York: American Council on Education/Macmillan Series on Higher Education.

> Introduction to the topic of educational measurement. This article prefaces the book edited by Linn which is the latest edition of the standard handbook on educational measurement. An excellent reference book.

Martin, D.S. 1989. "Cognitive Assessment of Diverse Populations." *Kappa Delta Pi Record,* 35-38.

Messick, S. 1989. "Validity." In R.L. Linn (Ed.), *Educational Measurement (3rd edition)* (pp. 13-104), New York: American Council on Education/Macmillan Series on Higher Education.

> Thought provoking article discussing the subject of validity. While the discussion is not always easy for the novice to follow, the author is well respected for his thoughts on this important issue.

Neisser, U. 1967. *Cognitive Psychology.* New York: Appleton-Century-Crofts.

Nitko, A.J. 1989. "Designing Tests That Are Integrated with Instruction." In R.L. Linn (Ed.), *Educational Measurement (3rd edition)* (pp. 447-474), New York: American Council on Education/Macmillan Series on Higher Education.

> Moves beyond matching test items to behavioral objectives, making a strong argument for utilizing tests as educational tools that enhance the instructional process.

Norman, D.A. 1980. "Twelve Issues for Cognitive Science." *Cognitive Science, 4,* 1-32.

Perkins, D.N., & Salomon, G. 1989. "Are Cognitive Skills Context-bound?" *Educational Researcher, 18(1),* 16-25.

Schoenfeld, A.H. 1988. "When Good Teaching Leads to Bad Results: The Disasters of 'Well Taught' Mathematics Courses." *Educational Psychologist, 23(2),* 145-166.

Sewell, T.E. 1979. "Intelligence and Learning Tasks as Predictors of Scholastic Achievement in Black and White First-grade Children." *The Journal of School Psychology, 17(4),* 325-332.

Snow, R.E. 1982. "The Training of Intellectual Aptitude." In D.K. Detterman & R.J. Sternberg (Eds.) *How and How Much Can Intelligence Be Increased?* (pp.1-32). Norwood, NJ: Ablex.

Snow, R.E., & Lohman, D.F. 1989. "Implications of Cognitive Psychology for Educational Measurement." In R.L. Linn (Ed.), *Educational Measurement (3rd edition)* (pp. 263-334), New York: American Council on Education/Macmillan Series on Higher Education.

> Well-written, comprehensive paper on the implications of cognitive psychology for educational measurement. Highly recommended for any reader who wants the latest information on the subject.

Sternberg, R.J. 1981. "Testing and Cognitive Psychology." *American Psychologist, 36(10),* 1181-1189.

Sternberg, R.J. 1984. "What Should Intelligence Tests Test? Implications of a Triarchic Theory of Intelligence for Intelligence Testing." *Educational Researcher, 13(1),* 5-15.

> Easily read article introducing topic covered in his book.

Sternberg, R.J. 1985. *Beyond IQ: A Triarchic Theory of Human Intelligence*. London: Cambridge University Press.

   Sternberg expounds on his triarchic theory of intelligence. Contains many concrete examples of his theory, including innovative ways to measure incidental learning.

Sternberg, R.J. 1986a. *Intelligence Applied: Understanding and Increasing Your Intellectual Skills*. New York: Harcourt Brace Jovanovich.

   Using many practical examples, this book addresses both the increasing and the understanding of intelligence.

Sternberg, R.J. 1986b. "The Future of Intelligence Testing." *Educational Measurement: Issues and Practice, 5(3),* 19-22.

Sternberg, S. 1969. "Memory-scanning: Mental Processes Revealed by Reaction Time Experiments." *American Scientist, 57,* 421-457.

Vygotsky, L.S. 1986. *Thought and Language* (A. Kozulin, Trans.) Cambridge, MA: The MIT Press. (Original work published 1934)

Wagner, R.K., & Sternberg, R.J. 1984. "Alternative Conceptions of Intelligence and Their Implications for Education." *Review of Educational Research, 52(2),* 179-223.

   Brief but comprehensive review of various conceptions of intelligence discussed from the perspective of education.

# INDEX